D0730413

What do Environmentalists Want?

    Healthier workplaces.

    Healthier lifestyles.

    A voice in the political system.

    Wilderness, protected for future generations.

    Fuel-efficient transportation.

    Pesticide-free food.

    Solutions to ecological problems that help
    beat inflation while saving the world.

How are we going to get it?

    With the steps advocated in this book.

THE
NEW
ENVIRONMENTAL
HANDBOOK

Friends of the Earth
Principal offices

124 Spear Street
San Francisco, California 94105

530 Seventh Street, S.E.
Washington, D.C. 20003

72 Jane Street
New York, New York 10014

The New Environmental Handbook

Edited by
Garrett De Bell

Literary Editor
Aubrey Wallace

Assistant Editor
David Gancher

FRIENDS OF THE EARTH · San Francisco

Designed by Terry Down

Cover Design by Bill Oetinger

Friends of the Earth gratefully acknowledges permission to reprint from the following sources:

"Cirque of the Unclimbables," reprinted by permission of Sierra Club Books from *High and Wild*, by Galen Rowell, copyright © 1979 by Galen Rowell.

"What's Ahead in the 1980s?" reprinted from Mechanix Illustrated Magazine, copyright 1980 by CBS Publications Inc.

"Four Gas Savers that Really Work," reprinted from Mechanix Illustrated Magazine, copyright 1979 by CBS Publications Inc.

Managing Your Personal Food Supply, copyright © 1977 by Rodale Press, Inc. Permission granted by Rodale Press, Inc., Emmaus, Pa. 18049.

Desert Solitaire, © copyright 1968 by Edward Abbey. Reprinted by permission of the Harold Matson Company, Inc.

The Supermarket Handbook: Access to Whole Foods, revised and expanded edition by Nikki and David Goldbeck. Copyright © 1973, 1976 by Nikki Goldbeck and David Goldbeck. Reprinted by arrangement with The New American Library, Inc., New York, New York.

"The Ruination of the Tomato" is adapted from *Three Farms* by Mark Kramer, and first appeared in *The Atlantic Monthly*, copyright © 1977, 1979, 1980 by Mark Kramer.

Gary Snyder, *Turtle Island*. Copyright © 1972 by Gary Snyder. Reprinted by permission of New Directions.

The End of the Road: A Citizen's Guide to Transportation Problemsolving, David G. Burwell and Mary Ann Wilner (1977). Copyright 1977 National Wildlife Federation, Library of Congress Card No. 77–92318.

San Francisco Chronicle, 1979 and 1980. Reprinted by Permission.

Manufactured in the USA

Trade Distribution by:
    Friends of the Earth
    124 Spear Street
    San Francisco California 94105

Contents

Foreword

What Do We Want Anyway?

by Garrett De Bell

In 1970, when we published the first *Environmental Handbook*, it was fairly easy to be comprehensive. The issues were new, a small number of papers were talked about among all the groups that were considering an environmental philosophy, and the work of a few writers like Aldo Leopold, Garrett Hardin, Boulding, Ehrlich, and Thoreau comprised a more or less universally agreed-upon foundation. One tribute to the success of the environmental movement is that now the body of literature is so large that you could do five or ten different environmental handbooks with little overlap in the selection of authors and articles. Some of the pieces now come not from esoteric environmental books but from the popular press. The environment has moved from a special cause to a wide concern throughout the country.

We can see signs of the quiet revolution already going on in our personal lives: we are becoming increasingly exhilarated by good food and health; and "addicted" to exercise, like running, walking, or riding a bike. It's an addiction in that once it's established the person feels less well if he or she doesn't get the accustomed "fix" (one explanation is a hormone, called endorphin, that is released by the brain during vigorous exercise[1]); and it's a positive one in that you can't stay up late drinking the night before a workout (twenty million people could live for a year on the amount of grain used by our beer and liquor industry annually[2]), and if you work out you aren't as likely to overeat, just by a natural process of metabolism (in a world of starving people, 40% of Americans are clinically obese[3]).

The reason for an overconsumptive society is, in part, overconsumers—not just big bad Madison Avenue or corporate giants or self-serving politicians—though all of those things certainly exist and contribute. And as we each cut back here and there, as we begin for whatever reason—curiosity about aerobics, or the economy of biking to work, or the sense of well-being from getting into condition—we begin to see ways overconsumption has degraded our lives and we are beginning to think we would rather conserve

1

than continue to contribute to this erosion. Perhaps the next decade will bring the practices of business and politics into reality too, and there are indications that it may.

In 1970 I called for a 25% reduction of energy use in the next decade in the U.S. This was used as an example of the attitudes of "the anti-energy youth" by Nobel Prize-winning physicist Glenn Seaborg, who was chairman of the now-defunct Atomic Energy Commission, when he gave speeches calling for more nukes. This year a best-selling study from no less than the Harvard Business School recommends conservation as the cornerstone of energy policy. Quite a change in a decade.

In 1980 the growing scarcity and exploding cost of energy has become our biggest ally. The excessive use of energy and waste of energy that have been the cause of many environmental problems are coming to an end. The Petroleum Age is essentially over.

What Do We Want Anyway—for the 1980's?

1. *Energy*. There should be no further increase in the use of nonrenewable energy resources. A yearly, gradual reduction in the amount of nonrenewable energy we use can be achieved by eliminating waste: with improved energy efficiency throughout residential, commercial and industrial use; by recovering and using the waste heat generated in industrial processes, rather than burning new fuels; by substituting renewable fuels, including alcohol, from waste products; and by recovery of the energy in waste materials. Solar energy should be improved and the nuclear industry should be phased out; it is one of mankind's biggest mistakes.

2. *Transportation*. Today's better, smaller, more fuel-efficient (and safer, thanks primarily to Ralph Nader) cars are a decided improvement as long as they are used as part of an integrated transportation network. But the world cannot support its present population by driving fuel-efficient compacts, let alone the expanded population that even the most optimistic ZPG advocates see in the next century. Sustainable transportation can be based on urban transit, rail, bus or equivalent for the long hauls and commutes; and walking, bicycling, etc., for the short hauls. Cars are appropriate for the times, places, and types of transit that can't be accommodated efficiently and with a quality experience by public transit — in low density rural areas for instance.

3. *Agriculture.* We need more use of labor, less use of energy, more biological controls, more fertilizers from biological sources, and a limited use of chemicals for fine-tuned means of pest control.

4. *Housing.* We need a mix of restoration of the decayed inner city, and new construction where necessary, for multiple dwellings like townhouses, condominiums, etc. The detached residence can be generally restricted to existing subdivisions.

5. *Solid waste.* Recycling should be the way garbage is handled and there should be no need for garbage dumps.

If we accomplish this much in the Eighties we can concentrate on the rest of the details in the Nineties.

One gross embarrassment looms on the current scene: no Presidential candidate has an environmental platform of any consequence. No Presidential candidate has even been willing to stand up for beverage container deposits as a way to increase recycling of solid waste. Not one is willing to risk the loss of votes or political contributions by vested interests that profit from the presently lucrative but non-environmentally sound way that we handle beverage containers—and the rest of our business.

The goals of the environmental movement will only be achieved through a combination of individual and political action. The job of alerting people to problems has been done and a great many of the solutions are readily available. The movement is in its second generation. Over the past decade we have set up procedures and mechanisms; they still require participation to work. The fiery emotion of the new idea has cooled—but its glowing coals should be banked, and can never be neglected.

Garrett De Bell
April, 1980
near the site of John Muir's cabin
Yosemite National Park

---

1. According to Dr. Dorothy V. Harris, professor of health, physical education and recreation and director of Penn State's Center for Women and Sport.
2. Laurel Robertson, Carol Flinders, and Bronwen Godfrey, *Laurel's Kitchen*, Nilgiri Press, Petaluma, California
3. Ibid.

Introduction

The Beginning of a Better Future

by Anne and Paul Ehrlich

It is relatively easy to visualize an American life style not based on material growth and consumption, that would be pleasant and rewarding. Many young Americans, born and raised in affluence, have been turned off by the attitudes of their parents, who seemed to have abandoned earlier virtues of frugality, prudence, and valuing of people over possessions. These young people have rejected the affluent society and its trappings and have sought alternative life styles that emphasize human values over material ones. The new life style is termed "voluntary simplicity" and—as in other, sometimes less socially or environmentally beneficial trends—Californians are pioneering it.[1] But all over the country people have discovered that less resource consumption than the average American's in the 1960s and 1970s does not mean instant poverty and drudgery, indeed it is rewarding in many ways.

While it may be financial considerations that push people to buy small cars with high gas mileages, they soon find these cars are not only cheaper to buy, maintain, and fuel, they are often fun to drive. And it's fun not to have to visit the gas station (and wait in lines) so often. Well-insulated houses are more comfortable to live in than poorly insulated ones and result in much lower heating and cooling bills. Many people have rediscovered the warm pleasures of wood fires. Others have installed solar heaters for swimming pools and water heaters. Solar heating provides some independence from centralized utility services and less vulnerability to possible shortages.

Health consciousness combines with "voluntary simplicity," and many people are eating less meat and heavily processed foods. (This has created regional markets for more nutritious foods, and food companies in the western states have willingly responded.) They take exercise seriously and frequently substitute bicycles or shanks' mare for a car.

The desire for a better life and independence from

"the system" has led more people to do-it-themselves. They repair their own homes, service their cars, grow their own fruits and vegetables and often preserve them too, make their own clothes and furniture. They help organize and participate in projects to recycle paper, glass, and metals. And they enjoy it. (All these activities also save money, of course.)

According to a survey by two Stanford University sociologists, the majority of California households in the late 1970's were participating to some degree in this new lifestyle.[2] The authors of the study felt that the California trend was "a precursor of a future social movement in the United States" and that continuing problems with the economy and energy supplies were likely to speed its diffusion to the rest of the nation.

That so many people are consciously turning away from the consumptive life style is a hope for our future. A steady-state economy might be established in the United States by conscious social choice rather than as the result of an economic collapse or, worse, the outcome of a catastrophic war over diminishing resources (in which case there would be a subsistence economy, at best).

Americans in 1980 see their paychecks evaporating in rising grocery and heating bills, their savings losing ground against inflation, and mortgage rates going out of sight. And the *quality* of practically everything they buy—furniture, clothing, leather goods, cars, building materials and methods—seems to be deteriorating. Nor are they reassured by what they see on TV news programs: international confrontations and extortion, terrorism, gold prices soaring, constant hikes in the price of oil, gas shortages, unemployment, famines, and monsoon failures. Americans are accustomed to the idea that things will get better, but, as we and others predicted,[3] lately things seem to be getting steadily worse.

Many Americans, not understanding the causes of their dilemma, have looked for a scapegoat: oil companies, OPEC nations, "lack of leadership" in the government. Rarely has the finger of blame been pointed in the right direction—at themselves. The vaunted American way of life—as most still do not believe—is profligate, wasteful, and destructive. The ethic of the frontier and the myth of boundless resources still pervade American thinking, though they have been obsolete for three-quarters of a century.

The frontier is long gone, and resources are proving to have all too real bounds. That there are limits to nonrenewable resources is obvious — though many Americans seem to think quantities far exceed what can be used in the foreseeable future. That there are limits to renewable resources, too, is less obvious. Supplies of food, timber, fresh water, and good soil are finite, even though they are constantly renewed if agricultural and natural ecosystems are properly conserved. The capacity of those systems to maintain resource flows is being approached as the human population expands and increases in material "affluence", demanding a greater share of resources *per person*.

Everyone knows that "too many dollars (or marks, or yen) chasing too few goods" is a cause of inflation. But another underlying cause today is too many people with dollars competing for too few goods — and that cannot be cured by changes in monetary or fiscal policy (although faulty policies may exacerbate inflation or even cause it to "run away"). The Arabs, quite sensibly, keep raising the price of their oil in an effort to curb the demand for their valuable — and finite — resource and make it last as long as possible. They also know that high prices will encourage conservation and the development of alternative energy sources. This in turn will help to produce a stable Western economy, which would benefit us all.

That supplies of a finite resource like petroleum would eventually become tight after decades of expanding consumption was recognized decades ago. The subtler idea that productivity of "renewable" resources might also be constrained has not yet sunk in. That the constraints have begun to show has gone largely unnoticed. Lester Brown of Worldwatch Institute[4] has pointed out, however, that peaks of global *per-capita* production of several important commodities of biological origin seem to have been reached and passed.

The commodities and the year of peak per-capita production are: wood (1967), fisheries (1970), beef (1976), mutton (1972), wool (1960), and grains (1976). *Total* production of some of these items has continued to rise, but the supply available *per person* on a worldwide basis has declined since the peak year. It is too soon to say in some cases (grain and beef, for instance) whether these really are the final per-capita peaks and production henceforth will not keep up with population growth, but it does seem clear that ceilings—at least given current treatment of the primary resources (land, soil, fresh water) from which these commodities are produced—are being approached.

In the case of fisheries, the ceilings for *absolute* production may also have been passed. Unless overexploitation of fisheries and destruction of estuarine and oceanic environments are reversed, productivity of fisheries may well drop precipitously in the future. Per capita supplies certainly will continue to decline.

Maintaining annual increases in world grain production has proven more difficult over the past decade than previously. Grain is the mainstay of the diets of people in poor countries; it is the underpinning of meat and poultry production in rich countries. Three of the ten years of the 1970s — 1972, 1974, and 1979 — saw significant declines in total grain production over the preceding years. In each of those years, a population nearly two percent larger had roughly four percent *less* food to share than it had the year before — or six percent less food per person. In rich countries, such a production decline is followed by a slight rise in the price of bread, and large increases in meat prices. In poor countries, it is followed by famine.

Continuing to raise food production each year to keep up with the expanding population is likely to become more and more difficult during the 1980s and 1990s. Food supplies in many of the poorest countries—in Africa and South Asia particularly—have never in recent history been adequate, but on a per-capita basis they have been falling further behind since the early 1970s.[5] Most responsible projections of food production anticipate that this trend will continue and that other poor countries will have increasing problems in meeting their food needs. Greater imports from rich countries, especially the United States, are expected to make up the deficit, but there is good reason to doubt the ability of American agriculture to continue raising production at rates that prevailed in recent decades. We have had our green revolution, and our recent record on soil conservation has been far from perfect. Finally, our high yields are dependent on large inputs of fertilizer, pesticides, and fuel — all derived from petroleum.

Other food commodities have shown signs of reaching production limits. Mutton and beef are luxury foods, available mainly to the rich. Tightening supplies and rising prices of both meats reflect the limited quantity of suitable grazing land and tightening supplies of grain for feed. The trend is likely to continue. If beef supplies do expand very much, it will mean one or more of the following has happened: more grain that could feed the world's poor people is being fed to cattle; herds are being expanded on the available grazing land, which may result in overgrazing and desertification; new grazing land has been opened, which may or may not be suited for long-term grazing; or more efficient breeds of cattle have been developed. There is no question but that any of these changes except the last would have an adverse effect on the world's future food production, at least in the mid- to long term.

The production of wool, of course, is subject to the same constraints as mutton, and it has fallen victim to competition from cheap synthetic substitutes. The synthetics, however, are heavily dependent on oil for their production; some are made from petroleum-based substances. They will not be so cheap or abundant in the future, and there will be renewed need for wool.

Wood is almost a special case. In the overdeveloped countries it is effectively a renewable resource, although replanted trees are often inferior in quality to the original forest's products. In poor countries, tropical, subtropical, and (in South Asia) temperate forests are being rapidly cut down but rarely replanted. Much of the wood is used for fuel, and the disappearance of forests spells a severe fuel shortage for the local people. When wood is unavailable, the poor resort to burning dung and crop residues, which then are no longer available as fertilizers. Thus the disappearance of forests can lead to losses in soil quality and declining food production.

In Brazil, the Amazon forest is being cleared to open the way for "development" and exploitation of that region's mineral resources. By far the most valuable resource of the Amazon basin is the forest — but it will be destroyed by the year 2000 if current cutting rates are maintained, as will most of the planet's remaining tropical forests. If these forest resources were being used rationally and trees were being replanted, production of wood could certainly be maintained, if not increased, indefinitely.

A great deal more than wood is lost in the destruction of the world's forests, especially in the tropics. Tropical rainforests are by far the greatest reservoir of organic diversity. They are the world's most complex ecosystems, with millions of populations and as-yet unnamed species: many potential new foods, medicines, fibers, and other useful commodities.

Wholesale deforestation also results in the loss of the free services formerly provided by the forest ecosystem. Locally or regionally it could include changes to a less stable climate, greater frequency of floods and drought, accelerated soil erosion, and pollution of water supplies. If the bulk of tropical forests are destroyed worldwide, the ensuing climate changes may also be global in scale—which cannot fail to affect agricultural production.

What has all this to do with affluence? Plenty, and we have already seen the early consequences. Faltering grain production has led to rapidly rising food prices, especially of meats produced by grain-feeding. Depletion of oil reserves leads to higher prices of energy and of almost everything produced or manufactured. Prices of fish have risen in response to increased demand relative to supply—and so have prices of wood products and fibers of both natural and synthetic origin.

Since the early 1970s, Americans have seen their material standard of living slipping below what they took for granted ten years earlier. Americans don't fully understand the causes of their eroding material affluence, but they do seem to realize more slippage is coming. In recent polls, the majority of Americans have said they do not expect to be better off five or ten years hence. Many expect to be worse off.

It must never be forgotten, of course, that while Americans are having to settle for a little less, millions in tropical Africa, Asia, and Latin America are also suffering declines in their standards of living. And for them, *any* decline means hunger, perhaps even starvation and death — not just a smaller home and car, less red meat, and more modest vacations. For everyone, problems associated with population growth, resource supplies, and environmental impact can be expected to multiply, intensify, and become increasingly intractable.

Along with frustration of their material aspirations, Americans have become aware of other declines in the quality of their lives. Nothing is as easy as it used to be, from commuting to work to making a purchase to getting appliances repaired. Social problems seem to be increasingly impossible to solve, although taxes keep getting higher and higher, supposedly to pay for the solutions. The result is that people are more dependent on "the system" to do things they formerly did for themselves — usually better. Or to do things that once were unnecessary, such as controlling or cleaning up pollution or protecting the public from criminal attack in public transport.

MOST OF THE LUXURIES, and many of the so-called comforts, of life are not only not indispensible, but positive hindrances to the elevation of mankind.

Henry David Thoreau

Most Americans have noticed that "getting away from it all" is harder and harder to do. Finding a recreational area for hiking, swimming, fishing, skiing, or just communing with nature that isn't overrun with other people is no easy task. Crowding, pollution, and overdevelopment have ruined the charm of many resorts. These are among the personal options that are progressively being foreclosed. Small wonder the public supports protection of the remaining American wilderness areas. Even if you never visit a wilderness, it is part of the quality of your life to know the option exists. And a great many other options seem to have disappeared: breathing clean air in any city; using decent, safe, efficient public transport; walking alone at night in an urban area in safety; conducting any business transaction without hassling with government regulations, codes, and tax problems.

While most people approve the reasons for most regulations — to protect the environment, to protect public health, or to protect people against exploitation by the unscrupulous—the United States seems to be choking itself with overregulation of trivia, while major processes, like the rape of resources, are allowed to go out of control. This nation was founded on the principles of individual freedom and independence. What we have today is tightly restricted freedom and growing interdependence, congestion, and conflict. We are only too vulnerable to any disruption of communications, the transport system, and supplies of fuel, power, food, or water.

An alternative to material economic growth exists: the steady-state economy, which has been described in most detail by economist Herman Daly.[6] The idea, of course, goes back at least to John Stuart Mill, who clearly saw the social disadvantages of perpetual growth as a prime social goal.

Daly has concentrated on constraining the use of non-renewable materials and fossil fuels; the total quantities of each commodity flowing into the economy would be limited by an annual "depletion quota" system. Use of fossil fuels would be severely curtailed and phased out as soon as possible, with renewable (primarily solar) energy sources replacing them. The major supplies of minerals would come from recycling and reclamation from emissions. New materials would be mined or imported only in amounts necessary to replace the small recycling losses.

Daly says nothing about what would happen in parts of the economy outside the energy/materials sectors, nor about how the controlled materials would be distributed within the economy and among industries. These distributions can, of course, change through time. A steady-state economy is not necessarily a static economy. Rather it is likely to be characterized as having *dynamic equilibrium* — somewhat like a mature ecosystem.

Yet economists and business interests feel non-growth is equal to "stagnation" or even decline and death. The concept of "maturity" eludes them, as does the possibility that characteristics of maturity, such as stability, security, and strength, could apply to economic systems as well as to living organisms and ecological systems. A human being does not grow in size between ages 25 and 65, but in the appropriate circumstances he or she does grow in wisdom, experience, compassion, and depth of character. Similarly, an economy that does not grow in the total use of materials and energy might still have growth in services and in many industries and products.

This is not to say that the poor of our country must

continue to be left out. Some mild redistribution and reasonable conservation would allow them a decent standard of living within our present national energy and material budgets without penalizing the rest of us—if the nation were willing to apply them.

There are good reasons to accept the end of material growth in mature societies, even to *reduce* consumption of many things, including energy: to protect what remains of our environment, our resource base, and our people's health.

A further reason for overdeveloped countries to reconcile themselves gracefully to the end of material growth is that, unless they do, there is virtually no hope that the majority of the world's human population will ever leave the abject poverty they now endure. If we—the rich countries—continue to coopt the overwhelming bulk of resources (at ever-mounting cost to ourselves), what remains will be too little and too costly to help the poor. And the costs and consequences will include a horrendous, burdensome legacy for all our descendants: a planet whose carrying capacity for human life has been greatly reduced.

The practitioners of "voluntary simplicity" are headed in the right direction. If the majority of American citizens take up the idea, eventually business and political leaders might be persuaded to follow us and develop a new kind of economy and society not based on material consumption. The future could be a downhill trip, but it doesn't have to be. "A calamity is a time of great opportunity," according to an ancient Chinese proverb. Leading a planned transition to a sustainable world is an opportunity Americans cannot afford to pass up—a chance to help create a brighter future for all of humanity.

1. E.M. Rogers and D. Leonard-Barton, address to the American Association for the Advancement of Science, San Francisco, Jan. 1980.
2. See note 1.
3. *The End of Affluence*, Ballantine Books, 1974.
4. Resource Trends and Population Policy: A Time for Reassessment, *Worldwatch Paper 29*. May 1979. Worldwatch Institute, Washington, D.C.
5. UN Food and Agriculture Organization, 1978. *State of Food and Agriculture, 1977*. FAO, Rome.
6. *Steady-State Economics of Biophysical Equilibriums and Moral Growths*, Freeman, San Francisco, 1977.

Issues

Highlights from The Council on Environmental Quality's 10th Annual Report

Air Quality

• Overall, the nation's air quality is improving. Combined data from 25 major metropolitan areas show that the number of unhealthful days declined by 15 percent between 1974 and 1977 while the number of very unhealthful days declined 32 percent.

• Data from approximately 50 of the most polluted counties across the country show that violations of ambient air quality standards generally either stayed constant or decreased between 1974 and 1977.

• In 1977, the air in 2 of the 41 urban areas for which reliable data were available (New York and Los Angeles) still registered in the "unhealthful" range for more than two-thirds of the days of the year. . . . In 3 . . . air pollution appears to have gotten worse between 1974 and 1977.

• The pollutants that most frequently drove index readings into the "unhealthful" range in the 41 urban areas were carbon monoxide and photochemical oxidants (ozone).

• In January 1979, EPA announced its widely debated decision that the primary standard (designed to protect human health) for ozone would be relaxed from .08 parts per million to .12 parts per million.

• EPA also tightened limitations on emission of sulfur dioxide from new coal-burning power plants.

• Carbon monoxide has shown marked improvement between 1974 and 1977 in the counties monitored, with the greatest change evident in the East.

• States must have State Implementation Plans (SIPs) that spell out in specific detail how federal air pollution goals will be met. Most SIPs are currently in the process of being revised because the 1977 Clean Air Act amendments established deadlines later than those in the original 1970 legislation for attaining ambient air standards.

• The cut-off date by which states should have developed revised SIPs . . . was July 1, 1979. Although most states (44) submitted their plans by late July, only one state, Wyoming, had an approved plan in place by the . . . deadline. . . . However, EPA expressed confidence that most plans would be approved by the fall.

• Current pollution control systems are often found to be malfunctioning because of poor auto maintenance or owner tampering. The Congress has therefore mandated that auto inspection and maintenance programs be instituted in all regions of the country where an extension of the ozone standard attainment date from 1982 to 1987 will be required. . . . Inspection and maintenance programs have become a highly controversial aspect of national air pollution control programs. . . .

• Acid rain is a major environmental problem on both sides of the Atlantic Ocean. . . . In the eastern half of the United States, the acidity of rainfall appears to have increased about 50-fold during the past 25 years. . . . Sweden placed the economic loss to its recreational and commercial fishing industry due to acid rain at $50 to $100 million in 1973.

Water Quality

• Problems with water quality data collection and assessment are still numerous. But the available evidence, suggests that water quality in the United States, is at least not getting worse. . . . There has been little or no overall change in the levels of five major water pollution indicators [fecal coliform bacteria, dissolved oxygen, total phosphorus, total mercury, and total lead] over the 4 water years, 1975 through 1978.

• CEQ made a close examination of trends in water pollution at 44 selected cities on major rivers. . . . Of 149 comparisons of violation rates, 69 showed improvement in water quality, 41 showed degradation, and 39 showed no change.

• As many as two-thirds of the nation's lakes may have serious pollution problems. . . . An estimated 80 percent of more than 3,700 urban lakes in the United States are significantly degraded. . . .

• DDT . . . was banned in 1972 in the United States, but fish from Lake Michigan still contained more than agreed upon maximum safe concentrations of DDT in their flesh as late as 1976. Similar slow declines in fish tissue concentrations have been noted for PCBs and other persistent organic materials in the Great Lakes.

• Controlling pollution from toxic substances in the Great Lakes Basin will be a special challenge. Much of the information on the manufacture and use of toxic chemicals is confidential, so that compilation of a complete list of all substances manufactured in the Great Lakes Basin is very difficult. The IJC [International Joint Commission] has made a start at compiling such a list, which now contains more than 2,800 different compounds.

• Among the major ground water quality problems in the United States is contamination from surface and subsurface waste disposal and storage—including impoundment or burial of industrial wastes. . . . An EPA survey completed in June 1978 has identified more than 133,000 "ponds, pools, lagoons, and pits" used for treatment, storage, or disposal of wastes in the country.

• A special problem for many of the nation's older municipalities in meeting the goals set out in the 1972 water pollution legislation is that of combined sewer overflows. . . . EPA estimates it will cost $106.2 billion for construction and repair of municipal wastewater treatment facilities and sewers between 1978 and 2000. An additional $62 billion is needed for control of storm water runoff.

• Land treatment projects in two communities, Muskegon, Mich., and El Reno, Okla., show the reality and the promise of crop production as a method of treating wastewater. . . . Average grain yields in 1976, 1977, and 1978 on cropland in Muskegon irrigated with wastewater were about 80 bushels per acre, indeed remarkable considering that the sandy soil would otherwise produce only a few bushels of corn per acre. . . . The total crop income has averaged $900,000 during the past 3 years, which offset one-third of the costs of operations and debt retirement for the whole wastewater treatment system.

• The greatest number of public water supply systems in our country are ground water systems, even though a minority of citizens use them. . . . In the next few years, the nation will have to address three basic and difficult problems concerning safety of drinking water: carcinogens in source and finished water . . . drinking water supply in water starved areas . . . and aging distribution systems.

• The world's oceans have come under increasing ecologic pressure from ocean disposal of ordinary and toxic municipal and industrial wastes. . . . Municipal sewage sludge disposal has increased between 1973 and 1978, while industrial waste dumping has dropped by about 50 percent. Paradoxically, the rise in sewage sludge dumping is directly related to the national water cleanup effort.

Toxic Substances and Environmental Health

• There may be 32,000 to 50,000 disposal sites in the United States containing hazardous wastes, and of these, anywhere from 1,200 to 2,000 may pose significant risks to human health or the environment. Most of these dumps are still being used; perhaps 500 to 800 are abandoned.

• In August 1978, the N.Y. State Department of Health . . . investigating residents' complaints of abnormal numbers of miscarriages, birth defects, cancer, and a variety of other illnesses, found that hazardous chemical wastes had leaked from rotted drums buried in the old Love Canal into the basements of nearby homes and into the area's air, water, and soil. . . . Air monitoring equipment identified pollution levels as high as 5,000 times the minimum safe levels.

• In 1978, there was a rise in casualties from toxic transportation accidents, with 45 deaths and 1,411 injuries nationally.

• EPA estimates that only about 10 percent of hazardous wastes are being disposed of in a manner that would comply with regulations that the agency expects to adopt. The vast majority of toxic wastes (80 percent by weight) is being disposed of in nonsecure ponds, lagoons, or landfills. Another 10 percent is being incinerated in a manner that pollutes the air or does not completely detoxify the waste residues.

• EPA reported that 17 industries . . . spend approximately $155 million per year for hazardous waste management. Proper management in accordance with proposed regulations would raise that figure to $750 million annually (or one-quarter of 1 percent of the value of production—$267 billion— of the 17 industries). A survey by the Manufacturing Chemists Association reported only 1 of 475 industry surface impoundments containing hazardous wastes would meet new disposal criteria. . . . Preliminary estimates by the association indicate an expenditure of nearly $900 million would be required.

• No public agency has enough money to clean up all the inactive dumps, costs that have been estimated at $28.4 billion to as much as $55 billion. . . . In June 1979, the Carter Administration proposed a $1.6 billion fund to cover the costs of cleaning up emergencies like Love Canal, and to respond to emergency hazardous substances and oil spills. The fund would be financed through fees levied on the oil and chemical industries together with a federal appropriation.

• Even after adjustments for age, the rate of cancer mortality—deaths due to cancer—has been increasing by 0.5 percent annually in the United States and the rate of incidence—new cases—by 1.6 percent.

• It is very difficult to attribute with any degree of accuracy the observed incidence of cancer to specific factors—pollutants, manufactured chemicals, dietary components, or contaminants. However, a recent government estimate places the fraction of cancer that is related to occupational factors at 20 to 38 percent, for the present and the next several decades. . . . Previous estimates of the amount of cancer due to occupational exposure had been much lower. . . .

• With the constant discovery of new suspected carcinogens in various products . . . it may appear that about anything, if given in sufficient doses, will cause cancer. This is an entirely misleading idea. . . . The evidence so far indicates that substances either do or do not cause cancer. . . . As of 1977, it was estimated that about 1,500 suspected carcinogens had been investigated sufficiently to draw some conclusions. . . . About 600 to 800 had shown substantial, positive evidence of carcinogenicity.

• More and more people began seeking compensation in 1978 and 1979 from various government agencies for radiation damages they claimed to have suffered in the past. . . . About 600 residents of Nevada, Arizona, and Utah . . . have

filed suit against the Department of Energy (DOE). . . .
More than 500 former military men have filed claims with
the Veterans Administration (VA). The VA has turned
down 92 percent of all bomb-related claims because it will
only accept symptoms, diseases, or injuries that turn up
during service or within one year of discharge.

• On February 28, 1979, the EPA Administrator issued
emergency orders suspending the registration of certain
uses of two related herbicides—2,4,5-T and Silvex. . . . The
action was based on human evidence and animal tests, both
indicating that 2,4,5-T, Silvex, and their common contaminant . . . generally known as dioxin, have the potential for
causing miscarriages, birth defects, and other adverse reproductive effects.

• The Toxic Substances Control Act, passed by the
Congress in 1976 after 6 years of effort, represents one of
the most far-reaching, comprehensive, and complex regulatory programs ever attempted by the federal government. . . . Most of this agenda still has to be carried
out. . . . Two groups of chemical substances have been regulated to date under TSCA: polychlorinated biphenyls
(PCBs) and certain chlorofluorocarbons (CFCs).

• Recent studies cast doubt on the primacy of lead-
based paint as a cause of elevated blood lead levels in children. . . . Gasoline lead appears to be an important source
of lead in New York City children's blood.

Municipal Solid Waste

• Municipal waste, which rose at a rate of 5 percent a
year from 1960 to 1970, slowed to a rate of about 2 percent a
year from 1970 to 1978, but is still on the upswing. . . . Total
U.S. municipal waste was estimated at 154 million tons for
1978, the equivalent of 1,400 pounds per person.

• New EPA criteria to be used in identifying "open
dumps" . . . will be far-reaching in their effect. . . .
Facilities that allow open burning or facilities sited in wetlands, floodplains, habitats of endangered species, or recharge zones for principal sources of local drinking water
are generally defined as unacceptable under these regulations and will have to be phased out.

• Squeezed by increasing amounts of waste, disappearing disposal sites, and tightening restrictions on use of the
sites, many local government officials and businesses in-

volved in solid waste disposal have begun to consider alternatives to disposing of wastes in sanitary landfills.

• The two basic alternatives for recycling solid waste are source separation, which is based on sorting of trash in the home or business and appropriate reuse of its various components; and centralized resource recovery, which usually involves burning trash at a central facility for its energy value and may also include separation of some components for recycling.

• The United States converted less than 1 percent of its municipal wastes to energy in 1977. . . . Another 7 percent of the nation's municipal solid waste was being recovered for its material value by recycling centers and other source separation programs.

• In 1978, 40 cities had some kind of source separation and collection program for the full gamut of recyclables, and another 196 collected newspapers. More than 3,000 independent voluntary community recycling centers were in operation . . . and more than 500 offices have paper recycling programs.

IT IS DIFFICULT for people living now, who have become accustomed to the steady exponential growth in the consumption of energy from the fossil fuels, to realize how transitory the fossil-fuel epoch will eventually prove to be when it is viewed over a longer span of human history.

M. King Hubbert

• EPA has estimated that a maximum feasible source separation effort nationwide could result in the recycling of about 25 percent, by weight, of total gross discards.

• The cost of collecting, sorting, and baling recyclables generally exceeds the revenues from their sales. Source separation is an economically viable proposition for most towns that have instituted it because it is a cheaper way of getting rid of wastes than operating a sanitary landfill or town incinerator.

• The percentage of paper products made from recycled

fiber . . . was about 22 percent in 1977. . . . Less than 10 percent of all steel produced in this country is currently made from scrap steel that has gone through a cycle of use, and almost all represents industrial rather than consumer waste. . . . Only 3 percent of glass production uses recycled raw materials. . . . For source separation to grow as a waste disposal method in the United States, long-term markets will have to be found for the systems' products.

• Interest in centralized waste processing for energy recovery has grown. . . . The General Accounting Office was able to identify 20 trash-to-energy plants in operation and another 10 under construction at the end of 1977. Advanced planning had been completed for 30 more, and preliminary planning had begun on another 70 facilities.

• EPA estimated in 1973 . . . that the maximum possible energy yield from trash was about 900 trillion Btus . . . enough energy to meet the home and office lighting needs of the entire nation.

• Technological barriers are probably the least serious obstacle to wider centralized resource recovery at this time. Problems can be minimized by employing proven, relatively simple trash-to-energy systems now in use in both Europe and the United States.

• Trash-burning plants have certain very appealing environmental characteristics when compared with other energy facilities. They produce no radioactive wastes. Nor do they emit large quantities of sulfur dioxide.

• Nevertheless, trash-to-energy plants do emit measurable quantities of fine particulates, certain potentially hazardous organic compounds, viruses and bacteria, and toxic elements such as calmium, lead, and mercury. . . . Health hazards, such as harmful dusts and vapors, infectious disease and viruses, and excessive machine noise, may also occur inside the facilities.

• American political and business institutions are structually ill-adapted to centralized resource recovery. . . . Utilities, which might logically be the best market for the energy produced and are prime candidates for owning and operating recovery facilities, appear loath to get involved.

• Solely on the basis of the energy they produce, complex trash-to-energy facilities definitely are not yet economically competitive. . . . Resource recovery facilities are able to break even or turn a profit only because the revenue they receive from sale of steam or fuels is supplemented by the amount the municipality pays them for getting rid of the wastes, known as a "tipping fee". . . .

• Many people in fact now think that the best approach in developing a centralized recovery facility is to design the system to work in tandem with source separation at the outset.

• The Resource Conservation Committee, a special interagency Cabinet-level group, gave special consideration in its report issued June 1979 to a mandatory national system of deposits and refunds for beverage containers. . . . Staff studies . . . indicated such legislation would: Reduce litter volume by 35 percent; . . . Reduce the amount of solid waste by up to 2 million tons per year, or 0.5 to 1.5 percent; . . . Eliminate between 4,900 and 10,400 jobs in the glass container production industry and between 14,200 and 22,000 jobs in the metal can production industry over a 5-year period; . . . Create between 80,000 and 100,000 new jobs in the beverage distribution and retail sectors.

Energy

• In 1978 U.S. demand for energy increased slightly. . . . U.S. energy consumption in 1978 totaled 78.2 quadrillion British thermal units (QBtus), topping the consumption of 76.5 QBtus recorded in 1972. . . .

• An indication of increasing energy efficiency in industry is a continuing decline in the energy required per unit of national output. In 1978 the energy/gross national product (GNP) ratio declined 2 percent, to reach about 56,400 Btus per dollar of GNP (1972 dollars). By comparison, the ratio was about 61,200 Btus per dollar in 1972.

• Under law, the average fuel economy for each manufacturers' entire fleet of new cars for the year had to be 18 miles per gallon (mpg) by 1978, and 27.5 mpg by 1985. . . . Average new car sales-weighted fuel economy, as determined by EPA's Federal Test Procedure, has risen steadily from a low of 14.4 mpg in 1974 to 19.6 mpg in 1978. However, these improvements have not been fully realized in performance on the road.

• In November 1978 the President signed into law the National Energy Act, which culminated 18 months of intense congressional and public debate. . . . Several provisions of the National Energy Act of 1978 are expected to produce more efficient and productive use of energy and thereby reduce energy demand including . . . weatherization grants at an annual authorized level of $200 million; . . . [and] grants to states totaling $900 million to assist schools and hospitals, fund energy audits, and install energy conservation and solar measures. . . . In addition DOE is required to set energy efficiency standards for a wide range of appliances. . . .

• The possible environmental risks of converting coal and shale to oil or gas are significant. The possible hazards from toxic trace metals and organic carcinogens—both in the conversion process and in the oil and gas products—are troubling. . . .

• The effects of synfuel development on land and water must also be carefully considered. Assuming that the mix of domestic energy in 1990 includes about 1.25 million barrels per day of synthetic fuels derived from coal, about 25 plants would be needed . . . in the West, about 500 square miles of land would be strip mined over the 30-year lifetime of the plants. . . . If the energy mix also included 400,000 barrels per day of synfuels from shale, about 100 to 200 additional square miles would be required.

• The total water consumption of the synfuel industry outlined would be enough to irrigate roughly 100,000 acres of agricultural land per year. This much water may be physically available . . . in the West, but it may already be committed to . . . other purposes. . . . New towns to house plantworkers will put further pressure on water supplies.

• Worldwide use of all fossil fuels, including coal-based synthetic fuels, may have to be curbed if present concerns about the impact of carbon dioxide are confirmed. The primary concern with increased carbon dioxide emissions centers around the so-called "greenhouse" effect—the trapping of outgoing infrared radiation from the earth's surface.

• On June 20, 1979, President Carter delivered to the Congress the nation's first Presidential message on solar energy. . . . The President called for a combined effort by the federal government, state and local governments, industry, and private citizens, to achieve a national goal of meeting 20 percent of our energy needs with solar and renewable resources by the end of the century.

• The federal financial commitment to developing and commercializing renewable energy technologies were at a level of $358 million in fiscal year 1978, will rise to over $1 billion in fiscal year 1980.

• The most serious accident in the history of U.S. nuclear power began in the early morning hours of March 28, 1979 caused by a chain of what was thought to be highly improbable events. . . . Prior to the accident, the Nuclear Regulatory Commission had already taken a second look at the Reactor Safety Study (The Rasmussen Report), . . . widely quoted as concluding that the risk to the general population from light water reactor nuclear power plants was negligible. . . . The NRC announced that it was withdrawing any explicit or implicit past endorsements of the executive summary of the report. . . .

• In May 1979, President Carter reaffirmed his opposition to the construction of the Clinch River Breeder Reactor (CRBR) project.

• The Interagency Review Group on Nuclear Waste Management (IRG) made its final report to the President in March 1979. The report concluded that . . . "Existing and future nuclear waste from military and civilian activities . . . should be isolated from the biosphere. . . ."

Natural Resources

• *The Second National Water Assessment* of the U.S. Water Resources Council (WRC), released December, 1978, found shortages of surface water in several regions of the country, as well as overdrafts of ground water—resulting in declining water tables—in parts of the High Plains, Arizona, and California. The WRC report concluded that there is a special need for better conservation and management, particularly in irrigated areas of the West.

• In some areas, declining water tables will cause abandonment of water-depleting activities before the water is totally consumed because of the increasing cost of the energy required to bring it to the surface. This has already begun in the Trans-Pecos areas of Texas. . . . Abandonment of large irrigated areas began recently when prices for natural gas used to run the pumps made continued production uneconomical.

• Intensive irrigation-based farming is increasing the soil salinity on several hundred thousand acres in California's San Joaquin Valley. According to a recent federal-state study, some farmers have been forced to switch to salt-tolerant crops, and annual crop losses from saline soils now exceed $30 million per year.

• Despite an investment by the federal government of more than $20 billion in support of soil conservation practices since 1935, erosion of agricultural lands remains one of the nation's most serious problems. . . . The 1977 National Resource Inventory Estimates show a national average loss from water-induced erosion in excess of 4 billion tons.

• The nationwide loss of plant nutrients due to erosion is significant. . . . USDA estimates the annual cost of replacing all of the nitrogen and phosphorus and one-fourth of the potassium lost by soil erosion at . . . $18 billion in 1979 dollars.

• Although 48 of the 50 states have adopted farmland preservation measures, most states have dealt with the issue primarily through provisions allowing preferential property tax assessment. . . . Other types of preservation programs include . . . purchase of development rights, agricultural districting, and transfer of development rights.

• Debate continued through 1979 over the disposition of Alaska's vast wilderness. . . . on December 1, 1978, President Carter issued an historic series of proclamations invoking the Antiquities Act of 1906, which set aside 56 million acres as 17 national monuments in Alaska.

• The largest and most controversial wilderness issue of 1978 and 1979 was the Forest Service's Roadless Area Review and Evaluation Process (RARE II). . . . In the RARE II Final Environmental Impact Statement released January 4, 1979, the Department of Agriculture recommended that 15 million acres of National Forest land be designated as wilderness.

• The Bureau of Land Management, as required by the Federal Land Policy and Management Act, has begun a separate wilderness inventory and evaluation process on 174 million acres of its lands.

• The "Omnibus Parks" Act of 1978 added eight new river segments (a total of approximately 696 miles) to the National Wild and Scenic Rivers System. . . . The System now protects a total of more than 2,317 miles of 27 rivers.

• The "Omnibus Parks" Act also established the first new national trails since two initial national scenic trails were created . . . the Continental Divide Trail, spanning a distance of 3,100 miles along the Rocky Mountains from the

Canadian to the Mexican borders, and four National Historic Trials.
- An increasingly important national problem in the future may be overcutting of privately held forest land, particularly land held by large companies. A study released in January 1979 by the Library of Congress concluded that the Forest Service, farm, and other small rural landowners appear to be cutting their softwood timber at a rate closer to a long-term sustained yield level than timber companies. . . . In 1977, the timber industry's . . . cut exceeded growth by 21 percent.
- Serious conflicts continue to exist between ORV users and desert homesteaders, hikers, scientists, and environmentalists. . . .

Ecology and Living Resources:
Coastal Ecology and Shellfish
- Coastal waters . . . are the nexus of several major natural systems. They directly abut the land and are affected by activities there—not only on coastal lands in the immediate vicinity, but also on land great distances away. . . . Human activities have a profound impact on this complex system in ways that are sometimes difficult to unravel and often unexpected.
- Urban and suburban watersheds release more suspended and dissolved substances, including nutrients, into streams than do natural watersheds. . . . In addition, in an urbanized watershed, peak flows after a heavy rain are very high and pass quickly.
- Molluscs can be used as indicators of environmental quality both by measuring the amount of pollutants accumulated in shellfish tissue and by keeping track of harvest statistics.
- Two EPA studies . . . indicate that molluscs still contained DDT residues 4 years after the use of the chemical was banned in 1972. . . . The situation for PCBs, the manufacture and some uses of which have now been banned, is more alarming. . . . , Even molluscs in otherwise relatively clean waters show as much as 50 ppb. Far higher values—even above 600 ppb—have been observed in molluscs from . . . Boston Harbor, Narragansett Bay, R.I., and Rockaway on the south shore of Long Island. . . .
- Mussels have also shown the presence of radionuc-

lides, for the most part apparently a legacy of the weapons testing program of the 1950s and early 1960s. However, one sample from Plymouth, Mass., suggests that the mussels are concentrating effluents from a nearby nuclear reactor.

• Records of commercial catches of clams and oysters . . . indicate that the number of molluscs in coastal waters has been steadily declining during the years. . . . When government records and landings statistics were initiated in 1879, an annual harvest of 117 million pounds of oysters was being taken from Chesapeake Bay alone. This figure is more than five times what the bay now provides, and is more than double the present total U.S. consumption of oysters.

• Causes of declines include overfishing, habitat loss and deterioration, pollution, economic developments, natural diasters, and political and sociological considerations. . . . The Department of the Interior's National Estuary Study of 1970 shows an annual loss of estuarine habitat . . . that translates to 0.21 percent annually from 1950 to 1969. A study for the U.S. House of Representatives published in 1970, indicates an annual loss of 0.36 percent between 1947 and 1967.

• Even the building of a sewage treatment plant has the potential to adversely affect shellfish habitat by altering salinity. Trouble arose for the shellfish of Great South Bay when attempts were made to solve Long Island's sewage disposal and water quality problems.

• Intensified agriculture, urbanization, construction, and lumbering, have greatly accelerated rates of sedimentation . . . During a 36-year period, 6,000 to 7,000 acres of productive oyster reefs were smothered in Matagorda Bay, Tex.

• There is general agreement that pollution has been a major cause of the decline of molluscan shellfish within recent decades. It is the principal problem confronting the commercial hard clam fishery, and a major one for the soft clam and oyster fisheries.

• The most recent National Shellfish Register shows 4 million of the 14.6 million acres of commercial shellfish waters to be closed . . . Prohibited polluted areas (closed to shellfishing) have increased from 16.1 percent of all commercial and noncommercial shellfish waters in 1971 to 18.5 percent in 1974 . . .

• Several laws provide mechanisms for protecting the

coastal zone, especially its fisheries. These laws, if carefully implemented during a period of years, are adequate to protect the resource and should result in a healthy coastal environment. However, . . . complete implementation of these laws has so far not taken place, resulting in the continued deterioration of the resource, albeit at a lessened pace.

Human Settlements and Land Use
• In the 1970s two demographic trends have become particularly striking in all parts of the country: the trends toward small households and population dispersal in rural areas.
• In the 1960s, when population grew at 1.3 percent per year, new households were formed at the rate of 1.8 percent per year. But since 1970, with population increasing at 0.8 percent per year, households are being formed at the rate of 2.6 percent per year. Between 1970 and 1977, average household size dropped 10 percent, from 3.14 persons to 2.86 persons.
• Between 1970 and 1978, nearly 350 nonmetropolitan counties, containing about 8.5 million people, grew at a rate three times (16.7 percent) that of the nation—rates that are typically associated with developing nations, although there the growth is from high birth rates, not migration.
• The migration to rural areas represents a reversal of the previous decline in rural population, but not a return to a rural society. A continuation of the 1970 to 1975 rates to the end of the century would still result in a nonmetropolitan population proportionately less than that of 1950.
• Efforts during the past year to site three new energy facilities in coastal areas reveal many of the inadequacies of the current planning process for such plants, as well as the difficulty of evaluating numerous and varying environmental effects. . . . The proposed facilities were two major oil refineries on the East Coast—at Eastport, Maine, and Portsmouth, Va.—and a large liquified natural gas (LNG) storage facility at Point Concepción, Calif. . . .
• The siting and constructing of major inland energy extraction and production facilities is fostering rapid growth in certain rural areas.
• The vulnerability of coastal resources and the intensity of the land use conflicts there provided an impetus for creating a federal/state land management partnership under

the Coastal Zone Mangement Act of 1972 (CZMA). . . . Between 1974 and September 1979, $70 million was distributed to states to help them develop coastal management programs. . . . To date, 15 of 35 eligible states have received federal approval for their coastal management plans.

• The CZMA has encouraged states to improve the coordination and simplification of governmental regulatory procedures. . . . The federal consistency provisions under CZMA allow states to review federal agency activities (except those on federal lands), to insure that they conform to federally approved state coastal management plans.

• The accomplishments to date under the CZMA are significant, but weaknesses in this innovative land use management approach do exist, including variations in state programs and the fact that some states have no programs at all.

ONLY WITHIN the moment of time represented by the present century has one species – man – acquired significant power to alter the nature of his world.

It is ironic to think that man might determine his own future by something so seemingly trivial as the choice of an insect spray.

Rachel Carson

• The Chesapeake Bay illustrates many of these shortcomings all too clearly. . . . Toxics, such as the Kepone that still persists in the James River; municipal sewage, estimated at 400 million gallons per day; and oil from nearly 800 petroleum spills per year, have closed shellfish areas, reduced fish catches, and destroyed valuable wildlife. . . . Yet because of state inaction, the bay has no comprehensive, integrated multistate coastal management. . . .

• In many cities, young middle-class professionals are renovating buildings in rundown city neighborhoods . . . for residential use. . . . The impact of such change can be nega-

tive as well as positive. . . . A study of 30 cities found that
48 percent of the neighborhoods were predominantly black
before new middle-income residents moved in, while only 2
percent remained so afterwards. Other studies have shown a
similar displacement of renters, blue-collar workers, the un-
employed, and the elderly.
  • The National Commission on Neighborhoods, in its
March 1979 report to the President, urged public and private
actions to maintain neighborhood diversity and assist current residents.
  • During fiscal year 1980, Amtrak trains will run 34 percent fewer train-miles than the current system would have in
that year. However, the recommended system will retain
approximately 80 percent of the passenger-miles included in
the current system and will serve 91 percent of the passengers who would have used the system.

Noise
  • Noise is the most frequently mentioned undesirable
neighborhood condition in central cities. . . .
  • Perhaps the most serious consequence of noise exposure is its effect on hearing. . . . It is estimated that as many
as 20 to 25 million people—about 1 in 10 in the United
States—are exposed to noises of duration and intensity sufficient to cause a permanent reduction in their ability to
hear. Of these, 10 to 15 million are estimated to be workers
exposed to excessive noise on the job.
  • The idea that people become totally accustomed to
noise is a myth. Although we may get used to constant
low-level noise, the human body will make automatic and
unconscious responses when exposed to sudden or loud
sounds. . . . Growing evidence strongly suggests a link between noise and cardiovascular problems, especially hyper-
tension.
  • In the past decade the number of local noise control
ordinances has increased dramatically. In 1972 only 59
municipalities had some type of noise law. . . . Today, more
than 50 percent of the U.S. municipal population lives in
localities having some degree of noise legislation.
  • State and local noise control programs are often underfunded, which generally means that ordinances or other
regulations cannot be implemented. In 1977, 27 states had
enacted noise legislation, but only 20 states had budgets to

support legislation. Only 11 states were spending more than $0.01 per capita per year on noise control programs.
• The Noise Control Act of 1972 specifies that EPA shall regulate new products that are "major sources of noise". . . . Since 1972, EPA has identified 10 products as major noise sources: medium and heavy trucks, motorcycles, buses, garbage trucks, wheel and crawler tractors (used in construction), portable air compressors, pavement breakers (or jack hammers), rock drills, power lawnmowers, and truck refrigeration units.
• OSHA proposed a revised workplace noise standard in 1974 that would keep the former standard of 90 dB for 8 hours, but would tighten other parts of the existing regulation. This proposed revised standard has not yet been adopted. . . . Under authority of the 1972 Act, EPA recommended that OSHA adopt a more stringent standard of 85 dB for 8-hour exposures. . . .
• Hearing protectors have sometimes been advocated as an all-purpose alternative to engineering controls of noise, but they are an inferior alternative. Hearing protectors are by far the least expensive method for reducing noise exposure, but . . . workers resist wearing them, either because they need to hear the sounds around them for reasons of safety or communication, or because the devices are uncomfortable. In addition, their effectiveness in practice is limited.

NEPA
• The Council's new NEPA regulations . . . were promulgated in final form in November 1978. The new regulations . . . are binding on all federal agencies. . . . They are designed to produce more useful, readable, tightly focused documents and to reduce delays through a variety of changes.
• One of the most significant innovations in the new NEPA regulations is the "scoping" process. When a federal agency determines that a proposed action requires preparation of an EIS, it must take prompt action, at the very beginning of the planning process, to identify the important issues that require full analysis and to separate those issues from the less significant matters.
• Another important innovation is the requirement that when an EIS has been prepared, the agency must produce a

written record of its decision on the proposal. . . . The record . . . must state whether all practicable means for
mitigating environmental harm have been adopted and, if
not, why not.

• Impact statements must be analytic rather than encyc-
lopedic and must be written in plain language. The regulations state that EISs should normally have fewer than 150
pages . . .

• The regulations also address a long-standing
controversy—the possibility of conflicts of interest when
applicants for federal permit or funding approval participate
in the environmental analysis of the project. The regulations
require that the EIS be prepared by the federal agency or by
a contractor selected by the agency. . . .

• An important feature of the regulations is improved
integration of NEPA procedures with other environmental
review laws and federal permit requirements.

• One of the most difficult problems in NEPA implementation during the years has been integrating the EIS
process with the legislative process. The new regulations
streamline the procedures for legislative EISs by allowing a
single legislative EIS (instead of a draft and final) to be
submitted to Congress under certain circumstances.

• After 7 years of divided opinion in government, the
Carter Administration approached the issue of whether and
how NEPA applies to federal actions abroad in a way sensitive both to environmental and foreign policy concerns. . . .
Executive Order 12114 signed on January 4, 1979 . . . requires that federal agencies prepare environmental impact
statements for major federal actions that have significant
environmental effects on the global commons (e.g., oceans
and Antarctica). Second, under certain circumstances agencies must prepare concise environmental reviews. . .

• The Supreme Court's opinion in *Andrus* v. *Sierra
Club* lends strong judicial support to the new NEPA regulations and CEQ's continuing efforts to reform the EIS process. The Court quoted extensively from the regulations on
such diverse subjects as the purpose of environmental impact statements, the timing of EIS preparation, the definition of an EIS, and the definition of "major federal action."

• The decision of the First Circuit in *Public Service Co.
of New Hampshire* v. *NRC* continues and strengthens a
series of NEPA cases holding that substantive requirements

in NEPA's Section 101 and 102 (1) give agencies authority to minimize adverse environmental damage, even when the agency's statutory charter does not authorize affirmative measures to protect the environment.

• During 1978, there were 114 lawsuits challenging federal actions under NEPA. This continues the levelling-off trend in NEPA litigation observed over the past 3 years. The most frequent complaint in 1978 NEPA lawsuits, comprising 57 percent of all allegations, is that agencies should have prepared an EIS but failed to do so. The second most common allegation is that an EIS is inadequate.

• During the 9-year period January 1970 through December 1978 . . . lawsuits were filed [regarding] . . . less than 10 percent of all federal proposals for which an EIS was prepared.

• A review of these 1,052 NEPA lawsuits reveals that 103 cases involved specific energy projects. . . . of these . . . 103, only 17 resulted in temporary or preliminary injunctions related to NEPA issues. . . . NEPA litigation and preliminary injunctions have not presented a significant obstacle to the development of energy projects.

• Federal environmental laws other than NEPA have been the subject of increasing litigation. . . . Roughly two-thirds of the approximately 750 lawsuits pending against EPA at the end of 1978 have been industry challenges to regulations. By comparison, citizen lawsuits and mandatory court enforcement actions represent less than 15 percent of lawsuits against EPA.

The Global Environment

• Throughout the tropical world, forests are disappearing at alarming rates. . . . A United Nation's estimate, based on observation in 13 countries, puts the net loss at an area roughly the size of Virginia per year. Estimates from U.S. government agencies . . . indicate the losses may be closer to 20 million hectares (50 million acres) per year. If the latter estimate is correct, the world's closed forests . . . would decline from one-fifth of the earth's land surface to one-sixth of the land surface by the year 2000.

• Virtually all this loss of forests is taking place in or near the tropics. Environmental damage from deforestation in these areas can be extreme . . . Intensified ruinous flooding, which has followed denudation of mountain slopes in many countries throughout history, is occurring increasingly today in tropical watersheds.

• The soils and other conditions of tropical forests are quite unlike those of the temperate zone. In many places, the soil is so seriously degraded after deforestation that the original forest will not grow again, and the land cannot support crops or pasture for more than a few years.

• Tropical forests are enormously diverse. . . . But species may be of very limited geographic distribution, and because they have no means of wide dispersal, once they are gone, there is no recolonization from outside.

• The importance of this loss [of species] becomes obvious when one considers . . . that one-quarter of the prescription drugs dispensed in the United States today are either derived directly from wild plants or are invented using chemical clues derived from wild species. . . . as many as half come from tropical forests; of these, . . . The genetic resources of wild plants are also valuable for breeding new characteristics, such as disease or pest resistance, into food plants. They may even supply new food plant species. . . .

ONE LOOK at the rush-hour jam in the subway and you know why no one rides it any more.

John Ciardi

• The principal direct causes of tropical forest loss are clearing for agriculture, fuelwood gathering, and industrial timbering. But behind these immediate causes are more fundamental social and economic problems—lack of agricultural development, great inequalities in land tenure and income, rapidly growing populations, and rising unemployment.

• Industrial forestry is increasing rapidly, especially in Southeast Asia.

• The World Bank has altered its policy for forestry loans. The Bank announced in 1978 that instead of supporting only industrial forestry projects, it would also support environmentally protective forestry, rural development forestry (for example, establishment of village woodlots for fuelwood), and institution-building projects that emphasize education and research in forestry and agroforestry.

• Rapid deforestation in the tributary watersheds of the Panama Canal Zone is one of the complex of causes leading to lowered water levels in the canal system. If current trends continue, by the year 2000 the Republic of Panama might take over from the United States a "worthless ditch." Panama and the United States are aware of the danger and are planning cooperative action to restore and stabilize the capacity of the canal.

• At its July 1979 meeting, the International Whaling Commission . . . voted to: Halt whaling from factory ships on the high seas (except for hunting of the relatively numerous minkes) . . . Reduce killing of the commercially valuable but jeopardized sperm whales by more than three-quarters; . . . Establish a whale sanctuary in most of the Indian Ocean.

• The possibility of global climate change induced by an increase of carbon dioxide in the atmosphere is the subject of intense discussion and controversy among scientists. . . . Many scientists believe that the amount of CO_2 in the atmosphere could double over the hundred years ending in the middle of the next century. . . . The result could be a 2° to 3° Celsius rise in temperature in the middle latitudes, with larger increases in the upper, lower, and polar regions.

• These CO_2-induced changes could conceivably affect the exent and stability of Greenland and Antarctic ice with consequent rising sea levels and inundation of low-lying coastal areas and changes in the productivity of ocean fisheries. Precipitation and growing seasons for crops could be greatly altered, possibly disrupting world agriculture.

• With increasing competing demands for land available for disposal of low-level radioactive waste, several more nations are looking toward the oceans as an alternative to land burial. . . . The countries most active in disposal of radioactive wastes at sea have been Belgium, the Netherlands, Switzerland, and the United Kingdom, with the greatest share of the radioactive waste coming from the United Kingdom.

• The worst oil spill in history began June 3, 1979, with the blowout of IXTOC No. 1, a well being drilled in the Bay of Campeche by PEMEX, Mexico's national oil company. Estimates of the oil spilled ranged from 10,000 to 30,000 barrels per day. . . .

• Convening in Paris in May 1979, the OECD environment ministers reported improved environmental protection over the past decade, at affordable cost. . . . They note that the short-term net employment effects have been positive; the impact on inflation has been on the whole moderate, averaging 0.1 to 0.3 percent per annum; and the effect on the rate of economic growth in the short run has been neutral, perhaps even slightly positive. Overall, expenditures by OECD countries on pollution abatement amounted to 1 to 2 percent of GNP.

• A fundamental factor shaping the quality of the environment for humankind is the spectacular growth in human population in this century. In 1930, the world's population stood at 2 billion, but by 1975—only 45 years later—it had doubled to 4 billion. . . . According to the estimates, world population may stabilize at 8 to 11 billion early in the 21st century.

Economics

• It sometimes appears that regulation, or any other government action for that matter, is judged with reference to one narrow national economic goal—lower prices.

• Although environmental regulations can contribute to inflation, they—or any other programs—must be judged on broader grounds.

• Private costs of production are those the producer actually bears—labor charges, the cost of capital, rent, utilities, and so on. Social costs include . . . certain other costs that some producers in the past have been able to escape paying—for example, the medical costs incurred by those subjected to the air pollution from a nearby plant. . . . Environmental legislation was drafted in response to this divergence between private and social costs. It was based on the clear recognition that existing market prices were giving incorrect signals to consumers by understating what society was giving up to have these goods. . . .

• Although no one likes paying more for the same product, the higher prices that may result from regulation may improve the overall allocation of the nation's resources.

• Environmental regulation can also be viewed as adding to the size of the standard market basket. That is, regulation allows consumers to enjoy not only the same clothes, foodstuffs, housing, and so on as before, but also more environmental amenities.

• The criticism that environmental regulation slows down the rate of growth of GNP must be viewed with care. As in the case of inflation, environmental regulation may do just what it is accused of doing, but to the nation's overall benefit and with its complete, though tacit, agreement.

• A report to CEQ of existing studies found major divergencies among estimates of air and water pollution control benefits. . . . For example, even after expressing estimates in 1978 dollars and standardizing for a 20 percent improvement in air quality, the study found that estimates of the health benefits of controlling air pollution from stationary sources still ranged from $1.8 billion to $14.4 billion.

• Because the ranges identified in the report to CEQ were so large, the study went further and selected a "most reasonable point estimate" (the single, most likely value) for both air and water pollution control benefits. . . . According to the study, the annual benefits realized in 1978 from measured improvements in air quality since 1970 could be reasonably valued at $21.4 billion. Of this total, $17 billion represented reductions in mortality and morbidity, $2.0 billion reduced soiling and cleaning costs, $0.7 billion increased agricultural output, $0.9 billion prevention of corrosion and other materials damage, and $0.8 billion increases in property values.

• The total annual benefits to be enjoyed by 1985 as a result of the nation's water pollution control legislation are estimated at about $12.3 billion per year, with recreation benefits accounting for $6.7 billion. . . .

• Between 1970 and 1978, federal environmental legislation added, on the average, slightly more than three-tenths of one percentage point to the annual rate of increase of the CPI [Consumer Price Index]. . . . With much of the required pollution control equipment now in place, the future contribution of existing environmental regulations to inflation will shrink. . . . between 1979 and 1986, federal environmental regulations will add between one- and two-tenths of one percentage point to the annual inflation rate.

• Air and water pollution controls will serve to stimulate employment during the entire 16-year period 1970–1986. By creating jobs in the pollution control equipment industry and jobs for those who operate and maintain this equipment, environmental protection reduces the unemployment rate by an average of one-fourth of one percentage point per year.

• Federal air and water pollution programs have a mixed effect on real GNP. . . . Between 1970 and 1977, real GNP was higher because of the stimulus provided by pollution control programs than it would have been in their absence. In 1972, the difference was $14.4 billion, or 0.9 of 1 percent of real GNP. However, after 1977, air and water pollution control expenditures began to exert some drag on the economy. . . .

• CEQ estimates indicate that the cost of complying with all existing federal pollution control and environmental quality programs in 1978 was $26.9 billion. . . . Over the 10-year period from 1978 to 1987, total incremental spending in response to all federal environmental programs is projected at $477.6 billion.

• The resources devoted to pollution control are not inconsiderable. Thus, it is reasonable to ask whether the nation's environmental goals might be met in a less expensive manner. . . . Effluent charges and marketable permits are the two forms of economic incentives that have received the most attention when alternative kinds of environmental policy are considered. In principle, both save money, but in practice it may not always be possible to reap all the savings these methods appear to offer.

A Case of Tired Geology

by Daniel Yergin

In the 1970s, the United States followed the path of least resistance and became increasingly addicted to imported oil. Our oil imports went from 20 percent to about 50 percent of our consumption. And, indeed, our imports doubled since 1972, at the very time when the declared policy was to decrease our oil imports.

This is an alarming and dangerous situation economically, and we can see it in terms of reduced growth rates, in terms of inflation, in terms of unemployment. And it is an alarming political situation, because of what it means for American foreign policy, what it means for our vulnerability to events in a very unstable part of the world. The question that we face in "Energy Future" is, what is the alternative to imported oil?

Most people who know the situation will agree we are overly dependent on imported oil. The real disagreement is what to do about it. We examined the conventional energy alternatives and came to the conclusion they don't provide much of an alternative to the extra barrels of imported oil that we see the United States using. Because we think the United States is on a track today where it could go from 8½ to 9 million barrels of oil imports to the point a decade from now where it will be importing 14 million barrels a day. Of course, it's very unclear how we could possibly pay for that oil, whether our dollar would be worth anything by that point, and where we could possibly get the oil. So we can see that the track we're on really is a track that leads to disaster.

We think that everything should be done to increase domestic oil and gas production. But the real challenge is to prevent American gas and oil production from slipping further. It has slipped dramatically in the 1970s, despite the increasing incentives for new oil and new gas. We do have a case in the United States of tired geology. If we wanted to maintain our oil production at its current levels, by the end of the 1980s we would have to find 4 billion barrels of oil reserves in the United States every year between now and 1990. There has been only one year in the last 30 when we found more than 3 billion barrels. So the prospects for oil and gas being a major alternative to those extra barrels of imported oil look slight at this point.

We do think there might be some growth in coal, that coal might grow as much as 50 percent in the 1980s. And that will provide a small alternative to those extra barrels of imported oil. Synthetic fuels will not make any impact at all until the 1990s.

On the other hand — and to our surprise — we came to the conclusion there really are two alternatives to extra barrels of imported oil that are very promising.

One is what we call conservation energy, which we think will be America's major new energy source in the 1980s. It's the quickest, it's the cheapest, it's the most abundant, it's the safest, and it's the most accessible. We call it conservation energy so that one can see that we can buy so many BTUs of energy by investing in the North Slope of Alaska — or we can buy them by investing in housing insulation. We think that we've only begun to scratch the surface in the United States, and that the potential is huge.

And when I talk about conservation energy I'm not talking about cutting back, scarcity, rationing, or sacrifice at the expense of economic growth — the bad image of conservation. I'm talking about greater efficiency in the use of energy. Just as we increase the productivity of labor, so we can increase the productivity of energy.

People used to think you had to have an increase in energy consumption to have an increase in growth. We argue strongly in "Energy Future" that the relationship is now reversed. The more energy we use, the more it will penalize economic growth. The best way to protect economic growth is through energy efficiency. It's really a choice between exporting dollars to buy oil and letting somebody use those dollars to buy gold, or investing those dollars in the United States: in new factories, in homes, in new automobiles, in creating jobs, and improving our standard of living.

It's possible at an outward barrier that the United States today could be using 30 to 40 percent less energy than it does — and have the same or higher standard of living. I'm not saying that that is what's going to happen. We've seen, however, in the industrial sector, that this is possible.

Gillette since 1973 has reduced its energy consumption in absolute terms by 30 percent, while its sales are up 34 percent. We have IBM, which in 1973 set out to reduce its energy consumption in 34 major facilities around the country by 10 percent. Accidentally it found it reduced its energy consumption by 50 percent — and with remarkably little investment. Neither IBM nor Gillette are exactly hippie companies. They show us in a hardheaded, practical, good business way that the possibilities of using less energy with very little penalty indeed are possible. IBM saved well in excess of $100 million. So this also is a way to fight rising costs and inflation.

What we really should be thinking about in the 1980s is whether we should have a goal of zero energy growth in the United States or even a goal of reducing our energy consumption by 20 percent by the year 1990. That's what our politicians should be debating, when they talk about energy in the political campaign. And seeing that as the best single thing we can do to encourage economic growth.

Beyond that, in the 1990s, we see a growing potential for so-called solar or renewable energies. It's possible that by the year 2000 we could be getting as much energy from various forms of solar energy as we get today from all of our imported oil. I say it's possible. We know pretty definitely that conservation energy can really deliver the goods. The solar renewables are less certain. We need to know more. But there is at least enough reason to think that that potential is there, that we should be doing what we can to give solar a chance now. We should be encouraging solar and conservation — not for ideological reasons, not for moral reasons, not for altruistic reasons, but for that most honorable reason of self-interest.

Synthetic Fuels: A Wrong Answer to the Energy Question

by Ron Rudolph

After a few martinis, anything seems possible, even spending the combined assets of the nation's three largest corporations. But even the most loaded New Year's Eve reveller would have a hard time believing the United States Congress would use such unprecedented sums of tax money to build blanks to fight the moral equivalent of war.

The dawning of the 1980s saw Congress and President Carter overwhelmingly agreed on a common, dramatic signal we would send the world. The US would get tough with the energy crisis. Conservation, though widely hailed as the cheapest, cleanest, quickest, safest, and surest way to create new energy supplies and cut oil imports, was considered not quite bold enough. Skeptics bellowed, "America did not conserve its way to greatness; it produced." Thus, amidst gas lines, turmoil in Iran, OPEC price increases, and a national "malaise," Congress settled on an ambitious program to create a synthetic fuels industry by the end of the decade. The plan, financed by the windfall profits tax, would dwarf the Apollo moon project, ultimately drawing up to $88 billion from the Treasury.

Will the plan work? Certainly not as expected. None of the synfuel technologies is now producing fuels for sale in the US market place. Many have not been tested beyond laboratory scale models. Moreover, the products they produce may unbearably strain our pocketbooks and would ravage the environment. Yet Congress hopes that in 10–15 years synfuels will be a cornerstone of the nation's energy supply.

The author greatly appreciates the advice and encouragement he has received from his friends and colleagues, David Masselli, FOE's Energy Policy Director, and Kevin Markey, FOE's Colorado Representative, without whose help this paper would have been impossible.

Synfuels are commonly defined as any liquid, gaseous or solid hydrocarbon that could be used to substitute for petroleum or natural gas, and is derived from coal, oil shale, tar sands, or biomass. We will focus on the history of synfuel development, the technologies (particularly oil shale and coal conversion), and their environmental and economic effects.

A Quick History of US Synfuels

Nineteen forty-seven was the last year the US exported more oil than it imported. Since at least 1943 Congress had recognized the need to plan for a petroleum-scarce world; producing new supplies has long been favored over increasing energy efficiency. By the oil embargo year of 1973–4, imports supplied about 36% of US demand for oil. By 1979, imports rose by 25% to about 8.5 million barrels per day (b/d). Today nearly 50% of the oil we use is imported, at a cost of $1.5 billion a week.

Oil addiction has put the US in a precarious economic and political position. Inflation is at a 35 year high and the 1980 Presidential election hangs on the whims of terrorists. Militarily the energy production and transportation systems we depend on are indefensible. As Senator Henry Jackson put it, we face

an unprecedented threat to our national security. Our bill for imported oil contributes heavily to our balance-of-payments problem and puts pressure on the dollar in international markets. Our dependence on foreign oil also exports jobs and potential profits away from American business.

The first synfuels program passed Congress in 1944. It lasted eleven years and went nowhere.

Synfuels finally hit it big in 1979. Legend has it that the latest and most successful push was hatched over lunch by two well connected Washingtonians, Eugene M. Zuckert, former Secretary of the Air Force under Presidents Kennedy and Johnson, and Paul R. Ignatius, Secretary of the Navy under Johnson and former president of the Washington *Post*. They envisioned synfuels as the way to supply the US with petroleum-like products in an oil-short world. What resulted from their conversation was the Carter Administration's proposed $88 billion program, aimed at producing two million b/d by 1990.

Senator William Proxmire, Chairman of the Senate Banking, Housing and Urban Affairs Committee, viewed the genesis of the program this way:

As lunches go, I would not be surprised if the lunch had been pretty well lubricated, and as they got into the first martini, this might have been $20 billion. At the second martini, maybe it went up to $40 billion. At $88 billion, the only way you can explain it is by the quality of martinis in this town—particularly when the vermouth is of low quantity and the gin is of high quality. It is clear that these gentlemen were flying high when they moved into $88 billion.

The massive crash plan of Zuckert and Ignatius, aided by Lloyd Cutler, Washington attorney and Carter confidant, gained steam during the first half of 1979. The clincher came with the long gas lines of late spring (which were caused by the Department of Energy's botched fuel allocation system). On June 26th, as OPEC ministers met to discuss new price hikes and gas lines in metropolitan Washington commonly stretched over one-half mile, the House overwhelmingly (368–25) passed a bill mandating a 2 million b/d synfuel program by 1990. In July President Carter descended from Camp David and proposed, among other things, the $88 billion plan and the creation of a federal corporation to dole out the goodies. The Senate gave Carter an early Christmas present when it approved a modified version of his synfuel package in November.

It now appears that the US will create a synfuels corporation to spend $20 billion during 1980–5 to build four or five commercial-sized demonstration plants using various oil shale, coal liquefaction, or coal gasification technologies. The remaining $68 billion will be allocated pending results of the first phase and a determination of which technologies will give us the most bang for the buck.

Congress and President Carter obviously were convinced that synfuels would produce affordable energy compatible with our needs and at an acceptable level of risk to human health and the environment. Critics claim synfuel technologies, demonstrated at best only on small pilot facilities, may not work when expanded to commercial plants, will cost too much, cause grave environmental damage, and do very little to reduce oil imports. Dr. Mel Horwitch, one of the authors of the Harvard Business School's

Energy Future, characterized the massive synfuel plan as

a conceptually simple technocratic solution for what is a complex
societal problem. . . . There is a strong likelihood that a massive
synthetic fuels program would follow the same . . . pattern as the
SST or nuclear power.

Failure of synfuels to live up to their advance notice
could cause people to lose faith still more in the government's ability to grapple with energy issues. Public trust, as
nuclear proponents have found, is not easily regained and
any chance for a national concensus on energy policy could
be lost for quite a while.

Will The Technologies Perform?
At the start of the 1980s, the US had no commercial
synfuel plants operation. There are only two commercial
plants in the world, a coal liquefaction plant in South Africa
and a Canadian tar sands facility. To meet the 1995 goal (the
goal slipped five years) would require building about 30
commercial sized plants. The Senate Banking Committee
wrote:

Enactment of a law which declares that synfuel technologies are
ready for commercialization will not alter the fact that many synfuel technologies are in a relatively primitive and untested state of
development.

It would be like turning a few fishing skiffs into a naval
armada.

The center piece of the US program is coal liquefaction. Based on DOE figures, coal liquids will provide at least
twice as much oil substitute as any of the other liquid
synfuels—about 600,000 b/d by 1995.

The Senate Energy Committee, which originated the
Senate's version of the 1979 bill, found that coal liquids (and
to a lesser extent shale oil), are

obviously the sole near-term opportunity to reduce the transportation sector's dependence upon petroleum. . . . In the near term
. . . a major objective of the synthetic fuels program will be to
provide liquid fuels for transportation uses to meet the exacting
specifications for vehicular and aircraft uses, and while [being]
capable of delivery through existing marketing facilities.

As we shall see, the Committee's optimism is unfounded.

Coal Liquefaction

The addition of hydrogen to coal is the main trick in turning coal into fuel liquids or gases. Coal contains only 2–6% hydrogen by weight, crude oil and gasoline contain 12–16% hydrogen, and natural gas 25%.

Hydrogen is added in two ways. Indirect liquefaction technologies operate by gasifying coal into a mixture of carbon monoxide and hydrogen (synthesis gas) and then chemically converting the gases into liquid products with the aid of a catalyst. The direct method skips the gaseous coal phase.

Using coal liquids to run automobiles, trains, planes, buses and the like is not a new idea. It was first tried in Germany in the 1920s. Adolf Hitler instituted that country's comprehensive synfuel program because he felt synfuels were needed for the engines of war.

According to information obtained by the German Document Retrieval Project of Texas A&M University, there were three small synfuels plants operating in Germany when the Nazis gained power in 1933. At its height in early 1944, the German synfuel effort produced about 100,000 b/d from 25 plants, approximately 16% of that country's domestic and military needs for liquid fuels.

Synfuel supporters have pointed to the German experience to support a massive crash program for the US. The German success, however, cannot be easily applied here. First, the Germans did not undertake a "crash program." Theirs developed over 22 years. Second, the German synfuel industry produced relatively small amounts of fuel. Dr. Richard E. Wainerdi, senior vice president of 3D International and former member of the German Document Retrieval Project, told a House subcommittee, "In eight days we would use up all the fuel that Germany produced in World War II, at the rate that we use fuel in America." Third, the great majority of German synfuel was produced by a technology that has yet to be fully reproduced. Perhaps the secrets will be found among the half million war documents dealing with coal conversion, but most of them have yet to be translated.

There are three direct liquefaction processes under development: Sovent Refined Coal (SRC-II), H-Coal, and Donor Solvent. SRC-II, H-Coal, and Donor Solvent. All produce a variety of liquid fuels.

DOE does not expect these direct liquefaction technologies to contribute commerical quantities of synthetic liquids until after 1990. The scale and operating experience of them gives some idea of how far the US has to go before we could rely on significant quantities of synthetic petroleum.

One day I was walking along Tinker Creek thinking of nothing at all and I saw the tree with the lights in it. I saw the backyard cedar where the mourning doves roost charged and transfigured, each cell buzzing with flame. I stood on the grass with the lights in it, grass that was wholly fire, utterly focused and utterly dreamed. It was less like seeing than like being for the first time seen, knocked breathless by a powerful glance . . . I had been my whole life a bell, and never knew it until at that moment I was lifted and struck.

Annie Dillard

The largest operating direct coal liquids facility is Gulf Oil's SRC-II plant near Tacoma, Washington. It processes 50 tons of coal a day to produce 150 barrels of oil. An SRC-II plant capable of producing 20,000 b/d from 6,000 tons of coal is planned for construction near Morgantown, West Virginia, in 1981.

Dynalectron, Inc.'s H-coal process is used at a 2.5-ton-per-day test facility. A pilot plant capable of turning 250 tons of coal a day into 625 b/d of "syncrude" (barely enough for a single gas station) is at least a year behind schedule and will cost about four times as much as expected.

Exxon's Donor Solvent process has been tested under laboratory conditions using a half ton of coal per day. A 250 ton-a-day pilot plant is under construction.

Coal liquids produced from direct hydrogenation cannot directly replace transportation fuels and other conventional petroleum items. They first must undergo extensive upgrading and refining—but very little is known about the costs of yields or the refining process. It is bound to be expensive.

The only coal liquefaction technology ready for commercial development is the Fischer-Tropsch process—an indirect liquefaction method— developed by the Germans in 1923. The world's only commercially operated coal liquefaction plant, in South Africa, uses the Fischer-Tropsch method. The government-owned African Coal, Oil and Gas Corporation (SASOL are its Afrikaans initials) runs the SASOL-I plant, which was completed in 1955. It can produce 15,000–20,000 b/d of a wide variety of petroleum products including gasoline, ethane, propane, home heating oil, diesel fuel, and residual oil. SASOL-II has been designed for ten times SASOL-I's output and has recently begun producing synthetic liquids. A third SASOL plant should be ready by the mid-1980s.

The Fischer-Tropsch process can also produce methanol, which can be used directly as a transportation fuel in specially designed engines. Up to 50% by volume can be added to conventional gasoline to stretch gas supplies, however the mixture separates at low temperatures and a conventional engine would be harmed by the non-homogeneous liquid. Methanol could be used in fleets of vehicles specially equipped to burn it or as a boiler fuel.

There are no plants, not even a pilot or demonstration plant, that use the coal-to-methanol process. There are five licensed methods to perform the task, but they all use methane (the main constituent of natural gas), not coal, to produce methanol. Coal was used until the early 1950s. A report commissioned by the Senate Budget Committee found the coal-to-methanol technology "could probably be developed to commercial readiness in five years."

Mobil Oil has developed a way to turn methanol into premium gasoline. The catalytic process has been tested on a four b/d facility that did not use coal as the feedstock. A demonstration plant will not be built until at least 1985.

Indirect liquefaction has a limited potential in the US. Two years ago, DOE did not consider it potentially significant. The Fisher-Tropsch process can only use non-agglomerating western coals and lignite. Other indirect liquefaction methods that could use eastern coals are still being tested in the laboratory.

In summary, it appears that the 600,000 b-d coal liquids goal is very optimistic. Even if the production and refining hardware could be built there is doubt that the objective of the program—to replace fuel in existing transportation systems—could be met. Upgrading and refining may make the fuel prohibitively expensive; so would the redesign of our transportation system to run on methanol. In the end, synfuels' only contribution to transportation may be in the form of very expensive paving tar.

Coal Gasification

It is hoped that coal gasification can reduce oil imports by about 400,000 b/d by 1995. The synthetic gas could be used as a boiler fuel, a chemical feedstock, or an intermediate product that could be converted to coal liquids using indirect liquefaction techniques.

Coal gasification was used extensively throughout the US and Europe for over 100 years during the 19th and early 20th centuries. It is estimated that by the middle of the 1920s the US had 11,000 coal gas plants producing low-Btu gas. Over 90% were in industrial facilities such as steel plants, glass manufacturers, and metallurgical and chemical plants. About 1,000 gasifiers were used by utilities to produce "town gas" for home heating, lighting, and cooking. Natural gas, which can be extracted and delivered to the point of consumption for only a fraction of the cost, eventually replaced coal gas.

The basic gasification method reacts the pulverized coal with steam under high temperatures to produce carbon monoxide, carbon dioxide, hydrogen and methane. As with coal liquids, the addition of hydrogen is the most important step. Depending on the technology used, the synthetic gas product will have a low-Btu (less than 2000 Btu per cubic foot), medium-Btu (200–500 Btu), or high-Btu (900–1000 Btu) content. Natural gas contains approximately 1000 Btus per cubic foot.

Several low-Btu projects are in various stages of construction. At present, low-Btu gas cannot be stored or shipped economically.

There are over one hundred medium-Btu gasifiers operating around the world, but none in the US. Medium-

Btu gas can be used as a boiler fuel, chemical feedstock, in indirect liquefaction plants, or for the production of hydrogen used in direct liquefaction facilities. Kodak has announced plans to use the gas to produce the chemicals for its film base.

Proponents believe the production of high-Btu gas is necessary to supplement and eventually replace natural gas. A process that depends on the gasifier in the Fischer-Tropsch process, a fixed-bed Lurgi gasifier, is the leading contender in the high-Btu market. A consortium led by American Natural Gas Company plans to build the nation's first high-Btu plant in Mercer County, North Dakota. The plant is designed to produce 125 million cubic feet of gas a day, enough to heat around 365,000 homes a year. Other high-Btu proposals have been on the drawing boards for years.

The fixed-bed Lurgi gasifier has a major drawback. It can use only lignite (the fuel to be used in the North Dakota plant, similar to the brown coal used by the Germans) and subbituminous coals found in the western part of the country. Eastern "caking" coals cannot be used by the Lurgi gasifiers.

Meeting the national coal gasification goal—400,000 b/d—appears unlikely, particularly with respect to high-Btu gas. The Congressional Research Service predicted that high-Btu production would be less than 250–300 million cubic feet a day (about 50,000 b/d equivalent) by 1990, even with substantial incentives. Low and medium-Btu prospects look better but increasing optimism about natural gas supplies would delay their widespread use.

Oil Shale

Under 17,000 square miles of northwest Colorado, northeastern Utah, and southwestern Wyoming lies approximately 600 billion barrels of potential oil reserves. The oil, in the form of a solid organic compound called kerogen, is locked in fine-grained sedimentary rock called oil shale. Oil shale is closer to commercial use than any other synthetic fuel. Environmental concerns aside—but only for the moment—there is a good chance that the national goal of replacing 300,000–400,000 b/d of imported oil with oil shale by 1995 can be met.

The US government will play a major role in developing oil shale. About four-fifths of the oil shale is on public lands. In 1974, the Department of the Interior leased four tracts of federal oil shale land in Colorado and Utah to various major oil companies under the Prototype Oil Shale Leasing Program. The Department of Energy's FY 1979 oil shale budget authority for research, development, and demonstration, was $53.5 million and the department expects to spend $511 million between 1980 and 1984.

There are two basic methods for obtaining shale oil from rock, surface retorting and modified in situ retorting. Both involve mining, fracturing, and heating the shale to decompose the kerogen into oils and gases. The resulting liquids have a slightly lower hydrogen-to-carbon ratio than crude oil and a much different chemical structure. They must undergo extensive upgrading to make it suitable for pipeline transportation and for refining. Upgrading entails adding hydrogen to break up the long hydrocarbon chains, and the upgrading must reduce the nitrogen, sulphur, and oxygen content of the fuel and remove arsenic and other impurities.

The basic design for surface retorting has remained unchanged for the last 20 years. In the last decade five different surface retorting methods have been tested.

Modified in situ retorting works by releasing the oil and gasses in the oil shale while the rock is still in the ground. The technology is still experimental, but two plants are under construction.

Shale oil must be refined before it can be used to replace petroleum products. Its inherent molecular structure and the cost of refining will dictate the characteristics of the refining products. (Costs will be addressed in a later section of this chapter.)

Tests done by Chevron showed that three-quarters of the refined shale oil consists of mid- to heavy distillates (those fractions of the oil that boil at medium to high temperatures) such as jet fuel, diesel fuel and home heating oil. Gasoline accounted for 17% of the output with the rest split between various light and heavy residuals.

There are no refineries able to handle shale oil. However, the nation's refining capacity will change in the 1980s and beyond as the demand for gasoline drops and the demand for diesel fuel and other middle distillates rises. The change will be hastened as the quality of crude oil stocks shifts from petroleum supplies that yield proportionately greater amounts of gasoline and other light distillates to supplies that produce more of the middle and heavy fractions. This will enhance shale oil's attractiveness to refiners.

The national oil shale goal appears to be the most technically feasible of all the synthetic fuel targets. The Interior Department estimates that 280,000–863,000 b/d will be on line by the early 1990s. The two plants under construction and two others that have received some permits would produce approximately 185,000 b/d by the mid-1980s.

Health and Environmental Effects

A major synfuel effort poses environmental and health risks as great as any other energy technology. The immature status of most synfuel technologies makes accurate appraisals of their effects virtually impossible. Most health and environmental assessments will not be finished until the mid-1980s, but preliminary studies indicate synfuels may cause grave damage to human health, especially to those people working in synfuel industries, and that synfuels may permanently harm land and water resources.

A single 50,000 b/d surface plant processing moderately rich oil shale will consume about 25 million tons of rock a year. A modified in situ plant would mine and bring to the surface about 15 million tons/year. By comparison, the largest coal mine in the country in 1977 produced about 13.5 million tons and the four largest coal mines combined barely equalled the capacity required for one surface shale oil plant. President Carter's shale oil goal of 400,000 b/d will require a mining effort more than a quarter again the size of the entire coal mining industry, but it would produce only one twentieth of the energy in the coal.

Enormous quantities of hazardous wastes are left after the oil is cooked out. The spent shale expands to 120% of its original volume. A surface plant will produce up to a whopping 22 million tons of waste a year, enough to bury a square mile of land 17 feet deep. Some of the waste will fill the mined out area, the rest would fill in canyons on the Piceance and Uinta Basins of the Colorado Plateau.

DOE has labelled disposal of spent shale one of the two "showstoppers" that could be an "absolute constraint" on the development of certain synfuel technologies. Large areas of land will require "special isolation" with little chance for reclamation; toxic substances will accumulate in vegetation, and contaminate surface water and ground water. Oil shale wastes contain benzo-a-pyrene, a known carcinogen, and varying amounts of trace elements such as fluorine, boron, molybdenum, nickel, vanadium, zinc and cobalt; a standard sized plant would produce up to 136 tons of arsenic each year. The US Geologic Survey found "disposal of heavy metals in these quantities, especially arsenic, poses grave questions for public health."

Toxic waste materials will spread through the environment through leaching of spent shale storage piles and abandoned in situ retorts. How quickly, how far, and to what degree the hazardous wastes will spread is uncertain. There are no control strategics.

Waer quality will be particularly hard hit. DOE researchers admitted:

The potential of long-term hydrological disturbances in arid areas or the introduction of toxic or carcinogenic materials into drinking water aquifers is in itself sufficient to preclude large-scale development until these concerns are resolved.

The serious salinity problem of the Colorado River basin will undoubtedly be worsened. The Colorado and its tributaries serve 17 million people in seven states and Mexico. In 1976 the river exceeded EPA's salinity guidelines for drinking water by 65%. If leaching is controlled 99%, a 400,000 b/d surface oil shale program could increase salinity in the Colorado by up to 30 micrograms per liter. Based on Bureau of Reclamation estimates, the increase would cost agriculture and domestic consumers over $10,000,000. The US is already spending about $275 million for salinity control projects on the Colorado to meet our treaty obligations with Mexico.

Effects on ground water would be the most serious environmental effect of oil shale. Ground water is an important source of water for the cities, industries, and agriculture of the arid southwest. Introducing trace metals and other toxics could render large quantities of it unusable. Contaminated groundwater will eventually pollute surface water and spread the problem. The damage could not be reversed.

DOE has concluded that "if groundwater is present, contamination is highly likely" from leaching of abandoned in situ retorts. The agency suggested "if retort(s) cannot be abandoned without adverse water quality impacts, modified in situ oil shale could be considered an unacceptable technology." And to date "means have not been developed for preventing contamination of ground water aquifers." DOE's warnings have gone unnoticed. The oil shale program will be well under way before possible solutions to these problems are developed.

Workers could be the real victims of oil shale. Little risk analysis has been done, but what has been learned is alarming. DOE wrote "the potential clearly exists for uncontrolled emissions of both toxic and carcinogenic materials." Miners in in situ facilities will be faced with a "unique environment . . . subject to exposure to many toxic materials" for which "proven health protective measures do not exist," according to DOE. The agency hopes that adequate controls for worker protection will be developed by 1983–4.

The national oil shale program would produce prodigious amounts of more conventional air pollutants. On an annual basis 19,000 tons of particulates (excluding dust from haul roads), 11,600 tons of sulphur dioxide, 8,700 tons of nitrogen oxides, and 2,100 tons of hydrocarbons will be produced, if oil shale production is split evenly between surface and in situ plants. The increased smog will be concentrated in five counties near many nationally important recreation areas, notably Dinosaur National Monument (a focal point of the mid-1950s energy battles that left us with Glen Canyon Dam) and the Flat Tops Wilderness Area of Colorado. It will worsen the increasing problem of acid rain in the Colorado Rockies and impair visibility all over the region.

Coal Conversion

Coal liquefaction and gasification also require moving great chunks of earth. DOE estimates that a 50,000 b/d facility requires mining 10 million tons a year for an SRC-II plant, and 6 million tons/year, for an H-Coal plant. There are no reference data for the Donor Solvent process. The coal derived portion of the synfuel program would increase US coal mining by 10–15%.

Disposal of wastes from coal-liquid plants will be a formidable task. A 50,000 b/d SRC-II plant would generate about four millions tons per year, an H-Coal facility about 600,000 tons/year. While the volume of wastes is less than oil shale, the toxic materials, particularly carcinogens, are more concentrated. According to DOE documents, the solid wastes include "mineral residue, sludge from water treatment, baghouse particulates, char, heavy tar residues and process reagents."

As with oil shale, leaching of coal liquid wastes poses a major environmental risk. DOE's analysis predicts "silicates, trace metals, in some cases hydrocarbons, nitrogen containing compounds and polynuclear aromatics" will be in the leached material. The trace elements include arsenic, barium, cadmium, lead, mercury, selenium, silver, copper, nickel, and zinc.

Workers' health and safety is of great concern. Many hazardous materials are used or formed in coal liquefaction processes. Known cancer causing compounds including benzo-a-pyrene, dibenz (a,h) anthracene, chrysene, 7-methylbenz (c) acridene and aromatic amines, are formed in the coal conversion process. The National Institute for Occupational Health and Safety has reported that workers in the SASOL-I plant often complain of rashes and other skin ailments.

The other potential "showstopper" identified by DOE are the heavy distillates from coal liquids. These possess mutagenic and carcinogenic potency "well above other products and the replaced oil products." Strategies to minimize public exposure are, according to DOE, "in their infancy."

Carbon Dioxide

A major synfuel development will accelerate the buildup of carbon dioxide in the atmosphere. Synfuels emit much more CO_2 per unit of energy than any other fossil fuel.

There is wide consensus that a doubling of CO_2 will occur by the middle of the next century. It would increase

---

AFTER YOU have exhausted what there is in business, politics, conviviality, and so on – have found that none of these finally satisfy, or permanently wear – what remains? Nature remains.

Walt Whitman

world surface temperatures by 1–3° C. The climatic effects of such a rise are uncertain but many scientists believe agricultural production is likely to drop at a time when an increasing world population is severely straining the limited agricultural resources of the planet.

The contribution of CO_2 from synfuels alone would be a relatively small amount of overall US emissions. However, the US should not be encouraging, even tacitly, the use of fuels that would cause a faster accumulation of CO_2 in the atmosphere.

What Will Synfuels Cost?

No one really knows the economics of synfuels. The proposed $88 billion represents the minimum amount that will be available for synfuels from the windfall profits tax, not a consensus on how much the program will actually cost. The lack of commercial-size facilities and the volatile world oil market make current estimates of consumer prices for synfuels, $25–50 per barrel, little more than guesses. Environmental uncertainties could also add to the synfuel price tag. For instance, DOE thinks that disposal of oil shale wastes could be "prohibitively costly."

The uncertainties of synfuel prices are directly related to the cost of building, operating, and maintaining synfuel plants and their transportation, refining, and waste disposal systems. The Rand Corporation found that the actual costs of building energy facilities based on new technologies have averaged 2.53 times the estimates. Threefold cost overruns were "not uncommon," and some plants have gone five times over estimates.

Using Rand's numbers and the Senate Energy Committee's estimate that a 1.5 million b/d synfuel effort will cost "in excess of $110 billion (in current dollars)", the real bill for synfuels could be from $220 billion to as high as $550 billion. Four hundred billion dollars were raised in the entire US economy in 1978.

Rand's study and one conducted for the Senate Budget Committee by the Pace Company Consultants and Engineers agreed that the single most important contributor to the rising cost of synfuels is increasing knowledge of specific engineering needs. For example, the Colony oil shale project saw its preliminary cost estimates soar 129% in one year following detailed engineering designs.

Labor and equipment shortages are sure to drive up synfuel capital costs. Building many synfuel plants will also severely strain the entire construction industry. "Hyperinflation" of construction costs will result, according to the Pace study. Building costs for all-new energy facilities will zoom upward. Pace concluded that

achievement of production levels even approaching the goals set by President Carter for synfuels would require a national commitment for diverting our resources into this activity, deprive other sectors of the economy, and lead to sharply escalating costs in the mining and construction industries and for certain types of materials and equipment.

Synfuel plant builders will have to acquire highly trained teams of engineers and construction workers and be guaranteed a smooth flow of essential materials. Pace examined possible delays resulting from equipment bottlenecks and found these too would increase synfuel plant costs:

The first few plants would contract for most of the available US manufacturing capacity for key items such as valves, pumps, compressors and high pressure vessels. As additional plants reach procurement stage, equipment suppliers will quote longer and longer delivery times. Longer delivery times also require higher price contingencies to cover unknown increases in supplier costs. Longer delivery times are death to large capital projects because time is money. We estimate almost half the total per barrel cost of synthetic fuels is simply the carrying cost of the capital investment project. Owners will therefore be willing to bid up the prices for crucial equipment in order to save time. A single week's delay may increase costs by millions of dollars.

Labor shortages can be expected in the synfuels stampede. There will be a great demand for managers, engineers, draftsmen and other professionals to design and build the plants. Pace estimated 24,000 such people would be required to meet the national synfuel goal while there are only 45,000 people qualified to work on synfuel plants in the entire construction industry.

If the word of wisdom for graduates in the 1960s was "plastics," for the 1980s it could be "synfuels."

In summary, a major synfuels program will create a menace to public health, air, land, water, and the economy. Much remains to be learned about the pollutants, and the solid waste problem alone could prove intractable. The wastes will remain poisonous forever and will have to be isolated from the environment forever. Proceeding with large-scale plants before waste disposal methods are perfected could lead to new tragedies like Love Canal. Workers will be asked to risk their lives against the known and unknown dangers of synfuels and against possible new epidemics of diseases like black lung and asbestosis. The incredible capital costs could tie up the whole American construction industry.

Yet despite these high risks that DOE and others have identified, the government is poised for a gung-ho charge after synfuels. The situation is obviously analogous to the early days of the country's ill-advised nuclear program. We could wind up in another no-win situation.

Senator Edmund Muskie succinctly made the case against an irrevocable commitment to synfuels:

Too often we have waited to observe the effects of long-term exposure to hazardous pollutants and only then recognized our mistakes. Too often we have tried to remedy those mistakes only to find that the effects on human health and on our environment are tragically irreversible.

We should not knowingly repeat those mistakes now. Yet that is exactly what we are being asked to do.

Before charging ahead and investing $88 billion and incalculably damaging our air, water, and, most important, health, we ought to find out whether these awesome expenditures will really buy us what we need.

Selected References

Subcommittee on Fossil Fuel and Nuclear Energy Research, Development and Demonstration, Committee on Science and Technology, U.S. House of Representatives, *New Technologies for Old Fuels*, November 1, 1977.

SRI International, *Environmentally Based Siting Assessment for Synthetic Liquid Fuels Facilities*, draft final report, December 1979

U.S. Environmental Protection Agency, *Compendium Reports on Oil Shale Technology*, January 1979

U.S. Department of Energy, *Synthetic Fuels and the Environment: An Environmental and Regulatory Impacts Analysis*, review draft, January 7, 1980

U.S. Department of Energy, *Environmental Analysis of Synthetic Liquid Fuels*, July 12, 1979

Congressional Record, November 5,7,9, pages S 15808–15899, S 16042–16097, and S 16181–16286, respectively

The Institute of Ecology, *A Scientific and Policy Review of the Proto-Type Oil Shale Leasing Program, October 29, 1973*

SRI International, *The Long Term Impact of Atmospheric Carbon Dioxide on Climate*, April 1979

David Masselli, "Proposals to Commercialize Synthetic Fuels,"statement before the Senate Committee on Banking, Housing and Urban Affairs, July 26, 1979

Kevin Markey, "The Costs of Oil Shale," FOE August 1979.

U.S. Department of Energy, *Environmental Readiness of Emerging Technologies*, January 1979

U.S. Department of Energy, *Environmental Readiness Document: Coal Gasification*, September 1978

U.S. Department of Energy, *Environmental Readiness Document: Oil Shale*, September 1978

U.S. Senate Committees on Banking, Housing and Urban Affairs, and Energy and Natural Resources, Report on Extending the Defense Production Act of 1950, October 1979

General Accounting Office, *Colorado River Basin Water Problems: How to Reduce Their Impact*, May 4, 1979

U.S. Geological Survey, *Synthetic Fuels Development: Earth Science Considerations*, 1979

"Energy is Eternal Delight"

by Gary Snyder

A young woman at Sir George Williams University in Montreal asked me, "What do you fear most?" I found myself answering "that the diversity and richness of the gene pool will be destroyed–" and most people there understood what was meant.

The treasure of life is the richness of stored information in the diverse genes of all living beings. If the human race, following on some set of catastrophes, were to survive at the expense of many plant and animal species, it would be no victory. Diversity provides life with the capacity for a multitude of adaptations and responses to long-range changes on the planet. The possibility remains that at some future time another evolutionary line might carry the development of consciousness to clearer levels than our family of upright primates.

The United States, Europe, the Soviet Union, and Japan have a habit. They are addicted to heavy energy use, great gulps and injections of fossil fuel. As fossil-fuel reserves go down, they will take dangerous gambles with the future health of the biosphere (through nuclear power) to keep up their habit.

For several centuries Western civilization has had a priapic drive for material accumulation, continual extensions of political and economic power, termed "progress." In the Judaeo-Christian worldview men are seen as working out their ultimate destinies (paradise? perdition?) with planet earth as the stage for the drama—trees and animals mere props, nature a vast supply depot. Fed by fossil fuel, this religio-economic view has become a cancer: uncontrollable growth. It may finally choke itself, and drag much else down with it.

The longing for growth is not wrong. The nub of the problem now is how to flip over, as in jujitsu, the magnificent growth-energy of modern civilization into a nonacquisitive search for deeper knowledge of self and nature. Self-nature. Mother nature. If people come to realize that there are many nonmaterial, nondestructive paths of growth—of the highest and most fascinating order—it would help dampen the common fear that a steady state economy would mean deadly stagnation.

I spent a few years, some time back, in and around a training place. It was a school for monks of the Rinzai branch of Zen Buddhism, in Japan. The whole aim of the community was personal and universal liberation. In this quest for spiritual freedom every man marched strictly to the same drum in matters of hours of work and meditation. In the teacher's room one was pushed across sticky barriers into vast new spaces. The training was traditional and had been handed down for centuries—but the insights are forever fresh and new. The beauty, refinement and truly civilized quality of that life has no match in modern America. It is supported by hand labor in small fields, gathering brushwood to heat the bath, well-water and barrels of homemade pickles. The unspoken motto is "Grow With Less." In the training place I lost my remaining doubts about China.

The Buddhists teach respect for all life, and for wild systems. Man's life is totally dependent on an interpenetrating network of wild systems. Eugene Odum, in his useful paper "The Strategy of Ecosystem Development," points out how the United States has the characteristics of a young ecosystem. Some American Indian cultures have "mature" characteristics: protection as against production, stability as against growth, quality as against quantity. In Pueblo societies a kind of ultimate democracy is practiced. Plants and animals are also people, and, through certain rituals and dances, are given a place and a voice in the political discussions of the humans. They are "represented." "Power to all the people" must be the slogan.

On Hopi and Navajo land, at Black Mesa, the whole issue is revolving at this moment. The cancer is eating away at the breast of Mother Earth in the form of strip-mining. This to provide electricity for Los Angeles. The defense of Black Mesa is being sustained by traditional Indians, young Indian militants, and longhairs. Black Mesa speaks to us through an ancient, complex web of myth. She is sacred territory. To hear her voice is to give up the European word "America" and accept the new-old name for the continent, "Turtle Island."

The return to marginal farmland on the part of longhairs is not some nostalgic replay of the nineteenth century.

Here is a generation of white people finally ready to learn from the Elders. How to live on the continent as though our children, and on down, for many ages, will still be here (not on the moon). Loving and protecting this soil, these trees, these wolves. Natives of Turtle Island.

A scaled-down, balanced technology is possible, if cut loose from the cancer of exploitation-heavy-industry-perpetual growth. Those who have already sensed these necessities and have begun, whether in the country or the city, to "grow with less," are the only counterculture that counts. Electricity for Los Angeles is not energy. As Blake said: "Energy Is Eternal Delight."

Recycling

by Garrett De Bell

America has been described as a nation knee-deep in garbarge, firing rockets to the moon. This phrase aptly points out the misguided priorities of the American government as well as the magnitude of the solid-waste crisis. Many solutions to the solid-waste, or trash, problem have been proposed—sanitary land fill, dumping waste into old mines, compressing it into building blocks, incineration, and dumping at sea. Even the best of these methods waste materials. The principle of recycling is to regard wastes as raw materials to be utilized; this is the only ecologically sensible long term solution to the solid-waste problem.

Recycling is a major part of the solution of many environmental problems. It is important to air and water pollution and to wilderness preservation. The core of the meaning of the word "recycle" is that resources be used over and over again and cycled through human economic-production systems in a way that is analagous to the cycles of elements (carbon, nitrogen, phosphorus, etc.) in natural eco-systems. This is directly contrary to the present produce and discard production system with its one-way flow of materials from the mine or farm through the household and into the garbage dumps, air, and water.

The benefits of reuse of materials (recycling) in our overcrowded world are obvious. Each ton of paper, aluminum, or iron reclaimed from waste is a ton less needed from our forests and mines, and a ton less solid waste in our environment. Recycling of many important materials is now technically feasible and major corporations are devoting some attention to it.

Aluminum is very easy to recycle because it need only be melted down for reuse. Because of aluminum's very high value, large-scale recycling operations are now feasible. Currently, scrap aluminum brings $200 per ton where scrap newspaper brings only $5 per ton. Reynolds Aluminum has been running ads stressing its interest in recycling aluminum cans; plants to accept used cans for recycling are now being built.

Paper and cardboard can also be recycled. Remember

the paper drives of past years? The price is now so low that scrap paper is not economical to reuse unless it is delivered to the mill in large quantities by very cheap labor. But demands on our forests have become so great that there is now pressure for more intense management of timber to increase annual production. Those of us who prefer wilderness and maximum areas of unmanaged forests would prefer that the demand for timber be reduced by increasing the percentage that is recycled. Current research on improving the techniques is being done by U.S. Forest Products Laboratories. More recycling of paper means less pressure for increased cutting in the forests.

At present, however, the reuse or recycling of solid wastes is not economically feasible for most materials. Since it is ecologically necessary to start recycling our solid wastes, our approach is to find ways to make recycling economical.

Suitable legislation can go a long way toward doing this. At the state or federal level, legislation should incorporate the cost of disposal of each product in its price in the form of a tax. By giving a competitive advantage to products with a lower tax, this tax would encourage the use of simple bio-degradable or easily recycled containers, such as those made out of paper, cardboard, and aluminum, and also reusable bottles and containers. It would discourage the use of plastic containers of types that cannot be recycled and of containers made of a mix of materials that are very difficult or impossible to recycle, such as paper and plastic laminated together or foil-covered cardboard.

The tax can be collected either at the factory or at time of purchase depending on the circumstances. The revenues gained from this tax would go into a fund to subsidize recycling of products. The amount of tax would be determined by the subsidy needed to make recycling economically feasible. For example, aluminum, being economically recyclable, would require no subsidy. Paper, if its recycling required a two-cent-per-pound subsidy, would carry a two-cent tax. Products that could not be recycled at all would carry a tax equal to the full direct and social costs of ultimate disposal after use.

To properly recycle our wastes will require an industry perhaps as large as the present automobile industry. Recycling-plants can provide people with socially useful jobs, increase the resource base, and improve the quality of life for everyone.

There are two major barriers to recycling wastes. The first is the problem of transporting the wastes to the site of the recycling. This is an economic problem which the subsidy will solve. The second is getting wastes sorted. The subsidy can be high enough to pay for this, or each city might establish a dual set of garbage rates, which people could choose between freely. One rate would be for unsorted garbage. The other rate would be for garbage separated into organic wastes, glass, and metal, and into plastic, paper, and cardboard. The difference in the two rates would simply be the cost to the municipality of sorting the garbage. There may be objection to having to sort or pay, but it is time to realize that this is one of the costs we have to pay for a decent environment.

This legislation represents a specific application of the economic theory of externalities. Instead of the usual practice of including only the cost of production in the price of a product, we also include any additional social cost—such as the cost in environmental deterioration—in the price of the product. This removes the incentive to industries to follow practices which save them money in the short run but produce environmental destruction in the long run.

Beyond the Recycle Principle

Normally the recycling concept means reuse of materials. Additonal steps outside this concept can be taken to reduce the rates of solid-waste production and resource depletion. In general, both legislation and citizens in their private lives can stress maintenance and repair of existing products rather than planned obsolescence. This will create less jobs on the assembly line, but more jobs for repairmen and renovators.

Note: this article has been recycled (reprinted) from the first Environmental Handbook. The problem hasn't gone away (as environmentalists say, there is no away) and the solution is still the same. In the last ten years we have seen recycling centers sprout up, but they are mostly out of the mainstream, frequented only by people with the most undying interest in the environment. It is still necessary for recycling to become the normal means of garbage disposal. This is one area that has progressed very little since 1970, although many states have passed "bottle bills" requiring a deposit on all soft drink and beer containers sold in order to maximize reuse and recycling. Over the next decade this movement should come to fruition with either a national law, or laws in each of the states.

The End of the Road

by David Burwell

Americans have a reputation for wanderlust. The majority of our ancestors making the leap to the North American Continent were motivated by the itch to move. Once settled along the eastern coast, their children lost little time exploring the western frontier. Their wanderlust is no less evident today with well over 40 million of us, a full 20 percent of our population, changing residences each year.[1] A bountiful land and a restless nature have made the search for "greener pastures" a full-time occupation for many Americans.

While the search was initially conducted by foot, wagon, and horseback, recent statistics confirm what a look out the nearest window reflects: the automobile is, overwhelmingly, the way we get around. The 133 million motor vehicles which zoom over our 3.8 million miles of highways constitute 50 percent of all the motor vehicles in the world.[2] Each of these vehicles consumes an average of 877 gallons of gasoline a year to travel an average of 10,000 miles per vehicle.[3] Every day about 10,000 new drivers obtain licenses and a net 10,000 vehicles (including motorcycles) are added to our highways.[4] In 1974 Americans spent $162.7 billion simply to move around, and private automobile travel accounted for $137.3 billion, or 84 percent of this outlay.[5]

But highways carry more than people; they are also the primary method of marketing the products of our $1.7 trillion economy.[6] As access to waterways created marketing centers in the eighteenth century and access to railroads created boom towns in the nineteenth, access to highways has played the dominant role in twentieth century marketing. By 1974, of an estimated total freight bill of $138.3 billion, truck transport accounted for $107.7 billion, or a full 77 percent of national freight costs.[7] Our transportation system, which accounts for 21 percent of our Gross National Product,[8] is uniquely dependent on highways. But why?

Highway construction stimulates the economy in several ways—at least temporarily. First, there is increased accessibility to markets. This is a real benefit since accessibility encourages trade which might not have occurred at all if the road had not been built, thereby increasing our total economic output and, presumably, our standard of living. Second, roads dramatically increase the value of adjacent commercial land, as long as access to the road is provided (this is less true with residential land). The city or town that attracts development by building highways also obtains the benefits of increased employment and tax revenue, and highways are often constructed for these benefits alone.

Finally, highway construction is big business. In the short term, it provides temporary jobs for many local construction firms. Nationally, highway construction provides a market for the use of our resources. In 1956, when exploitation rather than conservation of our natural resources was a national goal, the Portland Cement Association enthusiastically declared that the 40,000-mile interstate system would require, among other things, pavement area equalling 400 square miles, excavation that would bury Connecticut knee deep; sand, gravel, and stone that would build a wall around the world fifty feet wide and nine feet high; and culverts and drain pipes equalling the combined water and sewer systems of six Chicagos.[9] In the long term, the consumption potential of highway transportation is even more intriguing, due to the stimulating effect it has on car usage. As early as 1932 a highway enthusiast remarked: "Think of the result to the industrial world of putting on the market a product that doubles the malleable iron consumption, triples the plate glass consumption, and quadruples the use of rubber! . . . as a consumer of raw materials, the automobile has no equal in the history of the modern world."[10]

These economic benefits of highways are real and enduring. If you don't believe it, ask a stockholder in Firestone Tire and Rubber Co., a landowner at an interstate exchange, the owner of a trucking company, or a financier of equipment used for road construction. Of the ten largest corporations in the United States, eight have a direct interest in motor vehicle transport.[11] In a country that equates growth in the Gross National Product with progress, the close correlation between auto usage and the Gross National Product does not go unnoted by highways proponents. Between manufacturing, marketing, and servicing auto needs, one out of six jobs in our economy depends on the continued use of auto transport.[12]

Privacy, comfort, safety, mobility, and status are important amenities of automobile ownership but, being subjective, they are difficult to quantify. Enclosed cars, for example, are lockable, provide a rare refuge of privacy, protect passengers from rain and dust, and now come with radios, televisions, telephones, and even refrigerators. Even though more than 5,000,000 people are killed or injured in automobiles each year, 4,000 pounds of steel gives passengers a sense of safety. In an increasingly fast-paced society, cars are a scarce refuge of privacy. Models such as "Regal," "Grand Prix" and "Riviera" indicate that cars are still status indicators. Moreover, highway development and car usage has had a stunning effect on mobility. People caught in the cities have been able to escape to the beaches, mountains, and recreation areas for weekend trips, to the national parks for longer vacations, and to the suburbs permanently. Conversely, people down on the farm have been able to benefit from the cultural opportunities in the cities. As a Muncie, Indiana housewife said when asked why her family had a car but no bathtub, "You can't go to town in a bathtub!"[13]

Recent history has shown that highway construction is a good way to generate political capital. For example, the federal interstate program, launched in 1956, was inspired by the military effectiveness of Germany's Autobahn, and is actually called the National System of Interstate and Defense Highways. In the height of the cold war to vote against such a program was politically unwise. Ironically, the system has bridge clearances which are so low that many of our military vehicles cannot fit under them. As a result, the defense rationale has largely disappeared.[14]

The real political advantages of highways, however, are an outgrowth of short-term, local economic benefits. Labor and construction interests support highway construction, and support politicians who vote for it. Politicians also feel that large public works projects give the general population the impression of an aggressive, progressive administration. Moreover, public works construction, especially when heavily subsidized by the federal government, is an adrenalin shot to a sluggish economy that is much easier to apply and receive credit for than tortuous tax reform or government re-organization measures which may be more long-lasting solutions.

These do not encompass all highway benefits, but they do reflect the very real psychological and political as well as economic dependence that has blossomed around motor vehicle transport. In fact, the very state of dependence is used as a primary argument for continued dependence, much like saying that addiction is presumptive justification for continued addiction. Overlooked in this rationale, however, is cost, and highways have very real costs.

The American Reality: Highway Costs

The claim that highway construction incurs costs has never been denied. We are just now realizing, however, how extensive these costs really are. For many years after the passage of the first Federal-Aid Highway Act in 1916, perceived costs included only two items—capital and maintenance. These costs were assessed, not on society generally, but on the car owners who paid "user taxes" on gasoline, oil, tires and other automobile services. Since private users assumed these costs, highway proponents argued that society generally was the windfall beneficiary of privately financed construction projects. Even into the mid-sixties some highways analysts argued that, as far as society generally was concerned, highways have no costs, just benefits.

Acting on this "no-cost" theory of highway impacts, Congress in 1956 established the Highway Trust Fund, segregating gas tax revenues from general revenues, and specifying that they be used solely to amortize highway construction costs. At the same time the lawmakers added an interstate highway system to the growing list of highway-related projects these taxes funded. No sooner had almost all the transportation eggs been placed in the highway basket, however, than the true costs of highway construction began to surface.

In 1959 the New Haven Railroad, for many years a very lucrative industry in the industrialized Northeast, went into the red for the first time in its history. By 1961 it was bankrupt, and by 1968 had merged into the Penn Central. By 1973 the Penn Central and six other railroads in the Midwest and Northeast were hopelessly bankrupt. Railroad passenger miles, which hit a peak of 47 billion in 1920, had decreased to just 9.5 billion in 1975, although total passenger miles had more than quintupled for all modes.[15] By 1975, railroads accounted for only 0.7 percent of intercity passenger miles.[16] The railroads' share of total transportation revenues, freight and passenger, dipped from 72.3 percent in 1947 to 32.0 percent in 1973.[17]

To be sure, much of the blame for the railroads' present predicament can be placed at the industry's doorstep, both for its byzantine accounting system and poor management. But equal responsibility, if not more, must be attributed to the preferential treatment of highways. Specifically, highways are publicly owned and maintained, and as such are not tax-assessed. Railways, however, are owned and maintained by railroad companies, and taxes are collected on some property, such as terminals and switching areas. Also the trucking industry, through regulation of competition, high load limits, gas tax rebates, and low users' fees, has not paid its share of highway costs, thereby increasing its competitive advantage over railroads. Preferential treatment to highways has made it necessary for the government to pump $1.2 billion in grants and several billion more in loan guarantees into the fast-failing rail industry between 1971 and 1975.[18] Moreover, about 6,000 miles of rail lines have been slated for abandonment in the Northeast alone, stranding businesses located along these lines. These abandonments and subsidies are properly placed in the "cost" column of highway transportation.

The displacement of families is another impact of our national highway program. Many of the interstates have barrelled right through urban centers. In order to minimize land acquisition costs, the highway planners routed the highways where land costs were lowest—through low and middle-class neighborhoods. Destroyed were many multi-family units, at a time when our national housing goal was "a suitable living environment for every American family."[19] Between September, 1966 and June, 1971, 77 percent of all housing units destroyed by highways were low to moderate-income units.[20] Between 1956, the start of the interstate program, and 1967 more urban housing units were destroyed by highways (approximately 330,000) than were constructed by our entire national public housing program (239,374).[21] The dollar costs in community disruption, relocation expenses, and secondary government support for displaced families, although hard to quantify, have been enormous; the social and psychological damage to the affected communities is irreparable. While Congress has attempted to address this problem through relocation assistance, the permanent cost of community disintegration as a result of highway bisection remains.

While highways were seen as an economic boon to cities, hidden costs soon became obvious. Tax revenue from the land taken for highway purposes was lost. Businesses were displaced as a result of takings, and many folded rather than move to a new location.[22] Displaced residents were often maintained at public expense.

HEAVEN is under our feet as well as over our heads.

Henry David Thoreau

Cities were also forced to absorb the cost of municipal services (snowplowing, police, traffic lights, air pollution controls, etc.) that were needed to accommodate the daily commuting traffic. Maintaining the urban auto has been variously estimated to cost cities from 60 cents[23] to two dollars[24] per urban vehicle mile travelled, or five times the cost of maintaining subways. Finally, urban arterials allowed the more affluent urban residents to move to the suburbs, leaving the urban poor to assume a disproportionate share of municipal tax burdens. As suburban shopping malls developed to accommodate these suburban commuters, cities were further drained of their economic vitality. When all these costs are aggregated it appears that arterial highways in already industrialized cities may be net liabilities, not assests.

The ability of highways to promote development and tax revenues is highly praised by highway proponents. Overlooked, however, is the equal tendency of highway construction to promote land use patterns that increase the cost of providing community services—telephone, sewer and water lines, to name a few. These patterns are characterized by intense land use along strips of highway, the elimination of access to other land, and the encouragement of residential construction on large lots. Such development has been estimated to cost these "sprawl" communities 15 percent more than planned communities in road and utility

costs alone.[25] Moreover, as a look out the car window tells
us, sprawl destroys open space, eliminates important
wildlife and vegetative habitats, and is often less attractive
than a mix of high density housing and open space.

The impact of highways on fish and wildlife has been
murderous. An average of four animals are killed per car,
per year (or close to 500 million kills in 1976).[26] Many highways intersect with migration routes, mating grounds, and
wetland refuge areas. Highway fences in the West in some
winters are lined with starved and frozen antelope which
died attempting to migrate to grazing grounds. Salt from
roads runs into streams, reservoirs and lakes, killing plant
and fish life. In the Central Prairies highway ditches are
draining water from productive prairie potholes, our best
remaining breeding areas for ducks and migratory waterfowl. In nineteen counties of Western Minnesota alone,
100,000 acres of valuable prairie wetlands have been drained
into roadside ditches.[27] Ecological systems, like highway
systems, depend on continuity for survival. Just as a highway would be rendered useless without bridges to traverse
rivers in its path, many fish, wildlife, and wetlands cannot
survive bisection of their life cycles by highways. Sliced to
ribbons by highway pavement, these systems die.

The tremendous pollution of our air and water, and the
assault on our eardrums, caused by highway construction
and use is becoming increasingly unacceptable to a growing
percentage of our population. Nationwide, transportation in
1969 contributed an estimated 73 percent of the carbon
monoxide, 52 percent of the hydrocarbons, and 47 percent
of the nitrogen oxides in the ambient air.[28] Air pollution can
reduce the amount of sunlight entering a city as much as 16
percent, and in 1971 alone caused an estimated $10.1 billion
loss in damage to buildings, materials, and reduced property
value.[29] Annual death rates from heart disease rose from 137
per 100,000 in 1900 to 362 in 1970, while those from cancer
rose from 64 per 100,000 to 163.8.[30] Environmental pollution, much of it coming from motor vehicles, is considered
the prime suspect for these escalating figures.

Highway construction can also be very damaging to
drinking water supplies. Highways built in watersheds
which provide water to our surface reservoirs are often the
source of silt and salt contamination. If untreated, silt and
salt can reduce the oxygen content of the reservoir, increase

turbidity, facilitate the transmittal of viruses in drinking water, and cause the gradual decay (eutrophication) of the
water supply. Oil runoff from daily usage and spills is a
danger, as are asbestos tailings (from brake linings) and
poly-chlorinated biphenyls (PCBs—from brake fluid), both
of which are carcinogenic.

Most environmental effects of highway construction
cannot be quantified. Noise, for example, from both the
construction and use of highways, has been documented to
affect human blood pressure, digestion, and one's ability to
concentrate and to rest. There is no way to put a price tag on
a sleepless night, or a sore throat; they are nonetheless real
costs.

The most recently perceived, but arguably the most
important, consequence of auto dependence is its effect on
energy consumption. In 1975 motor vehicles consumed
more than 76 billion gallons of gasoline to travel 1.028 trillion vehicle miles, an average of 13.5 miles per gallon[31] (this
compares to 25.8 mpg in Italy and 20 to 26 mpg in other
European countries.)[32] The United States uses approximately 3.7 times more energy per capita in the transportation sector than does West Germany, a country as industrialized as the United States and with an approximately
equal standard of living.[33] Since transportation accounts for
about 25 percent of the total energy budget of the United
States, this energy gluttony is significant.[34]

Our intense use of energy per capita is partially due to
the fact that we are a large and mobile country—it takes
more energy for people in New York to visit relatives in Los
Angeles than for similar trips within any European country.
But the *way* we travel, primarily by car and air, is particularly energy inefficient. People travelling by car in urban
areas spend almost three times as much energy to go the
same distance as people who travel by rail transit (assuming
the statistical average of 1.6 people per car and 40 percent
occupancy rate per transit vehicle).[35] Air travel uses even
more energy: it takes more than five times as much energy
to transport a person from Washington, D.C. to Miami by
air than it does by bus (assuming a fifty percent occupancy
rate for both modes).[36] However, sprawled-out land use patterns have locked us into dependence on the automobile to
get around: few urban areas have sufficient population den-
sities to support rail transit systems.

Besides being wasteful, expensive and dirty, unrestrained car travel has contributed to the creation of severe national problems, including a large balance of payments deficit, dependence on energy sources we cannot control, and the possibility of international conflict over the use of dwindling reserves.

Highway proponents argue that roads are getting safer, not more dangerous. To support this argument they quote the declining death rate per vehicle miles travelled (from 5.58 deaths per 100 million vehicle miles travelled in 1966 to 3.47 in 1975).[37] But a proper question may be—safer than what? In absolute terms, it is more likely than ever that you will die or be injured in an automobile accident. During the 1960's traffic deaths increased 47 percent although the population only increased 11.7 percent.[38] There were 5,140,000 injuries involving moving vehicles in 1975, including 45,674 deaths,[39] with societal costs of an estimated 37.59 billion dollars. Once again, the total costs in human suffering are incalculable.

The predilection of public officials to pass public works legislation in order to stimulate the economy is well known. "Pork barrel" projects, often of doubtful economic value, are a convenient means of generating jobs for supporters "back in the district". The pork barrel includes, among other things, dams, waterways, armories, courthouses—and highways. The problem, however, is that highway projects don't given as much "bang for the buck" as they used to. Once done by pick and shovel, highway construction is now done with huge machinery that needs less manpower to do the same work. In 1950, 130,637 man-hours were required to do a million dollars worth of highway work (using constant 1967 dollars), but the same amount of work could be done in 60,364 man-hours in 1975.[40] While this trend is applauded by some as increasing labor productivity, it also means fewer jobs. On the other hand, transit construction as done in cities, requires more specialized work, and is not conducive to the use of big machinery. It is therefore more labor-intensive than highway construction, creating an estimated 3.2 percent more man-hours of work per million dollars spent than highways.[41] Rail rehabilitation is even more advantageous from an employment-producing standpoint, being an estimated 47 percent more labor-intensive than highway construction. Since public transportation also generates more permanent jobs (for operation) than highways (for maintenance), the conclusion is inescapable that highway construction, as an employment stimulus, is a questionable investment.

There are other costs. For example, the sky-rocketing out-of-pocket expenses of car ownership (gas prices, sale-price increases, registration fees, insurance, and repair) all have roots outside, but connected to, our dependence on automobiles. We are all paying: in increased commuting time; in higher prices for sales; in higher bills for repair; in fewer recreational areas; in acrid smells and watery eyes that accompany increasingly frequent traffic tie-ups; in sleepless nights; in devalued property next to freeways; in increased respiratory diseases; in community disruption; in strip-development pollution; in fewer waterfowl, deer and other wildlife; in lost wilderness areas; in oil spills; and, yes, in increased dependence on Saudi-Arabian oil, South-American rubber, and Japanese Toyotas. The list is endless, and includes every indicie of what is generally called our "quality of life."

Two important points merit emphasis. First, if you feel that highway costs are excessive, don't feel you have to justify your position with a trenchant cost/benefit analysis or intricate econometric models; the unquantifiable costs will suffice. Second, don't feel defeated by highway proponents' common argument that "highway users pay their costs, so what are you complaining about?" Highway costs pervade every level of government and affect all of our services and resources. Capital and maintenance costs barely scratch the surface of true costs, and it is these true costs for which we must all be held accountable. The time is long overdue for us as a nation to step back and evaluate whether the highway game is really worth the total ante.

---

1. J. B. Rae, *The Road and the Car in American Life* (MIT Press, Cambridge, Mass., 1971), p. 145.
2. Federal Highway Administration, *National Highway Transportation: Statement of Policy*, 41 Fed. Reg. 54090, 54091 (December 10, 1976).
3. Statement of Robert M. Kennan, Jr., *Hearings on Future Highway Needs, H.R. 5573, Before the Subcomm. on Transportation of the House Comm. on Public Works*, H.R. Doc. 93–5, 93d Cong., 1st Sess. 480 (1973).

4. *Id.,* at 480.
5. Transportation Association of America, *Transportation Facts and Trends* (Supp., Oct. 1976), p. 3.
6. Joint Committee on Economic Affairs, *Economic Indicators,* Govt. Printing Office (Dec. 1976).
7. *Facts and Trends, supra,* note 5 at 3.
8. Transportation Association of America, *Facts and Trends* (Twelfth ed., 1976), p. 3.
9. K. R. Schneider, *Autokind v. Mankind* (Schoken Press, New York City, 1972), p. 124.
10. *Id.,* at 123.
11. The companies are Mobil, Exxon, Texaco, Gulf, General Motors, Chrysler, Ford and U. S. Steel; See B. Kelly, *The Pavers and the Paved* (Donald W. Brown, Inc., New York City, 1971), p. 4.
12. American Motoring Association, *Automobiles of America,* p. 256. Kenneth Schneider estimates that in 1968 the figure was closer to one in five, *supra,* note 9 at 81.
13. F. L. Allen, *The Big Change* (1953), p. 121.
14. Karl Detzer, "Our Great Big Highway Bungle," Reader's Digest (July 1960) p. 45.
15. Trans. Assoc. of America, *Facts and Trends* (Twelfth Ed., 1976), p. iv.
16. *Id.,* at 18.
17. *Id.,* at 6.
18. U.S. Dept. of Transportation, *Study of Federal Aid to Rail Transportation Report of the Secretary of Transportation to the United States Congress pursuant to Section 902 of the Railroad Revitalization and Regulatory Reform Act of 1976* (Jan. 1977).
19. Housing Act of 1949, 42 U.S.C. 1441, *et seq.* (1970). This goal was reaffirmed in the 1968 Housing Act, 42 U.S.C. 1401 (1970).
20. Low income in 1971 was considered $60 per month or less (rental) or less than $6,000 valuation (house), moderate income $60-$110 per month (rental) or between $6,000-$15,000 (house). Secretary of the Department of Transportation, *1972 Annual Report on Highway Relocation Assistance* (1972), cited in P. W. Sly, *In the Path of Progress: Federal Highway Relocation Assistance,* 82 Yale L.J. 373, 377, n. 27 (1972).
21. Figures from *Report on the National Commission on Urban Problems to the Congress and President of the United States, Building the American City,* 91st Cong., 1st Sess., H.R. Doc. No. 91–34, at 81, 130 (1969). *See also* Sly, *supra,* note 6 at 377, n. 26.
22. A Texas study of relocation under the Relocation Assistance Act of 1970 found that over 50% of the businesses that were dependent on the local area discontinued operations rather than relocate. Overall, about 75% of the businesses were able to successfully relocate. Federal Highway Administration, *Social and Economic Effects of Highways* (1976), p. 16.
23. Statement of Brian T. Ketchum, Citizens for Clean Air, before the Metropolitan Transportation Authority (New York City), Jan. 5, 1977.
24. D. G. Wilson, *"Estimates of Pollution from U.S. Non-Freight Highway Transportation,"* 6 Intn'l. Jl. Environmental Studies, 35, 48 (1974).
25. Council on Environmental Quality, *The Costs of Sprawl* (1974), p. 8.

26. K. R. Schneider, *Autokind v. Mankind* (Schoken Press, New York City, 1972), p. 163. Mr. Schneider cites 1968 figures (365 million kills). 500 million is a conservative extrapolation based on increased car usage 1968–1976.

27. U. S. Department of the Interior, Fish and Wildlife Service, "Task Force Report on Effects of Road Construction on Wetland Wildlife Habitat" (1975). Available from Fish and Wildlife Service, Federal Building, Fort Snelling, Twin Cities, Minn. 55111.

28. Council on Environmental Quality, *Environmental Quality: The Second Annual Report of the Council on Environmental Quality (1971)* p. 212.

29. Council on Environmental Quality, *The Costs of Sprawl* (1974).

30. Council on Environmental Quality, *Environmental Quality: Fifth Annual Report of the Council on Environmental Quality (1974)*, p. 10.

31. Federal Highway Administration, *Highway Statistics* (1976).

32. Russell E. Train, "The Urgent Need to Curb Gasoline Waste," *Washington Post* (March 6, 1977), p. C1.

33. *Id.*, at C5.

34. "Transportation Energy Conservation: Opportunities and Policy Issues," *Transportation Journal* (Spring 1974); The Mitre Corporation, *Energy and Environmental Aspects of U.S. Transportation* (Feb. 1974).

35. "Transportation Energy Conservation Policies," *Science,* April 2, 1976, p. 16.

36. *Id.*

37. National Highway Traffic Safety Administration, *Traffic Safety '75* (1976), p. 1.

38. George W. Brown, Speech given at the Third National Conference on the Transportation Crisis, Washington, D.C., June 10, 1972.

39. Traffic Safety, *supra,* n. 23, at p. 1.

40. U. S. Dept. of Transportation, "Price Trends for Federal-Aid Highway Construction" (Third Quarter, 1976), p. 11.

41. Roger Bezdek and Bruce Hannon, "Energy, Manpower, and the Highway Trust Fund," *Science,* Aug. 23, 1974.

Wilderness

by David Gancher

Wilderness is the bedrock of the environmental movement. Before there was recycling, before there was an anti-nuke movement, before there were tax-credits for solar retrofitting, before synfuels or pollution—there was John Muir. The mystical old Scot, wearing a black suit and an overcoat—one pocket stuffed with bread, the other stuffed with tea—traveled the Sierra Nevada and Alaska, lived in Yosemite in ecstasy and bliss, and was utterly at home in the wilderness. Out of his enthusiasm for wilderness and his concern for its protection came the Sierra Club—and eventually today's environmental movement.

Though wilderness seems an issue without the drama and controversy of, say, synthetic fuels, it is still the heart of the environmental movement. If you don't believe me, go backpacking for a week and reconsider.

We sometimes think that the battle for wilderness is essentially over, that we've won and that the general public is so environmentally aware that the threats to wilderness are slight and fragmented.

Unfortunately, nothing could be further from the truth. Congress recently considered legislation that is the most sweeping and dangerous effort to block wilderness preservation yet—and it has strong, active and sophisticated backing by timber and mining interests. The proposed *non*-wilderness legislation is an attempt to shut the door once and for all on all forest additions to the National Wilderness Preservation system. In very brief terms, this legislation is "release" legislation. It says that whatever is not designated as wilderness before a certain arbitrary deadline will never become wilderness.

Before this new approach, Congress had established (in the 1964 Wilderness Act) a process for area-by-area consideration of lands for possible protection. The process was, at times, tediously repetitive, but it did ensure that the area received minute, specific consideration. Each year additional candidate areas have been considered in Congress—and in public hearings—to investigate the wilderness attributes, the resources tradeoffs and the specific boundaries of areas. Often, Congress has assembled a legislative package of such specific areas and passed them together, as an "omnibus" bill.

But in the 1970's, conservationists and industry people both sought a new approach to the problem of considering wilderness. So RARE II (Roadless Area Review and Evaluation) was developed. It was a Forest Service program between 1977 and 1979 to inventory, analyze and recommend the ultimate fates of some 62 million acres of roadless, undeveloped land in the National Forests. At first, RARE II went well—but industry political pressure resulted in a Carter Administration policy of doing the work hastily, and therefore inaccurately and haphazardly. Much of the analysis was done badly, by computer. The recommendations were predictable: 15.4 million acres were recommended as wilderness, another 10.6 million acres recommended for further study and 36 million acres were "released" from further consideration and made available for uses other than wilderness. Uses like mining and logging. Conservationists agreed, of course, that many of the 36 million acres weren't really suitable for wilderness. But conservationists disagreed hotly over other areas—and have been insisting that Congress reconsider the controversial areas.

Industry, however, has little patience for this deliberate, area-by-area approach. Wilderness opponents have now been urging once-and-forever legislation to deal with roadless areas. This particular legislation died a well-deserved, hasty, and emphatic death. By promoting a single, nationwide bill, they hope to bury the details in a superficial debate over the quasi-issue of "certainty." This has been the watchword of the industry—they want to know, once and for all, which lands will be wilderness and which will be open to logging, roads and development. It sounds reasonable, but it could prove disastrous—for it doesn't give anyone a chance to change their minds about wilderness. And they're not making it anymore, you know.

This "I want it all now" strategy is new to industry. And even conservationists admit that it's a clever strategy—they're clearly getting sneakier. A retired Congressman from Washington, Lloyd Meeds, now an attorney who lobbies for timber interests, explained the strategy thus: "We really need to begin to deal in a different ballgame. It is not fighting one wilderness here, or fighting wilderness there—that is what they [us—environmentalists] want us to do. We really need to recognize that our strength in industry. . . lies in creating a single package . . ." He summarized the anti-wilderness goal succinctly: "We need to get into the 36 million acres, and see that it is damn well returned and returned quickly to multiple-use management." The term multiple-use management, it should be noted, is misleading. It implies that everyone—industry and campers, hikers and loggers—should be given access to forests. But who wants to camp in a clearcut? Once logging starts, other uses are affected.

Industry's strength lies in its ability to make centralized decisions and wage media attacks on the "red tape" of wilderness preservation. But conservationists' strength lies in their ability to muster public opinion for these special, specific places. We do want Congress to continue to consider wilderness on an area-by-area basis and not to give it

Back from the Brink

During recent years, there have been some large successes in the return of a number of species of animals from near extinction (although the California condor is closer to the brink). The California gray whale, the southern fur seal, the southern elephant seal, the brown pelican and other animals have risen from precarious positions to healthy breeding populations that look like they'll be with us for a long time.

The gray whale, fur seal and elephant seal had been overhunted; under protection (begun a few decades ago) they were able to come back—the simplest form of wildlife management. The cases of the brown pelican and peregrine falcon were more complicated, tied into the proliferation of DDT and other chlorinated hydrocarbon pesticides, which made reproduction almost impossible for the birds. When these chemicals were cut back drastically the pelicans began breeding successfully again and we now see young pelicans in the offshore waters of California. Even the peregrine falcon—in dire jeopardy a few years ago—seems to have staged the beginning of a comeback.

GDB

away because of pressure from exploiters.

The battle for wilderness is taking place on two levels now. The various national environmental groups—the Sierra Club, Friends of the Earth, The Wilderness Society—are working with conservationist members of Congress to defeat this first stab at sweeping "release" legislation. Though the first bill proposed was defeated, the anti-wilderness forces will not stop their efforts.

The battle for wilderness will be a long one—you can help simply by joining one of these groups, by volunteering to help lobby, write letters, visit your Representative and Senators. You can help by applying pressure.

On a more local level, you can help by adopting a non-designated wilderness. Find one (or more!), learn about it—experience it—and with friends form your own informal task force. Through local efforts—articles in newspapers, letters to editors, public hearings—you can work to preserve your own wilderness by getting it designated as official wilderness. It is this local, individual, patient effort that will be the one that ultimately counts. Legislation comes and goes, but individual witness and effort abideth forever. Amen.

The Serpents of Paradise

by Edward Abbey

The April mornings are bright, clear and calm. Not until the afternoon does the wind begin to blow, raising dust and sand in funnel-shaped twisters that spin across the desert briefly, like dancers, and then collapse—whirlwinds from which issue no voice or word except the forlorn moan of the elements under stress. After the reconnoitering dust-devils comes the real the serious wind, the voice of the desert rising to a demented howl and blotting out sky and sun behind yellow clouds of dust, sand, confusion, embattled birds, last year's scrub-oak leaves, pollen, the husks of locusts, bark of juniper. . . .

Time of the red eye, the sore and bloody nostril, the sand-pitted windshield, if one is foolish enough to drive his car into such a storm. Time to sit indoors and continue that letter which is never finished—while the fine dust forms neat little windrows under the edge of the door and on the windowsills. Yet the springtime winds are as much a part of the canyon country as the silence and the glamorous distances; you learn, after a number of years, to love them also.

The mornings therefore, as I started to say and meant to say, are all the sweeter in the knowledge of what the afternoon is likely to bring. Before beginning the morning chores I like to sit on the sill of my doorway, bare feet planted on the bare ground and a mug of hot coffee in hand, facing the sunrise. The air is gelid, not far above freezing, but the butane heater inside the trailer keeps my back warm, the rising sun warms the front, and the coffee warms the interior.

Perhaps this is the loveliest hour of the day, though it's hard to choose. Much depends on the season. In midsummer the sweetest hour begins at sundown, after the awful heat of the afternoon. But now, in April, we'll take the opposite, that hour beginning with the sunrise. The birds, returning from wherever they go in winter, seem inclined to agree. The pinyon jays are whirling in garrulous, gregarious flocks from one stunted tree to the next and back again, erratic exuberant games without any apparent practical

function. A few big ravens hang around and croak harsh
clanking statements of smug satisfaction from the rimrock,
lifting their greasy wings now and then to probe for lice. I
can hear but seldom see the canyon wrens singing their
distinctive song from somewhere up on the cliffs: a flutelike
descent—never ascent—of the whole-tone scale. Staking
out new nesting claims, I understand. Also invisible but
invariably present at some indefinable distance are the
mourning doves whose plaintive call suggests irresistibly a
kind of seeking-out, the attempt by separated souls to restore a lost communion:

Hello . . . they seem to cry, who . . . are . . . you?

And the reply from a different quarter. Hello . . .
(pause) where . . . are . . . you?

No doubt this line of analogy must be rejected. It's
foolish and unfair to impute to the doves, with serious concerns of their own, an interest in questions more appropriate
to their human kin. Yet their song, if not a mating call or a
warning, must be what it sounds like, a brooding meditation
on space, on solitude. The game.

Other birds, silent, which I have not yet learned to
identify, are also lurking in the vicinity, watching me. What
the ornithologist terms l.g.b.'s—little gray birds—they flit
about from point to point on noiseless wings, their origins
obscure.

As mentioned before, I share the housetrailer with a
number of mice. I don't know how many but apparently
only a few, perhaps a single family. They don't disturb me
and are welcome to my crumbs and leavings. Where they
came from, how they got into the trailer, how they survived
before my arrival (for the trailer had been locked up for six
months), there are puzzling matters I am not prepared to
resolve. My only reservation concerning the mice is that
they do attract rattlesnakes.

I'm sitting on my doorstep early one morning, facing
the sun as usual, drinking coffee, when I happen to look
down and see almost between my bare feet, only a couple of
inches to the rear of my heels, the very thing I had in mind.
No mistaking that wedgelike head, that tip of horny seg-
mented tail peeping out of the coils. He's under the doorstep
and in the shade where the ground and air remain very cold.
In his sluggish condition he's not likely to strike unless I
rouse him by some careless move of my own.

There's a revolver inside the trailer, a huge British Webley .45, loaded, but it's out of reach. Even if I had it in my hands I'd hesitate to blast a fellow creature at such close range, shooting between my own legs at a living target flat on solid rock thirty inches away. It would be like murder; and where would I set my coffee? My cherrywood walking stick leans against the trailerhouse wall only a few feet away but I'm afraid that in leaning over for it I might stir up the rattler or spill some hot coffee on his scales.

Other considerations come to mind. Arches National Monument is meant to be among other things a sanctuary for wildlife—for all forms of wildlife. It is my duty as a park ranger to protect, preserve and defend all living things within the park boundaries, making no exceptions. Even if this were not the case I have personal convictions to uphold. Ideals, you might say. I prefer not to kill animals. I'm a humanist; I'd rather kill a *man* than a snake.

What to do. I drink some more coffee and study the dormant reptile at my heels. It is not after all the mighty diamondback, *Crotalus atrox*, I'm confronted with but a smaller species known locally as the horny rattler or more precisely as the Faded Midget. An insulting name for a rattlesnake, which may explain the Faded Midget's alleged bad temper. But the name is apt: he is small and dusty-looking, with a little knob above each eye—the horns. His bite though temporarily disabling would not likely kill a full-grown man in normal health. Even so I don't really want him around. Am I to be compelled to put on boots and shoes every time I wish to step outside? The scorpions, tarantulas, centipedes, and black widows are nuisance enough.

I finish my coffee, lean back and swing my feet up and inside the doorway of the trailer. At once there is a buzzing sound from below and the rattler lifts his head from his coils, eyes brightening, and extends his narrow black tongue to test the air.

After thawing out my boots over the gas flame I pull them on and come back to the doorway. My visitor is still waiting beneath the doorstep, basking in the sun, fully alert. The trailerhouse has two doors. I leave by the other and get a long-handled spade out of the bed of the government pick-up. With this tool I scoop the snake into the open. He strikes; I can hear the click of the fangs against steel, see the stain of venom. He wants to stand and fight, but I am pa-

SOMETHING of the wild and primitive should forever remain instinctive in the human race. All the joy of the senses lives in this law.

Zane Grey

tient; I insist on herding him well away from the trailer. On guard, head aloft—that evil slit-eyed weaving head shaped like the ace of spades—tail whirring, the rattler slithers sideways, retreating slowly before me until he reaches the shelter of a sandstone slab. He backs under it.

You better stay there, cousin, I warn him; if I catch you around the trailer again I'll chop your head off.

A week later he comes back. If not him, his twin brother. I spot him one morning under the trailer near the kitchen drain, waiting for a mouse. I have to keep my promise.

This won't do. If there are midget rattlers in the area there may be diamondbacks too—five, six or seven feet long, thick as a man's wrist, dangerous. I don't want *them* camping under my home. It looks as though I'll have to trap the mice.

However, before being forced to take that step I am lucky enough to capture a gopher snake. Burning garbage one morning at the park dump, I see a long slender yellow-brown snake emerge from a mound of old tin cans and plastic picnic plates and take off down the sandy bed of a gulch. There is a burlap sack in the cab of the truck which I carry when plucking Kleenex flowers from the brush and cactus along the road; I grab that and my stick, run after the snake and corner it beneath the exposed roots of a bush. Making sure it's a gopher snake and not something less useful, I open the neck of the sack and with a great deal of coaxing and prodding get the snake into it. The gopher snake, *Drymarchon corais couperi*, or bull snake, has a reputation as the enemy of rattlesnakes, destroying or driving them away whenever encountered.

Hoping to domesticate this sleek, handsome and docile reptile, I release him inside the trailerhouse and keep him there for several days. Should I attempt to feed him? I decide against it—let him eat mice. What little water he may need can also be extracted from the flesh of his prey.

The gopher snake and I get along nicely. During the day he curls up like a cat in the warm corner behind the heater and at night he goes about his business. The mice, singularly quiet for a change, make themselves scarce. The snake is passive, apparently contented, and makes no resistance when I pick him up with my hands and drape him over an arm or around my neck. When I take him outside into the wind and sunshine his favorite place seems to be inside my shirt, where he wraps himself around my waist and rests on my belt. In this position he sometimes sticks his head out between shirt buttons for a survey of the weather, astonishing and delighting any tourists who happen to be with me at the time. The scales of a snake are dry and smooth, quite pleasant to touch. Being a cold-blooded creature, of course, he takes his temperature from that of the immediate environment—in this case my body.

We are compatible. From my point of view, friends. After a week of close association I turn him loose on the warm sandstone at my doorstep and leave for a patrol of the park. At noon when I return he is gone. I search everywhere beneath, nearby and inside the trailerhouse, but my companion has disappeared. Has he left the area entirely or is he hiding somewhere close by? At any rate I am troubled no more by rattlesnakes under the door.

The snake story is not yet ended.

In the middle of May, about a month after the gopher snake's disappearance, in the evening of a very hot day, with all the rosy desert cooling like a griddle with the fire turned off, he reappears. This time with a mate.

I'm in the stifling heat of the trailer opening a can of beer, barefooted, about to go outside and relax after a hard day watching cloud formations. I happen to glance out the little window near the refrigerator and see two gopher snakes on my verandah engaged in what seems to be a kind of ritual dance. Like a living caduceus they wind and unwind about each other in undulant, graceful, perpetual motion, moving slowly across a dome of sandstone. Invisible but tangible as music is the passion which joins them—sexual? combative? both? A shameless *voyeur*, I stare at the lovers, and then to get a closer view run outside and around the trailer to the back. There I get down on hands and knees and creep toward the dancing snakes, not wanting to frighten or disturb them. I crawl to within six feet of them and stop, flat on my belly, watching from the snake's-eye level. Obsessed with their ballet, the serpents seem unaware of my presence.

The two gopher snakes are nearly identical in length and coloring; I cannot be certain that either is actually my former household pet. I cannot even be sure that they are male and female, though their performance resembles so strongly a *pas de deux* by formal lovers. They intertwine and separate, glide side by side in perfect congruence, turn like mirror images of each other and glide back again, wind and unwind again. This is the basic pattern but there is a variation: at regular intervals the snakes elevate their heads, facing one another, as high as they can go, as if each is trying to outreach or overawe the other. Their heads and bodies rise, higher and higher, then topple together and the rite goes on.

I crawl after them, determined to see the whole thing. Suddenly and simultaneously they discover me, prone on my belly a few feet away. The dance stops. After a moment's pause the two snakes come straight toward me, still in flawless unison, straight toward my face, the forked tongues flickering, their intense wild yellow eyes staring directly into my eyes. For an instant I am paralyzed by wonder; then, stung by a fear too ancient and powerful to overcome I scramble back, rising to my knees. The snakes veer and turn and race away from me in parallel motion, their lean elegant bodies making a soft hissing noise as they slide over the sand and stone. I follow them for a short distance, still plagued by curiosity, before remembering my place and the requirements of common courtesy. For godsake let them go in peace, I tell myself. Wish them luck and (if lovers) innumerable offspring, a life of happily ever after. Not for their sake alone but for your own.

In the long hot days and cool evenings to come I will not see the gopher snakes again. Nevertheless I will feel their presence watching over me like totemic deities, keeping the rattlesnakes far back in the brush where I like them best, cropping off the surplus mouse population, maintaining useful connections with the primeval. Sympathy, mutual aid, symbiosis, continuity.

How can I descend to such anthropomorphism? Easily—but is it, in this case, entirely false? Perhaps not. I am not attributing human motives to my snake and bird acquaintances. I recognize that when and where they serve purposes of mine they do so for beautifully selfish reasons of their own. Which is exactly the way it should be. I suggest, however, that it's a foolish, simple-minded rationalism which denies any form of emotion to all animals but man and his dog. This is no more justified than the Moslems are in denying souls to women. It seems to me possible, even probable, that many of the nonhuman undomesticated animals experience emotions unknown to us. What do the coyotes mean when they yodel at the moon? What are the dolphins trying so patiently to tell us? Precisely what did those two enraptured gopher snakes have in mind when they came gliding toward my eyes over the naked sandstone? If I had been as capable of trust as I am susceptible to fear I might have learned something new or some truth so very old we have all forgotten it.

They do not sweat and whine about their condition,
They do not lie awake in the dark and weep for their sins. . . .

All men are brothers, we like to say, half-wishing sometimes in secret it were not true. But perhaps it is true. And is the evolutionary line from protozoan to Spinoza any less certain? That also may be true. We are obliged, therefore, to spread the news, painful and bitter though it may be for some to hear, that all living things on earth are kindred.

Mono Lake—
At the Other End of the Tap

by David Gaines

In the part of Los Angeles where I grew up, most homes had swimming pools and luxuriant landscaping. Leaves were hosed off driveways and sidewalks; kids played in the streams that coursed down the street-curbs into the gutters. No one knew or cared very much that the area was really a sub-desert, nor about what was happening at the other end of our taps in the watersheds of the distant Sierra. And from the year I was born, 1947, to the year I was graduated from high school, the city's population doubled. Meanwhile at the "other end," Mono Lake began dying an unnatural and needless death.

For millions of years clear, cold streams flowed from the flanks of the Sierra Nevada into this life-productive inland sea cradled by volcanos, glacier-sculpted canyons and snow-laden peaks. In 1941 some of the water in these streams was diverted out of the Mono Basin and into the Los Angeles Aqueduct. During the 1970's the diversions were dramatically increased. By 1980 the level of Mono Lake had fallen 43 vertical feet. Its volume had been halved and its salinity doubled. Clouds of alkali dust rise off 15,000 acres of exposed lakebottom, fouling the air for miles around. Mono is becoming a sterile sump and alkali dustbowl, the same fate that overtook Owens Lake half a century before. Looking across the sere Owens Lakebed, dust clouds rising from its surface, it is difficult to imagine steamboats plying its waters and millions of birds feeding along its shores. Only oldtimers recall the 20 miles of water that reflected Mt. Whitney and its neighboring Sierra summits in the days before the Owens River was siphoned to Los Angeles.

Must Mono Lake also be sacrificed to the seemingly insatiable water demand of an ever-increasing population? To be followed by San Francisco Bay, the Eel River, the Columbia, and on and on until every last marsh, wetland and free-flowing stream has been destroyed? Until the last waterfowl and last salmon follow the California Grizzly into oblivion, and even the Yukon is diverted? And we tip the balance of nature against our own children?

The plight of Mono Lake reminds us of the vital connections between our use of resources and the health of the earth. It reminds us there is beauty and life at the other end of our taps, and that soon there may be only dust.

Because we have forgotten these connections, and have yet to realize ultimate costs, we have been flagrantly careless and wasteful in our use of water and other precious resources. The installation of simple, inexpensive water-saving fixtures in every California household could save Mono Lake many times over.

Mono Lake is a warning about the earth's limited resources, and a signpost pointing out the path to responsible resource use. Let's consider what will be lost if Mono dies, and how we, in our everyday lives, can conserve enough water to save this lake, and our other remaining wetlands.

California's Inland Ocean

I first saw Mono Lake when I was 15 and treked from Tioga Pass to the summit of Mt. Dana in Yosemite National Park. There to the east, where I expected an unbroken expanse of sagebrush desert, lay an immense inland sea 10 by 14 miles wide, a disk of blue water with one black and one white volcanic island.

On that same trip I wandered for the first time along Mono's beaches. As far as the eye could see, every square mile of the lake was peppered with waterfowl, while thousands of shorebirds and gulls crowded the delta of Lee Vining Creek. For a moment, savoring the salty air and listening to the cries of the gulls, I thought I was at the seashore. But the White Mountains rising to 14,000 feet in the east, the sheer, snow-mantled Sierra Nevada to the west, the symmetrical volcanic domes of the Mono Craters to the south, the two starkly contrasting islands in the indigo lake, and the ornately sculptured tufa (mineral) towers rising above their reflections into the blue, belonged to a place apart, a grand and haunting landscape unlike anything I ever could have imagined.

Only a handful of organisms have been able to adapt to the unique saline and alkaline water of Mono Lake, but they occur in astronomical numbers. Microscopic green plants, phytoplankton, form the base of a relatively simple food web. They nourish the brine shrimp and flies on which the lake's birdlife depends. The abundance of invertebrate-feeding birds is directly related to the absence of fish, which cannot survive in Mono's brine. Without fish competing for the shrimp and flies, the birds have an essentially limitless source of food.

Because of this cornucopia, Mono harbors thousands of times more birds than freshwater lakes like Tahoe. About 95% of California's California Gulls raise their young on its islands. About 50% of the world's Wilson's Phalaropes, a colorful sandpiper, stop at the lake during their migrations. From August through October over a million grebes, ducks and shorebirds, amass on its waters. At few places on earth do so many birds gather at once.

Now the Lee Vining Creek delta, where I birdwatched as a teenager and where local duck hunters used to bag their limits, is dry and deserted. The receding lake has left an ugly "bathtub ring" of white, alkali-encrusted rocks and sand. Most of the tufa formations which once projected so dramatically fom Mono's surface are shipwrecked on its shores. The remains of docks and marinas lie bleached, high on the beaches. The State Fish Hatchery is a pile of rubble beside the dry bed and dying willows of Rush Creek, once Mono's largest tributary stream. The pools at the mouth of Rush Creek, where trout once fattened on Mono Lake flies, are only a memory. White shoals of alkali reach for two miles from Black Point to Negit Island and a strong wind can make the lake vanish in a cloud of chemical dust.

When I visited Negit Island in 1976, it was an avian madhouse of 38,000 adult California Gulls and an equal number of chicks. The pitch and intensity of life was overwhelming. When I returned in 1979, the island was silent and deserted. The shrinking lake had exposed a two-mile-long landbridge between Negit and the mainland and predators crossed the landbridge, annihilating the world's largest known colony of California Gulls. Only empty nests, scattered egg shells and partially eaten chicks remained.

If Mono Lake continues of shrink, its increasing salinity will poison all of its millions of birds and the brine shrimp and flies on which they feed.

These birds have nowhere else to go. Aquatic habitat is scarce in the arid interior of western North America, and birds depend on Mono Lake, Great Salt Lake and a very few other lakes for the food they need to cross hundreds of miles

Water Resources

The development of water resources is a frequent cause of
environmental battles. Rivers are dammed, water tables
pumped ever lower, water-using plants in desert regions are
cut down so the water will be available for use by people,
and vast canal schemes are designed to shift water from
where it is plentiful (and part of the natural scene and
wildlife habitat) to flush toilets elsewhere. Mono Lake, on
the east side of California's Sierra Nevada, is almost a prototype of the problem—and an example of common sense
conservation as the solution.

GDB

of desert. If Mono dies, bird flocks will dwindle, not only in
California, but from the Arctic to Argentina.

Moreover the unique species of brine shrimp and other
organisms which thrive in Mono's waters have evolved over
the millions of years of this ancient lake's existence, adapting to a saline habitat unlike any other on earth. An ecosystem, not just a species, will become extinct.

One can readily inventory these wildlife and scientific
values. It is infinitely more difficult to take stock of Mono
Lake's intangible esthetic and spiritual values. How often,
watching thousands of birds flocking along Mono's shores,
have I experienced a deep and comforting joy in the beauty
and bountifulness of creation? I feel the same way while
swimming in Mono's waters, buoyed by the heavy brine,
gulls wheeling overhead and millions of brine shrimp drifting
below. What is that feeling worth?

"I never dreamt this was here," said one of my field
trip participants, "I don't understand why this isn't a national park." Just about everyone who takes the time to
explore Mono's shores echoes this sentiment. The changes
occurring at Mono are akin to damming Yosemite or strip-
mining Death Valley.

If our consumption of water can only be brought into
harmony with the needs of our watersheds, Mono may not
become another Owens deathscape. An Interagency Task
Force, chaired by the California Department of Water Resources, has recommended a plan to restore Mono Lake to

its 1970 elevation of 6,388 feet. This elevation would protect the Negit Island nesting areas, alleviate the dust menace, and restore the lake's pristine scenic grandeur.

The Task Force plan calls for immediately reducing water diversions by 85,000 acre-feet per year. (An acre-foot is the volume of water required to flood one acre of land to a depth of one foot.) But how will Los Angeles obtain replacement water? Alternative sources are not only expensive, they would destroy other California environments.

Fortunately the Task Force has recommended a solution that does not hold San Francisco Bay, the Eel River or any other watershed ransom for Mono Lake's life: less wasteful use of our water resources. We have all been profligate in our use of water, and can get along comfortably with much, much less. The Planning and Conservation League has estimated that Californians can conserve at least 5 million acre-feet annually through urban and agricultural water conservation and wastewater recycling—enough to save Mono Lake almost 60 times over!

The choice is ours.

The Lesson of the California Drought

During 1976 and 1977, Californians weathered the worst drought in the state's history. With rainfall a fraction of normal and reservoirs reduced to puddles, people had to conserve. In 1977 urban water consumption dropped by 20 percent, saving 434,000 acre-feet statewide. The San Francisco Bay Area conserved 32 percent, while Marin County and some Sierra foothill communities conserved over 50 percent. More water was saved than anyone, especially the water agencies, thought possible.

The people of Los Angeles conserved 16 percent (97,000 acre-feet), more than enough to maintain Mono Lake—and no lawns withered, no swimming pools were drained, virtually no one complained of the hardships of sweeping leaves off driveways, or watering yards at night.

The drought exposed our water-wasteful ways, and taught us we could thrive on much less. When the rains returned, the lesson was not entirely forgotten. In Los Angeles, water consumption remained 9 percent below pre-drought levels. In parts of the Bay Area, it remained more than 20 percent below.

But, unfortunately, per-capita water consumption is again on the rise. Cries are being heard for more dams, more aqueducts, more dollar- and energy-expensive water projects that will sicken our environment and mortgage our future.

How can we nurture the water conservation alternative? Here are some suggestions:

1. Let people know that water, like energy, is a precious, limited resource that is running out, and that there are places like Mono Lake at the other end of our taps.

2. Set an example, in your own life, of frugal, responsible water use, and urge neighbors and friends to do the same.

3. Spread the word that water conservation is easy and rewarding, and that saving water saves energy.

4. Support and promote water conservation and wastewater recycling programs rather than new dams and water projects.

How does this relate to the 85,000 acre-feet of water per year that Mono Lake desperately needs to survive?

If all 20 million Californians installed water-saving devices in their faucets and showers, and placed plastic bottles or similar displacement containers in their toilets, they would save about 250,000 acre-feet of water per year. If 1.5-gallon-per-flush toilets were installed, these savings would jump to about 700,000 acre-feet per year.

Moreover all this water can be saved mechanically, that is, without altering in any way our actual water use *habits*. When we consider how much more can be saved through conscientous water use inside and outside our homes, the potential becomes well over a million acre-feet. At least another four million acre-feet can be conserved through statewide wastewater recycling and agricultural water conservation (agriculture accounts for 85 percent of California's water use).

Through installing these water-saving devices, turning off the tap when we brush our teeth, and in countless prosaic ways, we not only save water and energy, but we also connect our lives with the life of the earth, and assume responsibility for its (and our) well-being. We become watershed housekeepers, responsive to the needs of the land from which we draw our sustenance and health.

The choice to conserve is not enough. We must also choose to share, not only with Mono Lake, but with all the rivers and streams, lakes and marshes, bays and estuaries whose life is now in our care.

Population Update

by Judith Kunofsky

Most people now believe that the U.S. population has stopped growing, or is well under way toward stabilization.

This is not true.

While our goal is much closer than ten years ago, and many of our initial hopes have been more than fulfilled, population stabilization (or zero population growth) is neither here nor assured. The substantial success in lowering the birth rate itself over the past decade, and the tremendous increase in the extent to which individuals and families are able to control the numbers of their children, have not guaranteed an end to population growth.

In 1970, the population increased by more than 1,800,000, with 3.3 million births, 1.9 million deaths, and (net) legal immigration of perhaps 300,000. Illegal immigration adds an unknown number, with estimates ranging from 166,000 to over a million per year. The question of whether "current trends" are such as to lead to an end to growth depends on what one takes to be "current trends." Perhaps the following two examples will put the situation in some perspective.

The Census Bureau's lower projection assumes reproduction of 1.7 children per woman (i.e., 1,700 children per 1,000 women), and net immigration of 400,000 per year. From those assumptions, one can project an end to U.S. population growth at 253 million in 2015 (it is 222 million today), and the beginning of a slow decrease thereafter. This projection assumes a fertility rate about 5% lower than the current level and does not include illegal immigration.

Assuming a fertility rate of 2.1 children per woman, however, and total immigration of 800,000 per year (whether legal or illegal) yields a population of about 272 million in the year 2000, 331 million in 2030, and still growing at a substantial rate. The range of possible futures is still wider than these two examples indicate, because some demographers believe fertility may rise well above 2.1.

Coupled with the widespread belief that population growth is no longer a problem has been a decline in the attention paid to population by environmentalists. Environmentalists still think the right way, but their attention seems to be elsewhere. There certainly has been a lessening of activism and financial support.

Why?

In the early 70's, population fitted in well because much environmental thinking and discussion was at an abstract level. Most environmental battles, though, are over very specific, tangible things: they are fought to save particular pieces of land, to clean a river, to keep toxic substances out of the drinking water. But population is not an environmental "problem" in the way air pollution is. Population is a *cause* in the same way that wasteful technology and overconsumption are causes. It tends toward the abstract, and abstract issues are harder to work out than concrete ones. Even if Congress were to pass a bill declaring zero population growth as the goal of the country, we might not have the same immediate feeling of satisfaction we get upon stopping a dam.

And then people *see* environmental desecration in a way they don't see population growth. A two million increase in the number of Americans may not seem like much of a problem if your area has stabilized or is growing at a manageable rate. Our unconscious is quite capable of saying, let them live somewhere else.

Finally, as John Tanton observed, while he was president of Zero Population Growth, to a great extent, the future of population growth in this country will be determined by immigration policy rather than fertility. Even before the Indochinese refugees were admitted, legal immigration alone constituted 25% of the population's annual increase. The need to deal with immigration makes policy-making easier in one way. Immigration is (at least theoretically) a decision of the government, while fertility and reproduction are very personal decisions made by individuals. But in another way it makes the issues more difficult: To the extent that much of the environmental constituency was and is liberal on social issues, it can support family planning and increased opportunities for women for their own sakes, as well as because they help lower the growth rate. But immigration is a newer, more difficult issue for us. We need much more public debate to determine an immigration policy that will satisfy our desire for a rapid end to population growth while filling other needs that immigration serves.

It is important to remember that at the national level, the victories came in situations where population growth was rarely, if ever, mentioned by its own name. Family planning services are supported in order to improve health, expand freedom of choice for women and make every child a wanted child. Early teenage childbearing creates problems for parents and children. Abortion is (and should be) an individual's choice. Career and education opportunities for women are a matter of rights. The population argument might in many cases be superfluous—or even harmful—to the effort! Similarly, immigration is only now coming to be seen as a population issue, in addition to considerations of labor policy, brain drain, civil liberties, family reunification and refugees.

In other words, to clean up the air, we've talked about cleaning the air. But to reduce population growth it has been

---

The 60's and 70's: Lengthening the Fuse on the Population Bomb

The environmental movement began to pay attention to the population issue in the 1960s. Paul Ehrlich's *Population Bomb* (1969) and his appearances on Johnny Carson's show, along with newspaper articles, magazine features, courses, television programs, and the like, made population the subject of wide discussion. As the 1970s progressed, we won victories that slowed the rate of population growth. The political ones were remarkable:

• the establishment in 1970 of the first federal program to fund family planning services
• the conclusion by the Commission on Population and the American Future (1970–72) that the U.S. should welcome and plan for an end to population growth
• the decisions of the Supreme Court in January, 1973 legalizing abortion throughout the country
• the increase—although still woefully inadequate—in job and educational opportunities for women. These are regarded by many to be a major cause of a reduction in the birth rate

• the rapid and continuing proliferation of growth control movements

• establishment in 1978 by the House of Representatives of a Select Committee on Population, which concluded the U.S. has no capacity to plan for population change, whether to respond to change or coordinate those federal actions that influence change (family planning, pregnancy programs, immigration policies, job opportunities for women, etc.). Unfortunately, conflicts over jurisdictions with standing committees and a general budget cutting ended the Committee's life a year later

• the attention given to consequences of population change and, in particular, the effects of the current slower growth rate, by President Carter's budget messages in 1979 and 1980.

And the non-political victories have been even more substantial—and perhaps even more surprising:

• the decrease in the number of children young women want, from three in 1967 to just above two (on average) today

• the decrease in the actual rate of reproduction to about 1.8 children per couple in the last few years

• lessening social pressures to become a parent, as measured by the content of the media and other organs of public sensibilities

• the turnaround in public attitudes towards population. A Gallup poll in 1977 found that 87% of those polled would rather that the U.S. population not increase any more

• the change in local growth debates from focusing on encouraging population growth to *accommodating* the increase that is expected and that is supposedly outside a community's control.

Population growth aggravates all environmental problems. If per capita use of water, say, is halved but the population doubles, the total strain on water supplies is back where it started. If each individual drives half the number of miles per year and uses a car that gets twice as many miles per gallon, but the population increases fourfold, any gain is wiped out. No amount of conservation can keep up with an eternally increasing number of people, and population growth is even used to justify unsafe technologies. (One utility association has posters in major airports supporting nuclear power "for the sake of our children.")

J.K.

more effective to stress other arguments relating to fertility and immigration. This has exacerbated the already-substantial problem of getting political institutions to tackle developing a population policy.

Although the 1970's witnessed decreasing attention to population growth by environmentalists, this must—and will—change in the 1980's. The full impact of population growth on the environment will become more evident as the next decade passes:

• Americans have always wanted to move away from it all, find a little piece of ground somewhere, or a small town with trust and friendship. But the population boom has caught up with an awful lot of those places we once moved "away" to. One resident of Crested Butte, Colorado, who is fighting the proposed molybdenum mine there, said "I moved to Denver to get away from it all, then to Colorado Springs, then here to Crested Butte, and now there's nowhere else to go. I'm making my last stand." With statements like that, the frontier is really closed, with all that that implies for attitudes towards a growing population.

• Even in cities, the problems of population growth are getting more difficult to solve. Some parts of the country are experimenting with phased limits to urban development, boundaries within which urban services will be provided but outside of which they would be unavailable. There is growing awareness that this is only a temporary experiment—that we must begin to speak about permanent urban boundaries to save the economy of cities, to save energy, to save the agricultural land outside, to save money. And once you've established permanent urban boundaries, you must make the tradeoff among population, open space, and density. This necessary tradeoff will force us all to look once again at the inevitability and desirability of population increase.

• Housing prices are putting home ownership beyond the reach of most young Americans and the supply of both homes and rental units may not be keeping pace with people's desires. In part this reflects the post-World War II baby boom grown up and fueling demand; in part it reflects the economics of the housing industry and its dependence on the availability of mortgage money. But some developers are now confronting environmentalists with the need for housing and blaming *us* for the shortages. Our response is to call for more compact cities with lower costs and energy conservation, consistent with people's needs and desires in both short-term and long-term. But our point of view makes sense only when combined with an end to population growth. Just as we refuse to speak of taking garbage or toxic wastes "away," we should refuse to speak of accommodating U.S. population growth "somewhere else." One former commissioner of the Immigration and Naturalization Service commented that there was plenty of room for people in Alaska. *He* was from Texas.

LESS IS MORE.

Mies Van Der Rohe

Population projections are often used to justify development projects. Many are well aware of the often self-fulfilling nature of these projections: Forecast population increase on some farm, then tax it for development, build roads and sewers to accommodate the increase, and lo and behold here come the people! Or: forecast population increase in a region and then water shortages, build a massive water diversion project to fill those needs and (if you're lucky) the people come. Pretty soon the water shortage is as bad as it was in the first place. If you're not lucky, the demand doesn't increase fast enough and the project is a financial disaster.

I have run dozens of workshops on the use and abuse of population projections for communities. We discuss the ways these projections are often inflated and the question inevitably arises, "But aside from the slipperiness of the forecasts, isn't population increase real? What can we do about it?"

There are two really important answers.

We must ensure that the already-developed parts of America become or remain places worth living in. If people don't like their part of the country, they will move to yours. In other words, even those far from the cities need to support America's cities.

And we need a rapid end to national population growth Perhaps we're on the way there. Perhaps not.

Changes may need to be made in the social security system, education, transportation, housing, and the labor market in order to take advantage of the opportunities offered by a low—or even negative—growth rate and minimize any disadvantages. But unless the country makes an explicit commitment to ending growth and begins to make those adjustments, the U.S. is likely to have the same reaction as some of the other countries now close to or at zero population growth: futile efforts to increase the birth rate or massive programs to bring in foreign workers. The latter is a problem when those workers are kept as second-class citizens (as in some European, middle Eastern and North American countries today) or when they postpone the eventual day of reckoning.

Population change takes place over decades, and if we wish to see rapidly ending population growth, we must begin now.

How should the U.S. approach population stabilization? The first step is probably the development of a national population policy. The United States is often telling other countries they need one, but we have somehow ignored our own refusal to confront the issue politically. There are many varieties of population policies, among them the following.

• An explicit declaration by Congress that the U.S. welcomes and supports an end to population growth. Bills to this effect have been introduced over the years, but none has ever come to the floor of the House or the Senate for a vote. Such a bill might or might not include a recommended "path" to ZPG or a target population size, or date at which we would hope to have achieved population stabilization.

• A "structural" solution, setting up a policy development and coordination mechanism to analyze the various options for population trends, to point out the often contradictory effects of various federal programs that affect population, to provide a forum for debate on population policies.

• The politically easier approach is an implicit population policy. If all federal agencies were to plan for population stabilization, if research were conducted to evaluate those changes necessary to meet the population stabilization, if we all talked in terms of and acted in terms of an approaching zpg, we would in effect have a population policy.

How should environmentalists respond? First, there is the individual contribution: "stop at two" (children) is as important today as it was when ZPG coined the phrase a decade ago. But, just as environmentalists realize that individuals turning off lights makes up some, but not all, the solution to the energy problem, we must acknowledge the need for action as a society.

Some ideas:

• When participating in local growth debates, talk in terms of the final picture of development in your community. Acknowledge that while you are pro-progress and pro-people and pro-well-being and pro-full-employment, you are certainly a no-growther on population.

• Enter the current debate over the best population path for the U.S. to follow. How quickly do you think we should try to reach an end to population growth in this country? Be sure to figure out where you would advocate housing the population increase over today's 222 million.

• Support the few organizations working for a U.S. population policy. Also worthy of consideration are groups working on reproductive rights and immigration reform.

• Get groups in which you are involved to reiterate their philosophical commitment to zero population growth. If they're unwilling to be active on population, insist they support the efforts of those who are!

Is there cause for optimism? Yes. With a little help from our friends, the coming decade could easily be the time we come to grips with an official national population policy and head ourselves surely toward zero population growth.

Bibliography
John Holdren, "Population and the American Predicament: The Case Against Complacency," in *Daedalus,* Journal of the American Academy of Arts and Sciences, Fall, 1973
Leslie Corsa, "Population Policy in the United States," *Sierra,* May/June 1979
Sierra Club, "Population and the Sierra Club," from Sierra Club, 530 Bush Street, San Francisco CA 94108
Judith Kunofsky, "Population Projections, How They are Made . . . and How They Make Themselves Come True," *Sierra,* January/February 1979

John Tanton, "Rethinking Immigration Policy," available for $2.50 (postage paid) from FAIR, Box 57066, Washington DC 20037

Zero Population Growth, 1346 Connecticut Ave., NW, Washington DC 20036
  "A U.S. Population Policy, ZPG's Recommendations"
  "A Basic Case for Zero Population Growth"
  "World Prospects for ZPG"
  "U.S. Population Fact Sheet"
  "U.S. Immigration and Population"
  "ZPG and the Economy" "The One-Child Family," and others
  (publications list free on request)

Lester R. Brown et al, "Twenty-Two Dimensions of the Population Problem," Worldwatch Institute, 1776 Massachusetts Ave., NW, Washington DC 20036 March 1976

Lester R. Brown, "Resource Trends and Population Policy: A Time for Reassessment," Worldwatch Institute, address above, May 1979

Paul Ehrlich, Anne Ehrlich, and John Holdren, *Ecoscience: Population, Resources, Environment,* W.H. Freeman & Co., San Francisco 1977.

The Fundamental Things Apply . . .

Dwellings and Communities: Urban Environmentalism

by David Gancher

At the heart of the housing/settlements issue can be found many related issues. Housing should rely on renewable energy for heating and cooling; the energy costs will go down—and utility bills, too. Mass transit is essential to clean air and safer streets and is intimately related with—its patterns causing and being caused by—settlement patterns. More efficient packaging will mean less trash, cleaner parks, less annoying litter all over the place. The city—where most of us live—is the nexus of most of our environmental problems; it is where they come home to us. It is the focus of problems of pollution and just plain livability.

The goal of environmental planning for cities and housing is simple: good living. The term "decent housing" is not adequate—it has been used for decades to denote monolithic, crime-ridden tenements, entire neighborhoods of self-perpetuating despair.

The environmental city we envision is not one of those science-fiction fantasies-of-the-future envisioned in the 1920s through 1960s—their horizons dominated by gigantic skyscrapers laced together with arching bridges where tiny citizens watch individual helicopters flying about on unimaginable errands. As preposterous as these imaginary cities seem, they still dominate the thoughts of many city planners. The real-life application of these fantasies has been the fiasco called "urban renewal." In San Francisco, for example, many of the finest old neighborhoods were razed a decade ago to make room for housing projects. The financing fell apart, and since then much of San Francisco's most valuable real estate has remained empty—a fenced-off wasteland of weeds and rubble. Had the old neighborhood been permitted to remain standing, the natural process of revitalization would have begun; a deteriorating slum would have become a homey neighborhood of renovated, elegant two-to-four-story Queen Anne and Victorian houses and apartments.

The city we envision is probably more densely settled than many today. The construction of the future will tend to cluster—as condominiums, as apartments—to accomplish several things. First, clustered housing is cheaper to build, to service and to heat (or cool). If it's well-built and maintained—by no means an automatic assumption these days—individual units will have maximum privacy and sound insulation. Second, building—say—50 units in a cluster requires much less land than building 50 single-family homes on 50 lots. Moreover, the land that is saved can be kept as open space—a grove of trees, perhaps, with a brook or a meadow full of wildflowers—instead of becoming 50 lawns, 50 backyards, 100 sideyards, 50 driveways and so on.

Accordingly, most urban development should take place as what planners call "infill"—on vacant lots, underused land. Some stretches of tiny, inefficient homes might be razed to make room for cluster developments and open space.

Infill development also allows the preservation of greenbelts and of agricultural land near cities. This must be protected by zoning laws, otherwise, that suburban land will probably be converted from agriculture to housing. This makes the urban/suburban transportation problem much worse and forces farms onto marginal land, which requires the use of more fertilizer, imported water, energy-wasteful practices, and erodes the soil faster. This in turn drives up the price of food. It also tends to drive the small farmer out of business by making all agricultural land more expensive. And it separates the city dweller off even more from a sense of where food comes from.

Neighborhoods

The key to livable cities is cohesive neighborhoods, where residents know each other and cooperate on a number of projects of mutual interest.

Government policy tends to mitigate against strong neighborhoods. For example, in many government housing projects, it is illegal—for one reason or another—for residents to maintain the property. But involvement is exactly the main point in building and maintaining a pleasant urban environment: involvement with neighbors, pride and personal, emotional investment in the place where people live. When residents can take charge of their neighborhoods, the net result is an improvement in the quality of life in very specific terms. Some of the methods that will work are:

- Neighborhood associations funded by trickle-up taxes.
- Giving tax breaks to police and firemen to live in the cities where they are employed. Today this is often difficult, because these public servants are badly underpaid for the very services that make cities secure and livable.
- The establishment of neighborhood gardens to provide healthy, affordable vegetables and flowers—and a place where people can meet and work together. Gardens are more than small vegetable factories; they are a social occasion.
- Neighborhood child and old-age centers.
- Neighborhood schools.

One of the growth movements in the 1980s will be the rebirth of grassroots organizing and planning for the improvement of urban America. Small groups, like the Institute for Local Self-Reliance, have made a good start, but they cannot do it all; the forces of decay are simply too great to overcome with only enthusiasm and dedication. National groups, like Friends of the Earth, must use their own resources and organizing skills to help local residents to draw up neighborhood plans, organize to beautify neighborhoods, and set up food co-ops, child-care and old-age centers, and so on.

Sweat equity programs have already made the notion of government giving away housing look not so radical. It is already happening in the most decayed and abandoned neighborhoods—most spectacularly in the South Bronx.

In addition to urban homesteading, other approaches to revitalizing our cities may be successful. Neighborhood Housing Services, founding in 1968 in Pittsburgh, is a coalition of citizen groups, financial institutions, and governments. It collects money to provide mortgage loans for rehabilitation projects in neighborhoods that can still be rescued. This approach tends to work best in neighborhoods with a high percentage of owner/residents. They aren't as likely to move away as renters are; they are eager to maintain their property and its surroundings; they can easily see the personal and financial benefits of cooperation.

A new pilot program in California is aimed at the middle-class; people not living in slums, people employed but still unable to come up with the price of a house. The program, called HCD (for Housing & Community Development, the agency that will administer it) is really homeownership assistance. Using state funds, HCD will provide up to 49% of the purchase cost of a dwelling unit. The state department will be a silent, invisible partner. The homebuyer will be responsible for property taxes, insurance, maintenance and so on. In return for putting up the money, HCD will share in the eventual profits when the home is sold or refinanced, or when the homeowner is in a position to take over the full payments. The state presumably uses its profits and payments to keep the program operating and expanding. Attractive enough for obvious reasons, the HCD California program could reduce the impact of real-estate speculation on people with fixed incomes.

The 1980s will undoubtedly see the proliferation of different types of neighborhood organizations. This variety is both inevitable and healthy, for without massive federal bureaucracies, the organization can be flexible and can serve the particular needs of given places—be they transportation, gardens, police services, traffic regulation. The

---

THE CITY's effort to quell noise turned out to be loudly characteristic. To the existing din the city added a large yellow truck, filled with flashy newspaper reporters and decibel detectors, and hired two taxicabs to roar across its path, blowing their horns continuously. The heavens boomed with anti-sound.

E.B. White

---

role of the larger environmental and urban institutions should be to provide information and expertise—and to help with the initial organizing and with the difficult processes of grant-proposal writing and other funding necessities.

The goal is the sort of living you, or I, or anyone would want: well-designed, well-maintained houses and apartments in mixed neighborhoods with trees, parks, good shopping, gardens and adequate transportation. These are for everyone—not only for the middle class. The problem:

how to get there? The solution will not be a comprehensive plan of any sort—in fact, many of today's urban problems are the inadvertent result of trying to solve urban problems, which tended to be many, particular and localized, with grandiose bureaucratic theoretical solutions. The real solution is the traditional one of muddling through. But among the mix of solutions, a few basic principles recur.

Principle 1:
The Poor Are With Us Always

It is not worthwhile to assume that because of some wonderful plan or theory, poverty will soon be abolished, obviating the need to provide housing for people who happen not to be rich. At one time in American history, even poor people could afford to buy houses. With housing prices in attractive areas rising quickly, this is no longer true.

Even the most sensible housing plans cannot eliminate poverty, but that does not remove the obligation to make poverty more bearable. The traditional approach—that of "doing something" *for* the poor—has not worked. The usual solution, skyscraper-prisons stuffed with poor people, only exacerbates the problem and ruin inner-city neighborhoods in the process. Besides being poorly designed and often maintained very poorly, typical "urban renewal" projects are delivered "turnkey," with only minimal citizen participation and a very high unit-cost. Recent projects average around $40,000 per family unit in 1978 dollars. At this scale and cost, only a tiny fraction of inadequately housed people can be helped.

There are several alternative approaches.

The one that has received the most publicity is Sweat Equity: residents gain the ownership of housing by renovating abandoned tenements or houses. First started in the early 1960s in Indianapolis, this program appeared in New Jersey, in the South Bronx, in California, and elsewhere. It solves several problems at once: it creates cohesive community bonds that can be used to affect other social and political processes. (If you've worked on a roof with people, chances are you can affect an election or zoning board with them.) It can also halt the process of neighborhood adandonment and blight. And most important, people end up with somewhere nice to live—something they did for themselves, by themselves.

The basic principle of resident involvement is important, even crucial, to improving the lot of poor people. One way of ensuring resident involvement is by transferring ownership of a building to the tenants. Currently, the federal (or state or city) government is the landowner, and the poor people are the tenants—a feudal relationship in many ways. The tenants never have an opportunity to gain equity in the building. And because they can't own it, they tend to trash it. But it would not be impossible to rectify the situation, if the government were to gradually transfer ownership of existing apartments to the tenants, in return for renovation and maintenance work. Mortgage payments would accrue to the government—instead of rent—as would tax payments on the property. Moreover, federal expenditures would be cut as maintenance and repairs become the responsibility of the tenant/owners. The tax revenues and the money saved on reduced expenditures could then be used to finance new construction and renovation of abandoned buildings which could be made available to poor people. The result would be a net reduction in poverty—since the tenant/owners would acquire equity in the property. But the realistic, final result would be a reduction in crime, in vandalism, and in poorly maintained buildings. People tend not to vandalize their own property—because vandalism is a protest of powerlessness, a political protest against domination by a faceless government.

But it is unfair and unrealistic to expect the government to be the only source of housing for the poor. The government tends to do it badly (another good reason for getting the government to give away its property) and to react relatively slowly to new social trends.

On Taxes

Taxes are a wonderful thing, quite one of humanity's most ingenious solutions to many problems. Sociobiologists have argued that taxation is the circulatory system of the meta-human organism we call society. Taxes epitomize software solutions to hardware problems of distribution. The problem, of course, is that tax policy is in the wrong hands. This opinion is the principal attraction and charm of the fiscal policies of the Republican Party—the perception that too much centralization of capital and bureaucracy is inefficient and inherently unfair. Resources cannot be intel-

Renovation

Many American cities have an unrecognized legacy of care, design and grace. Buildings of the late 19th and early 20th-century were built to last. While we have the chance, we should recycle them and shape them to our own needs.

Though sweat equity and urban homesteading programs have received a lot of admiring attention, they have not appreciably slowed the abandonment of buildings in New York and in the other old industrial cities of the Northeast and Midwest. As this abandonment picks up speed, it becomes increasingly difficult to reverse—perhaps some of the more innovative approaches toward financing renovation and renewing neighborhoods will make a larger contribution as more funds can be found.

One interesting new trend is toward the transformation of commercial buildings into residences—condominiums, cooperatives and apartments. This typically happens in declining downtown areas, where small or light industry has fled to suburbs or been shut down entirely because of imported products from nations or regions with lower labor costs. In New York, these loft conversions have had astonishing results. The converted spaces, large and difficult to renovate, have attracted very high prices from people who want to move into the city from the distant suburbs and thus to save on the time and expense of commuting. The same thing is happening in a few other cities—and it will undoubtedly become one of the hottest real-estate trends of the 1980s. It is important that these old buildings not be simply torn down and replaced by drab, modern commercial rectangles. The older buildings are well-built, generously-designed and can become high-quality living and working areas.

DG

ligently allocated because plans are too general, regulations too stifling. The quality of life is best protected, they say, by local governments which are familiar with specific local conditions and needs. If this is true—and as an idea it has considerable intuitive appeal—it should be reflected in tax policies. A few examples of how tax policies would improve the quality of life in cities:

TRICKLE-UP TAXES The big tax dollars—federal taxes—
are spent first on high-ticket, national-priority items. Some
of these—new parks, protecting resources, cleaning up air
and water and so on—are of undeniable value. Others—
building freeways that can only encourage gasoline consumption, ebarking on fabulously expensive weapons systems such as the MX missile—are more controversial. At
any rate, these large expenditures tend to starve out local
communities. To be sure, federal money does enter the
economy at local levels—if only in the forms of CETA
grants and construction subsidies for sewer systems. The
point is that local people have little control over the uses to
which these funds are put—though it is considered poor
urban etiquette to reject federal money for any purpose. The
use and flow of tax money is, however, a very important
question. The flow of energy through an organism creates
the patterns of adaptation, determines the structures that
the organism will use to survive. And cities are organisms: if
many neighborhoods seem chaotic, perhaps it is because
there is little flow of financial energy through the neighborhood. In more specific terms, nothing will create a
neighborhood organization quite as rapidly as having a
budget to administer.

Current tax policies reflect a curious set of priorities.
What remains underfunded are precisely those things that
people often indicate they have struggled so hard to achieve:
good schools, adequate child care, good neighbors, and desirable neighborhoods.

Suppose that a given fraction of all taxes—a rather
high fraction—were to be rebated to neighborhood or block
associations for purely local needs and projects. Most taxpayers would feel much better about paying $2000 in taxes if
they knew that even $500 would be spent right where it
could be seen. (Of course this is oversimplified—this would
keep poor neighborhoods from improving as fast as rich
neighborhoods—but the important details could be worked
out.) The main organizational problem lies in determining
the size of the unit that would spend the money. Too large a
unit will create essentially the same situation we have
today—with the exception that cities don't buy fighter
planes. If the unit is too small, then things like sewer sys-

tems are hard to fund. Let us say that this, too, is negotiable.

The kind of projects that trickle-up taxation might fund include

• Employing residents to become watchmen (goodby, burglary), thus freeing up regular police for the sort of activities they are best at.
• Paying for seeds, fertilizer, rototill services, etc. for neighborhood gardens, partly as a nutritional/economic source of well-being, partly as an opportunity for social interaction.
• Playgrounds, playing fields, small parks. If you are an urban parent, you already know how rare and bleak these facilities are—and how crowded the good ones are.
• Neighborhood transit: passenger vans for regular downtown expeditions, short-distance commutes, driving children around. The driver/organizer could also be a neighborhood employee.
• Child-care centers: an additional source of neighborhood cohesion and political power.
• Old-age facilities—preferably in tandem with child-care centers—to enable older residents (who feel like it) to participate in the lives of the youngest residents. These two groups, the older and the youngest, often appear to enjoy each others' company—for limited amounts of time.
• Food co-ops, group purchasing of such staples as cannot be grown: Environmentalists and consumer interests often complain about the deleterious effect that the large supermarket chains have had on the economy, the quality of nutrition and the effect of agribusiness. Organizing in smaller, but non-inconsiderable groups gives people the economic power to save money by buying wholesale—and the financial clout to encourage small farmers, organic orchardists, etc., thereby reducing dependence on chemical pesticides, fertilizers, etc.
• Local schools. Though a topic of considerable political controversy, they are a good idea environmentally. Less gas is wasted

---

I KNOW of no more encouraging fact than the unquestionable ability of man to elevate his life by a conscious endeavor.

Henry David Thoreau

trucking children around; a greater sense of social cohesion and convenience are possible. And a neighborhood can decide just how good its school is going to be—how small the classes are, etc. And the school can also serve as community center, food coop warehouse, child-care facility.

Parents who felt that the schools were still not adequately funded could get together with others of similar opinions and hire supplementary tutors—just as conscientious parents do today.

• Cultural resources. Drama, music and dance lessons, string quartets, musical-instrument banks.

• Neighborhood tree planting and urban forestry; nothing improves the look of a sidewalk like a row of maples or aspens, so long as their planter boxes are kept clean of litter.

• Painting houses. In every neighborhood there is one owner who is the target for complaints about how rundown his or her house is; now the neighbors could get together to help get all the property looking spiffy, while protecting it from the weather.

The list could go on and on. The point is a simple one: to recreate villages within the city, cohesive, important social structures of stability, significance, and conviviality.

Property Tax. A California Congressman, lobbying for passage of a tax-income plan, recently made an important statement. "Property taxes," said Representative Edwards of San Jose, "are a powerful tool—but to what end? As currently practiced, they are simply another means of gathering revenue. Particular attention is not paid to its source—housing itself. The tactic most often applied is designed to maximize revenues—not to encourage the prevalence of particular types of housing."

Revenue has traditionally been maximized by tying the tax rate to the valuation of the property. This has led many apartment building owners in New Jersey, in New York and elsewhere to abandon decaying properties Though this will, one hopes, be the renovated housing of the future, it is also an eyesore and exacerbates all sorts of social problems. What happened was that the money required to restore the property was far more than the landlords—be they poor immigrants or callous slumlords—were willing to pay. The buildings were appraised at low values; so taxes were low. The landlords stayed afloat while they could, collecting rents before the rats, cockroaches, safety codes and sheer entropy took over completely. The city could have the building.

But cities could use the tax structure to encourage different types of housing. If taxes were lowest on a perfectly maintained building, then it would be increasingly expensive to let properties decay in the first place. If taxes on substandard buildings were very high—and if federal, state or local tax revenues were available to assist in renovation—then the stock of acceptable housing could be gradually increased. If we extend this idea to stipulate that taxes will be the lowest possible on a building that is 1) completely up to code, with a garden already installed; 2) equipped with renewable-resource energy supply where possible—that is, solar heat and cooling, possibly windmill-generated electricity, and so on; 3) completely occupied, with residents paying low rent. Conversely, the highest tax rates would be charged to the owner of a vacant building that doesn't meet the codes. If such an owner defaults, the building would revert to public ownership and would be made available for such programs as sweat equity or urban homesteading.

The goal of this tax innovation will be to maximize the number of pleasant apartments and houses that would still be available to people of different descriptions and to families of different sizes. San Francisco is often pointed to with a sort of pride—lots of beautiful renovation and retrofitting goes on there. But while the stock of desirable housing has increased, the numbers of people (and the numbers of kinds of people) who can afford the housing has decreased, so that the population of San Francisco is becoming increasingly white, wealthy, single, employed and status-conscious. What is lost is diversity—and interest.

The property owners might not benefit so spectacularly from real-estate speculation under the system of taxation herein proposed. But since one of the goals of improving the quality of life in American cities must be the reduction of extractive, exploitive real-estate speculation, it is just as well. The responsible property owner will not lose profits; the property will continue to appreciate since it is well-maintained and fully occupied. The benefits to the tenants should be obvious—they have a pleasant building with a nice garden and an accessible landlord more than willing to listen to suggestions, especially if complaints lead to reassessments of taxation rates. This scheme would build ethics into the tax rate—rewarding stewardship rather than profit taking.

It is important in all things, most environmentalists agree, to keep construction on an "appropriate" scale. The quality of life people want is generally predicated on humane surroundings. Think about the kind of neighborhood you think is ideal, and you'll probably conclude that small is beautiful. This, though perfectly obvious, is unpopular thinking in planning circles, and something subtle has been lost in "efficient" developments—important but subtle. It is this sense of scale, of fitting in. And it is a sense of connection with landscape—of knowing where the creeks run, where you might see an owl. Or why the Indians called this "mussel beach." This sense of connection with landscape is the basis of all environmentalism and is probably the one identifiable human urge that will permit our species to survive. Finally, it is this sense of place that people associate with a "quality" environment.

"Expect poison from standing water."
–William Blake

Toxic Substances in the 1980s

by Marc Lappé

The individual and global impact of chemical and physical pollutants will intensify and become even more apparent in the 1980s. The 1970s saw a dramatic increase in the numbers and kinds of chemical agents introduced into the biosphere, but the 1980s will likely see the syncrgistic, combined impact of literally thousands of these chemicals as they find their way into the ecosystem.

Concerned epidemiologists in the 1970s monitored the effects of only a few major water pollutants in episodes of contamination that occurred, for example, in Long Island, New York, and Dade County, Florida. But in the early months of 1980, health officials in California had already charted wells with water contaminated by more than 25 different chemicals with organic molecules—more than half of which are known to be hazardous to human health. Possible additive, potentiating or synergistic effects of these contaminants on human health are unpredictable, but dangerous in their potential scope and impact. The plain truth is that we're introducing thousands of chemicals, not monitoring their uses or disposal—and are only beginning to learn, with considerable horror, of the dimensions of the threat to human health.

Episodes of regional pollution such as those of Minimata, Japan (mercury), Seveso, Italy (dioxins), or Love Canal, New York (toxic wastes) are likely to proliferate over wider and wider areas. The extraordinary heavy-metal pollution of Minimata Bay in Japan and the resulting epidemic of Itai-itai disease (a severely incapacitating nervous-system disorder) was not unique. In the U.S., lead pollution along U.S. highways and in urban ghettos is widespread, and many health officials believe that such lead contamination is likely to cause central nervous system damage to tens of thousands of children—an epidemic barely noticed. Nor is there only one Love Canal. The Environmental Protection Agency has plotted fully 3383

EVERY GENERATION is one of transition, but our own time portends bigger changes in the organization of the planet than we have had in at least five hundred years. A crisis of values has swept across both the capitalist and the socialist world. . . .

Richard J. Barnet

hazardous-waste sites. Another 12,000 are probably lost forever—closed, abandoned and forgotten. Many of these lost dumps will generate future environmental episodes like the mysterious outbreaks of disease in Memphis, Tennessee, that may be related to the offbase disposal of military wastes twenty years ago. The EPA estimates that 762 million tons of hazardous waste are dumped each year, and at least 600 million tons of them are potential health hazards. To make matters even worse, the current practices of waste disposal range from barely acceptable to truly appalling. These wastes are often dumped into ponds or pits, and easily leach into water supplies, ending up in nearby wells and reservoirs.

The global effects of such wastes, rather than the relatively circumscribed effects of spills or leaching from dump sites that we saw in the 1970s, will become the rule in the 1980s as wastes diffuse from individual sites. Whole aquifers, for example, in the Central Valley and in southern California have been found to be contaminated with DBCP, a chemical that sterilizes humans. (The California Department of Health Services found 193 of 527 ground samples taken from 24 counties to be contaminated.)

Water systems along the length of the San Gabriel Valley are contaminated with trichloroethylene, which causes cancer in animals. Accidental spreading of hazardous substances is not the only way that global pollution may result. International trade also brings the hazardous byproducts of developed nations to less developed—and unpolluted—countries. At least one U.S. corporation had contracted, with a $25 million advance, to ship and process hazardous wastes in Sierra Leone. Some corporations are realizing that cleaning up dumps and enduring close regulation of disposal practices are likely to prove extremely expensive. Simply exporting the hazards may be cheaper. And who cares if a relatively insignificant third-world nation complains? The reasoning may sound cynical—it is—but it is the reasoning that will result in the final distribution of toxic substances becoming global, affecting dramatically larger populations in the 1980s than in the preceding decade.

Biological Consequences

In the 1980s scientists will discover that toxic substances have increasingly deleterious effects on three previously unappreciated targets: the exquisitely sensitive nervous system of higher animals; the photosynthetic activities of lower organisms; and the centerpiece of life itself, DNA. Our failure to anticipate the toxic consequences of environmental exposure to chemicals is the result of the very newness of the problem—and the insensitivity of our diagnostic tools. More than 1000 new chemicals are introduced into the environment annually. The majority of the 50,000 to 70,000 manmade chemicals that now confront living systems have been introduced only within the last 30 to 40 years; plastics, resins, rubber products and halogenated solvents are newcomers to the chemical scene.

The newest wave of epidemiological evidence suggests that the toxic effects of many industrial chemicals on the human nervous system have been underestimated. For example, polybrominated and polychlorinated biphenyl compounds (PBBs and PCBs), previously thought to be free of measurable acute toxic effects on humans, are now prime suspects for long-term neurological damage. Such herbicides as 2,4-D have only recently—and controversially—been recognized as neurotoxins for the peripheral nervous system. Solvents in widespread use in modern industrial processes, such as *n*-hexane and methyl *n*-butyl ketone, have been only recently discovered to be potent nerve-damaging agents, capable of producing irreversible injury to peripheral nerve axons. Concentrations of other neurotoxic agents such as cadmium and lead are increasing in the environment. All have demonstrably harmful effects on the developed nervous systems of grown humans and higher animals; they are just now being tested for their possibly harmful effects on developing central nervous systems.

A whole new field of behavioral teratology—abnormal development—is likely to burgeon in the 1980s. Researchers in this new discipline are plotting the subtle, long-

Toxic Iceberg

Love Canal is only the beginning, the tip of the iceberg. Ill-conceived waste dumps from the past continue to emerge, as they gradually move through water tables and reach a water supply used by people, or as building takes place near an old, sometimes forgotten dump, or as waste containers age and begin to leak. Nuclear wastes, which have leaked at Hanford, Washington, and other places, are the worst of the wastes because of their extremely long life and the impossibility of destroying them. But wastes from the pesticides and chemical industries are almost as troublesome because when they combine many of them produce even more dangerous poisons.

What's the Solution?

This problem isn't easy, particularly regarding soil and groundwater that's already contaminated. Each incident will have to be solved case by case: replacing water systems, closing some lands to agriculture and habitation, etc. We have to prevent any new "Love Canals." We have to establish the principle that manufacturers have a responsibility toward the final disposal of their product. A product which is hazardous after use and for which there is no safe disposal should not be produced. The sort of environmental impact analysis that is now done on major federal projects should be done on all new (and many old) potentially harmful products. Safe, environmentally sound disposal should be a prior condition for going into production.

A system of disposal for hazardous wastes needs to be developed stressing the reclaiming and reuse of wastes as first priority (recycle mercury, lead, etc. out of waste chemicals). Second priority should be incineration where possible to detoxify the waste. The "safe landfill" should be last priority after recycling and incineration, just as sanitary landfills should be the last resort solution for ordinary wastes.

What can you do as an individual?

Avoid those hazardous materials that can be avoided. Any hazardous wastes you have around the garage, garden or home should ideally be disposed of in the new, proposed system. While it smacks of the tactics of the sixties I feel that the manufacturer is the key and that if everyone returned hazardous waste to the corporate headquarters of the manufacturer it might generate their support for a comprehensive, ecologically sound disposal system.

GDB

term consequences of exposing fetuses to agents that have nerve-damaging potential. Substantial numbers of retarded and brain-injured children are evidence of maternal exposure to heavy metals. The damage caused by toxic chemicals is likely to be detected through behavioral-analytic techniques still in their infancy.

The greatest possible threat to the fragile web of life would be an array of pollutants that directly or indirectly upset the process of photosynthesis in the top layer of the oceans. Since photosynthetic micro-organisms are the primary base of most major food chains on earth, any disruption of their ability to photosynthesize and/or survive could have long-lasting and dramatic ramifications. Herbicides such as 2,4-D can adversely affect both photosynthetic organisms and the next level on the food chain.

There are already signs that the proportion of carbon dioxide in the earth's atmosphere may be shifting in a way that will directly affect the process of photosynthesis and, through changing the net heat balance of the atmosphere, indirectly alter the rate of photosynthesis. Even more ominous is the discovery that many of the herbicides and chlorinated polycyclic hydrocarbon pesticides—like DDT—that were used in ever-increasing amounts in the 1970s could upset the delicate life system of phytoplankton, the tiny organisms that are responsible for most of the atmosphere's oxygen generated through photosynthesis.

Technical Innovation and Cancer

Many of the newest chemical and technical innovations threaten the structural integrity of DNA and correspondingly increase the incidence of cancer in exposed populations.

The exponentially rising curve of technological innovation mirrors certain changes in the incidence of cancer over the last 15 years. High cancer rates recorded from 1950 through 1969 in the heavily industrialized areas of the New York/New Jersey and Philadelphia corridor have begun to spread. According to detailed epidemiological studies conducted in the mid-1960s, the rates for the nation have begun to catch up with those in areas with historically high rates of the incidence of cancer.

Additionally, tumors in such organs as the skin, bladder and lung that are directly linked to environmental or occupational exposure have increased in incidence at a rate four times that of tumors not so linked (even after taking into consideration the contribution of cigarette smoking to such cancer rates). The annual rate of increase for tumors linked to the workplace or environment is calculated by Dr. Marvin Schneiderman of the National Cancer Institute at some 4% a year. Chemicals as diverse as hair dyes and flame retardants have proven both mutagenic and carcinogenic in animal tests.

Extraordinarily long and complex webs of causation link human activities with these alarming statistics. Just how chemicals cause cancer is largely unknown—and the causal relationship may not be established for years. But just one example of the global magnitude of the probable impact of human invention illustrates both the subtlety and the dramatic danger posed by chemicals in the environment.

In every nation where cancer statistics have been kept, the most dramatic increase in cancer incidence in recent times has been that of the pigmented skin tumor known as melanoma. Melanoma is extremely resistant to treatment, with an average five-year survival rate of less than 20%. Its incidence is directly correlated with ultraviolet light exposure, as reflected by latitude of residence.

The National Academy of Sciences has calculated that if fluorocarbon propellants are allowed to be used and disposed of without regard for their impact on the atmosphere's ozone layer—which protects us from ultraviolet exposure—as many as 100,000 new cases of squamous cell carcinoma and 2000 to 5000 cases of melanoma can be expected over the next decade. Such propellants are no longer used in the U.S., but they are widely used in other nations.

The present epidemic of melanoma appears to be signaling some other relationship, perhaps between solar exposure, chemical carcinogenesis and susceptible individuals. The fact that these relationships are largely unrecognized, even among cancer experts, is a bad sign. Melanoma is likely to be the miner's canary for the pollutants of the 1980s. The increase in melanoma portends extremely serious episodes of malignant growths in humans caused by continued use of chemical agents that, alone or in combination with natural radiation sources, continue to damage the genetic material of cells—leading to the development of tumors.

Protection of the Genetic Heritage of the Species

The environmental mandate for the 1980s will thus be to protect the genetic heritage of the world's species from damage and from further deterioration.

Heretofore, much of the attention to preserving the integrity of genetic material has rightly focused on endangered species, but many other animal and plant populations face possible irreversible damage to their genes. Diminished ozone layers in the stratosphere, nuclear reactors, isotopes, other manmade sources of radiation and wholesale diminution of the genetic variability of the stocks of plants and animal species pose parallel risks to the genetic complexity and variety of the environment.

The cumulative effects of the various threats to our genetic heritage are almost overwhelming; they include many pesticides in current use; diagnostic x-rays; and expoxides, formed from chlorinated short chain and polycyclic hydrocarbons. The list could go on and on; the inescapable conclusion is that the genetic makeup and evolutionary continuity of species are threatened by human activities. It is this threat that poses the single most important challenge to the world environment.

How Things Get Done

Decade of the White Whale

by Harold Gilliam

FROM ALL the look-backs at the 1970s that are appearing in the papers and magazines and on TV, we are led to believe that it was the decade of Watergate, TM, est, disco, various libs, Star Wars, gas lines, Muhammad Ali, Henry Kissinger, Woody Allen and King Tut. Perhaps. But these are flotsam on the surface of a deep historical current that gathered undeniable momentum in the last ten years and portended the direction of our culture for generations to come.

For Americans, at least, the decade of the '70s was the decade of the White Whale.

I believe it was Lewis Mumford who first suggested, 50 years ago, the symbolism of Herman Melville's classic, in which Captain Ahab was not content to "harvest" whales for the market but fanatically pursued Moby Dick, the White Whale, on his mission of vengeance, whatever the cost.

In "The Golden Day," Mumford wrote: "One may read 'Moby Dick' . . . as an epic of the human spirit and discover an equivalent of its symbolism in one's own consciousness. For me, the Whale is Nature, the Nature man warily hunts and subdues, the Nature he captures, tethers to his ship, cuts apart, scientifically analyzes, melts down, uses for light and nourishment, sells in the market, the Nature that serves man's purposes so long as he uses his wits and can ride on top. But with all this easy adventuring, there is another and deadlier Nature — the White Whale — a Nature that threatens man and calls forth all his heroic powers, and in the end defeats him with a final lash of the tail."

At about the same time that "Moby Dick" was in the

making, George Perkins Marsh, author of another classic, "Man and Nature," saw the ruins of ancient civilizations in Europe and observed that nature, treated with respect, can provide for man's needs but pushed too far will retaliate with devastation — floods, dust storms, erosion that destroys not only the soil but ultimately the civilization based on it. There were other warnings, later, in the mid-20th century, particularly in seminal books by Fairfield Osborn, William Vogt, Harrison Brown, Rachel Carson, Stewart Udall, Barry Commoner, Paul Ehrlich, and others, but it was not until the past decade that Americans on a large scale became aware of the limits to technology in attempts to master nature.

Call it conservation, ecology, environmentalism — at bottom it was the dawning realization that humans are able to organize nature for the production of wealth provided they show moderation, restraint and respect for nature's processes, but nature abused is the White Whale, unleashing destructive fury on its tormentors. Just as in Vietnam we learned something about the limits of our ability to exert military power, so as a result of the new environmental consciousness we are becoming aware of the limits of technology. There are still technological "hawks" who would escalate the war against nature to achieve total victory.

They are the Ahabs of our time, who would sacrifice the rest of us as well as themselves in their mad pursuit of absolute power over nature.

Among other things, we have learned in the '70s that wiping out "pests" with weapons of total war also destroys species essential to our own survival; that pouring industrial and automotive wastes into the air can cause lung disease and death; that the release of spray-can chlorofluorocarbons depletes the protective ozone layer, increasing skin cancers; that giant irrigation projects can destroy the soil by depositing salts; that spraying chemicals and dumping deadly wastes in waterways and natural sumps can lead to tragic birth defects; that dependence on fossil fuels creates excessive atmospheric carbon dioxide that could upset the global climate patterns, disrupt agriculture and flood coastal cities. Beware the White Whale.

If we give up the futile attempt to subdue nature by such means as these, the alternative is not to abandon technology and go back to the caves but to acquire a well-informed respect for nature's laws and act within the limits set by natural systems. The consequences of such a change in direction are likely to alter American ways of life as drastically as they were altered by the Industrial Revolution. After 300 years of attempting to conquer nature with all-out assaults by increasingly powerful industrial machinery, Americans have finally begun to learn during the '70s the necessity for new approaches, new technologies, new life styles compatible with natural systems. That discovery may be the most historic development of our time.

Although the movement had roots in the '60s and earlier, the environmental decade began chronologically with President Nixon's first official act of 1970, the signing of NEPA — the National Environmental Policy Act — on New Year's Day. Three months later on Earth Day tens of thousands of Americans participated in ceremonies that formally inaugurated the movement.

NEPA had seemed like a motherhood resolution and had passed Congress in December of 1969 with little opposition. But it contained a sleeper provision requiring environmental impact statements for all federal projects, from building dams to spraying forests to erecting post offices. States passed similar laws, and the courts later said the requirement applied to government agencies giving permits, to government contractors and to any programs in which federal or state money was used.

The best popular account I know describing the impact of the environmental impact statement and the entire environmental movement of the '70s was written by an insider, Robert Cahn. As the Pulitzer-Prize-winning science correspondent of the Christian Science Monitor, he recorded the origins of the movement in the '60s and was nominated by President Nixon to the Council on Environmental Quality, a three-man board set up by NEPA as the environmental arm of the White House.

In his book, "Footprints on the Planet," Cahn describes the Council's first meeting with the president, six months after it was appointed to advise him: "We left the meeting vaguely frustrated, feeling like outside visitors as the president handed each of us souvenir paperweights, pens, cufflinks and golf balls. The president had done most of the talking. He had not once sought our advice on anything."

Nevertheless, Cahn gives Nixon credit for taking stands for the environment when it was politic to do so — the creation of the EPA, support for expanded wilderness and urban parks (such as the Golden Gate National Recreation Area), curbing use of pesticides, and the dramatic act of cancelling a gigantic half-built barge canal across Florida, which would have destroyed watersheds and ecosytems on an appalling scale. It had been promised to the state in 1960 in a Chamber-of-Commerce campaign speech by John F. Kennedy.

Cahn gives Kennedy low marks for environmental awareness. Johnson fares better, having unleashed Ladybird in the natural beauty campaign that became environmentalism. Ford gets zero and Carter high marks for his first two years, although subsequent conflicts have developed with environmetalists over such issues as nuclear energy, Tellico Dam of snail darter fame, and synthetic fuels.

One gargantuan indication of our change of direction in the '70s, Herman Melville might be interested to know, is the whale. Commercial whaling has not yet been totally halted, but during the '70s it disappeared in the U.S. and diminished substantially elsewhere as world opinion affirmed the leviathan's right to live.

Although seldom mentioned in roundups of the past decade, our new respect for the most awesome of our fellow passengers on this planetary space craft is a gargantuan symbol of the historic change now under way. The Ahabs still among us, hunting the metaphoric White Whale, are anachronisms belonging to an age that is swiftly coming to an end.

Do Thy Patient No Harm

by Garrett De Bell

The solutions to environmental problems must be environmentally sound.

Over the next decade we will see more and more small scale technologies that are decentralized, inexpensive, and have a kind of democracy and individual participation to them that's very appealing. Some will be totally acceptable, some will be totally rejected and some will be appropriate in certain instances and not others. (There aren't many totally acceptable ones—except simple conservation of water, energy, and other resources.)

It's important that we be just as critical of the environmental impacts and overall implications of the small systems we propose as we are of the side effects and negatives of nuclear power plants, shale oil development, strip mining, and so on.

For instance, growing our own fruit and vegetables can reduce our dependence on chemical- and energy-intensive agribusiness that realistically should be a smaller part of the total food production system. While it makes sense to have large agriculture growing wheat, we can plant kitchen gardens and salad gardens—so long as we use natural fertilizers and cultural means of pest control along the lines suggested in *Organic Gardening and Farming* and similar publications.

Likewise, burning wood for heat is small scale and uses a renewable resource, but there is a right way and a wrong way to heat with wood. The stoves and fireplaces we select should be efficient, non-polluting, and safe, and we should not just automatically take "the best good dry oak." Instead we should be sure that the wood we burn is obtained in an ecologically acceptable manner, or is scrap wood or dead and down wood of a size that is not useful for wildlife habitat.

Solar energy is important and should become a mucn larger part of our total energy picture. Passive solar designs in homes and businesses basically work with nature to catch heat when you want it, reject it when you don't, and if possible, store it for use later. They have very few potential problems and should become part of our building philosophy immediately. But active systems can have problems. There is the aesthetic impact of the collectors and the area occupied by them. If we use large scale community solar collectors that cover a lot of ground their impact can be as serious as if the land were covered with an asphalt parking lot—and is to be avoided equally. Some of the ugliest scenic intrusions along the well-designed Highway 280 linking San Jose to San Francisco, a highway that has been commended for environmental sensitivity, are solar collectors on the hillsides. The collectors reduce the amount of area where rain percolates into the soil, thus theoretically contributing to soil erosion, and they simply occupy land that should have been left to grass and native plants. Placement of the same collectors on roofs or the sides of buildings would eliminate the intrusion, in this case.

Another concern in solar systems is for the heat exchange fluids used, particularly in cold areas where water freezes in the collector. It's important that the fluid or the system be such that we don't expose ourselves to poisonous chemicals in our effort to conserve energy. A toxic chemical in a solar collector is of equal concern to one used in agribusiness. The danger is in the chemical regardless of the intent of how or by whom it is used.

Saving water left after a shower, "gray water," for reuse can be desirable, particularly in a drought. It can greatly reduce our consumption of drinking quality fresh water for flushing toilets, and can be used to a limited extent in home gardens — if proper care is taken to ensure that infectious diseases aren't passed on. It would be prudent, in a house with a sick person, to use gray water only for flushing toilets.

Using the consolidated gray water from a building or community for agricultural purposes creates public health difficulties because it is inevitable that someone will have a communicable disease. The appropriateness of a gray water system is going to depend on location, type of soil, the ability of the ground to absorb water and transpire it through plant systems before the water reaches the water table and water supply, and other considerations.

The composting toilet is another solution which is often advocated and is probably safe, usable and appropriate in some places, and not appropriately usable in others.

Its benefits include reducing the amount of water needed to carry raw sewage and the need for sewage treatment plants. The drawback is potential spread of disease if the compost has not been thoroughly digested or if it has organisms that can survive through the humus-creating process. The best generalization that can be made is that the composting toilet is appropriate to rural situations where each household would have control over the complete system, including the plants that are grown with the material, so problems of disease transmission would be minimized.

In our enthusiasm to adopt solutions to environmental problems we can take a line from the Hippocratic Oath: "Do thy patient no harm." Which is to say, make sure the cure is at least no worse than the disease.

Citizen's Guide to Transportation Problem Solving

by David Burwell

Alternatives to single-passenger driving can be placed in two broad categories: those which use highways and those which do not. Both categories have the goal of (1) developing transportation systems which produce fewer of the negative consequences of auto dependency, and (2) providing, to the extent possible, the same kinds of benefits that make car ownership so attractive.

Highway-oriented alternatives have the advantage of avoiding the tremendous cost of constructing a completely different transportation system. Imaginative examples of such alternatives include:

• Six thousand Delaware residents are now served by a regular dial-a-ride system. Users purchase a book of tickets, call a dispatcher two hours before they need to go somewhere, and obtain door-to-door service at very reasonable rates. A similar "handyride" system serves residents of Denver.

• Students at Washington, D.C.'s Georgetown University initiated an inexpensive shuttle bus service for students, staff and faculty in 1974. The student government bought mini-buses, hired student drivers, and mapped out the routes. The project is a great success.

• Students in Berkeley, California, established a safe hitch-hiking system called "Transit Share-a-Ride." Both riders and drivers within a 100-mile radius of the campus are registered and issued identification which is shown when the ride is begun.

• The Citizen Association in Reston, Virginia, circulated questionnaires concerning commuting patterns and, with the results, contracted with a bus company for commuting service to Washington, D.C. Started in 1969, by 1975 the single bus service had expanded to three buses and the Association had a $4,500 operating balance.

Each of these alternatives used no public funds, was

self-planned, and took advantage of the availability of a highway network.

If you are interested in organizing a local public transportation project, approach local or regional transportation planning agencies for support. Ask for either financial assistance to do planning for the project, or the services of a planner to help determine the feasibility of the project. Regional planning agencies should perform this type of service as part of their statutory citizen participation obligations. Once the project is planned and accepted as feasible, ask your city or town to help raise the necessary capital to put the plan into effect.

The federal Urban Mass Transportation Administration (UMTA) periodically gives "demonstration grants" to promote innovative local public transportation projects. However, these grants are given exclusively to governmental units. You will have to be sponsored by your local government to apply. Your state Department of Transportation can assist you in applying for those grants.[1]

In communities where public transportation services already exist, citizens may prefer to participate in the effective municipal management of these services rather than starting one of their own. Here are some common public transportation services and suggestions for getting involved:

Buses

Many cities have publicly owned bus service, run by an operating authority within municipal governments. The ecological equation between buses and cars is approximately as follows:

$$2.5 \text{ cars } (congestion)$$
$$1 \text{ bus} = 2.4 \text{ cars} (energy\ consumption)$$
$$4.8 \text{ cars } (air\ pollution)$$

Obviously, with even a minimal amount of patronage, buses have the potential to yield substantial public benefits over single-passenger cars in cleaner air, less congestion, and energy conservation. They also provide mobility for people who cannot afford a car.

Three areas where citizens can participate in the efficient running of public bus service are fare structure, routing and scheduling, and quality of service.

• An optimal **fare structure** should be low enough to

attract patronage, be affordable to low-income users, yet cover costs of operation. However, due to a generally perceived commitment to provide at least some service at all hours to the complete system, revenues will not cover costs. The issues then raised include: What is an acceptable deficit? How much off-peak (non-rush hour) service should be provided? Will fare increases actually *reduce* revenues through loss of patronage? What about zone fares versus flat rates? How about free transit (total subsidization through taxation), or are free pass programs better (selective subsidies to the poor, elderly, handicapped)? These are all public issues which should be answered in light of community values and commitment to public transit service. As such, they need to be opened to public debate.

• **Routing and scheduling** are also public issues. An observer of the Boston bus system commented "These buses go from where people no longer live to where they used to work." With changing demographic patters, both the routes and the frequency of service must constantly change. However, these decisions are often made haphazardly, or by politicians wishing to satisfy particular constituents. Find out if your city bus company has a route and scheduling committee. If it does, investigate its method of decision-making. If not, push for one.

• The **quality of service** provided is of equal importance to the availability of service. A one-hour wait for a bus that is scheduled to run every fifteen minutes can lose a customer permanently. Over-heated (or freezing) buses, drivers who won't wait for people running to catch an empty bus, dirty stations and no schedules will all push people back into their cars. To better understand the problems users have with the system, some authorities have established "users' panels" of citizens who contribute directly to the management of operations.[2] How does your local bus authority handle complaints—by phone, or do they make you write? Do they keep records of complaints and seek to remedy persistent abuses or is it more of a "PR" effort? Consider the benefit of a users' committee. Such a committee should advocate service improvements which attract more users.

All of these problems deserve your attention. However, public transportation authorities rarely have official mechanisms for involving the public. If the transit service extends to several communities, there may be a council of community representatives that set policy and approve budgets. Ask your mayor or town manager to appoint you to that council. If service is only within your community, there usually is a board of non-paid appointees which reviews the operation of the agency. Ask to be placed on that board.

Effective citizen action, however, is not dependent on being appointed to act in any official capacity. Divide your citizen organization into three committees, investigate each of the problems outlined, write a report, and call a press conference. Your effectiveness will be a direct function of the quality of your work and your ability to focus public attention on the problem.

Taxis and Jitneys

Taxis and Jitneys (cars which share riders and often run fixed routes) provide mobility to people not served by public transit but who do not want (or cannot afford) a car. Jitneys, however, were outlawed by most cities fifty years ago because they competed with streetcars. With the demise of the streetcar a matter of history, it is time to reconsider jitneys as a legitimate means of transportation in urban areas. If prohibitions on such vehicles still exist in your community, ask your city council or state legislature to reconsider them.

Bicycles

The advantages of bikes are obvious. They contribute nothing to pollution. They place no development pressure on open space. They provide door-to-door service. They have low capital and operating costs. The only energy they use is what it takes to make the bike and feed the driver (with non-fossil fuels)—and they help keep people healthy in the bargain.

Bikeways are considered highways under *federal* law, thus qualifying states for federal reimbursement of 70%-90% of their costs.[3] Money in state highway trust funds generally qualifies for bikeway construction as a highway-related purpose. Check the language of your state statute or constitutional amendment establishing the trust fund. Some have extremely restrictive language. The biggest obstacle, however, is that many state planners refuse to take bicycle planning seriously. State administrators, who often have plans

EXERCISE IS BUNK. If you are healthy, you don't
need it: if you are sick, you shouldn't take it.

Henry Ford

designed for two or three times as many highways as they
have federal dollars coming in, refuse to allocate highway
funds to bikeways. To combat this bureaucratic antipathy to
bikes you can:

- Fight for legislation *requiring* highway funds to be used for
bikeways.
- Do your own bikeway planning, and then go to state administrators and politicians and request that the project be
funded.
- Pressure transit authorities for bike racks and storage
facilities at mass transit stations, and the right to take bikes on
trains and subways during non-rush hours.
- Pressure city officials for ordinances requiring parking garage and city facilities to provide safe bicycle parking
facilities.
- Monitor road improvements in your area to make sure the
improvements are safe for bicyclists (i.e., sewer drains constructed
perpendicular to the road rather than parallel).

In light of the present danger and inconvenience of
competing with cars on the open road, a relatively small
percentage of potential bicyclists actually ride a bike. This
circumstance in turn is used by highway officials to indicate
a "lack of demand" for bikeways. Don't be discouraged.
Studies in urban areas have indicated a tremendous latent
demand for bikeways—if facilities are provided they will be
used. Highway officials should be reminded that demand for
cars was also low—until there were paved roads on which
to drive them.

Light Rail

Light rail vehicles (trolleys) have one substantial
drawback: their routes are fixed. If commuting patterns
change, a line can't change with it. However, they have
many compensating advantages. They can be placed on or
beside existing roads. The cars can be hitched together,
thereby using fewer operators. If electrically powered, they

are non-polluting at the point of use. They last twice as long
as buses. They don't contribute to urban congestion if located on a separate track. They are substantially cheaper
than subway construction, while rivaling them in passenger
capacity.

Trolley lines were overbuilt early in this century by
land speculators who pushed up real estate prices by providing transit service to their property. When the property was
sold the lines were abandoned, leaving the cities to pick up
the cost of operation. If trolleys are to be revived, they must
be planned to benefit logical commuter corridors.

Heavy Rail

Heavy rail vehicles (subways) are quite expensive,
with capital costs approximating $1,000 per person in the
area served. One mile of underground construction can cost
$30-$40 million.[4] However, they are correspondingly efficient, fast, and do not conflict at all with road traffic. Subway vehicles have elephantine lifetimes, and one operator
can drive up to 700 passengers. They substantially increase
land values in the areas served.

Commuter Rail

Passenger rail service was marginally profitable in the
hey-day of private railroad companies; now it requires large
subsidies. However, it can provide fast, long-distance
commuting service to suburbs and neighboring cities, does
not require the buying of new track, is generally more comfortable than trolleys or subways, and can carry freight on
off-peak hours. Since commuter trains service a different
market than trolleys or subways, they compete only with
the automobile.

If your city provides light, heavy, or commuter rail
service, there are several ways your citizen group can participate:

• Get involved with issues of fare structure, scheduling, and
quality of service as described for buses.
• Since a capital expansion is expensive but politically attractive (the federal government picks up 80% of the capital costs),
monitor extensions to make sure they are both needed and desired.
When possible, push for service improvements over capital expansion.

• In several areas, commuter rails are being replaced by rapid transit. These two non-highway alternatives serve separate markets. Although the corridors used by commuter trains look attractive for rapid transit extension, one mode should not be sacrificed for another if both are needed. Protect the integrity of each mode. They all will be needed in the future.

• If lines are abandoned, protect the abandoned rights-of-way from sale to private owners. A commuting line, once carved up, is prohibitively expensive to reassemble. Converting these rights-of-way to bike paths both preserves their integrity and provides an alternative means of travel.

Trolleys, subways, and commuter trains cannot by themselves provide viable alternatives to auto use. The focus of citizen efforts should be: first, to prevent any additional deterioration of rail, trolley and subway lines and second, to make these alternative systems attractive enough to entice drivers from their cars.[5]

Auto Constraints

Measures which discourage or even prohibit car usage are called auto constraints. They are the "stick" that is sometimes necessary to change commuting habits. As discussed in Chapter Two, single-passenger drivers, particularly in urban areas, have not had to pay the full cost to the

WE ABUSE LAND because we regard it as a commodity belonging to us. When we see land as a community to which we belong, we may begin to use it with love and respect. There is no other way for land to survive the impact of mechanized man, nor for us to reap from it the esthetic harvest it is capable, under science, of contributing to culture. That land is a community is the basic concept of ecology, but that land is to be loved and respected is an extension of ethics. That land yields a cultural harvest is a fact long known, but latterly often forgotten.

Aldo Leopold

community of providing the roads, parking, traffic lights, traffic policemen, snowplowing, etc., which support such driving. Many auto constraints are simply attempts to lessen this subsidy to single-passenger driving. They can be regressive, however, in that a low-income driver with no alternative to driving to work pays as much as a high-income driver who may live next to a bus line. Constraints should generally be adopted only where alternative means of transportation are available. With this in mind, constraint strategies include:

• *Toll increases and parking taxes:* regressive; more acceptable if revenues are used to aid public transit. Problem: the authorities with the power to set tolls are usually separate from, and do not contribute to, other transportation systems.

• *Increased gas, oil, and vehicle registration taxes:* regressive; again helpful if revenues placed in general transportation fund rather than a segregated highway fund.

• *Parking permits:* issued to residents, or to commuters who pay a fee. Bans all other commuters. Possible constitutional problems. Of undetermined effectiveness in reducing car usage.

• *Parking freezes:* prohibits new parking facilities. May require existing facilities to maintain a fixed vacancy rate. Federal authorities are prohibited from imposing such requirements on states, but states and municipalities may adopt such measures themselves.

• *Auto-free zones:* limits access to service and freight vehicles. Pushes congestion elsewhere, rarely discourages auto use. Effective only if comprehensive. Grenoble, France, has decided to ban passenger cars from the entire downtown area by 1980.

• *Preferential lanes:* preferential highway lanes for buses and car pools are a constraint on single-passenger vehicles, which are denied the use of that lane. This is one of the most easily accepted strategies. It does not increase the cost of mobility (single-passenger vehicles pay in lost time, not money); and low-income users can car pool, making the strategy less regressive.

If you are in a city with an air pollution problem, the Environmental Protection Agency may have already attempted to impose some of these restrictions through a Transportation Control Plan. In these cities citizens can participate in the development and monitoring of such plans. What the federal government is prohibited from doing in terms of auto constraints, state and local authorities may adopt voluntarily. Contact your state Bureau of Air Quality and ask if such plans are being developed. Auto constraints are usually proposed where considerations such as air pollution demand more comprehensive measures.

Proposing and implementing these alternatives takes time, dedication, political expertise, and organizational ability. You may therefore want to begin your participation by advocating more modest, procedural reforms. If so, consider one of the following:

• Set up an *energy conservation task force*. With energy conservation now a primary national goal, local governments are looking for ways to save energy. An energy conservation task force, with public sponsorship, could look into many energy-saving projects, including transportation. In one county in Northern Virginia, a school superintendent estimates that if 25 miles of sidewalks were built so that students could walk to school, 87 buses could be eliminated.

• Get a *town transportation planner*. Most small to medium size communities have no person working full time on transportation issues. Transportation problems are taken care of by the Planning Board, or by the local highway department. Try to place a full time transportation planner on the public payroll who will have a broader outlook on transportation problems. If funding is a problem, state or federal public employment programs may be available.

• Establish a *bike commission*. With an estimated 100 million bicycle users in the United States, the demand for safe corridors on which to bike is on the increase. A local bicycle commission should be created to address the special problems of bicycle transportation—new bikeways, safer roads, the elimination of dangerous intersections, and safety education programs.

These are only a few of the options available to citizens concerned about transportation. Success in implementing these reforms, however, often hinges on a thorough knowledge of the transportation planning process, to which we now turn our attention.

Since the 1930s, when the automobile replaced indoor plumbing as the most desired household item, this nation has operated under assumptions about auto transportation that have largely lost their validity. Yet new highway construction rontinues, nationwide. Transportation alternatives flounder.

THE WORLD we have made as a result of the thinking we have done thus far creates problems that we cannot solve at the same level as the level we created them.

Albert Einstein

We are—in our minds, anyway—moving from the age of exploitation towards the age of conservation. We see now that, like a serpent eating its own tail, the more natural resources the car consumes the closer it comes to extinction. Yet Dr. Einstein's dilemma strikes close to home. Just as it takes very few people to create a nuclear reaction but a national consensus to control its use, it takes even fewer people to decide to build a highway but an entire political coalition to stop one. As a nation we must create the coalition—a permanent coalition reflected in national priorities that move us away from total dependence on the automobile to satisfy our need for mobility. That coalition already has deep roots. If enough citizens take up the challenge put forth in this book and get involved in controlling their transportation system, the system will change.

Good Luck.

---

1. You can learn more about these demonstration grants by contacting the Office of Management and Demonstration, Urban Mass Transit Administration, Department of Transportation, Washington, D.C. 20590.
2. The City of London, England, has a citizens' user panel. Also, the Metropolitan Boston Transit Authority is in the process of constructing such a panel. For further information on the Boston experience, contact Director, MBTA Office of Community Affairs and Marketing, 145 Dartmouth Street, Boston, Massachusetts 02114.
3. 23 U.S.C.§ 217 (Supp. 1977).
4. It is estimated that the 112-mile Washington Metro will cost $5.0 billion if fully constructed, or more than $44 million per mile.
5. An "Analysis of Alternatives" policy has been promulgated by the Office of Transit Assistance, Urban Mass Transit Administration, Department of Transportation, Washington D.C. 20590. This policy statement outlines the factors UMTA will consider in deciding whether or not to fund a transit proposal. *See* 41 Fed. Reg. 41512–41514, (Sept. 22, 1976).

How to Finance
The Energy Transition

by Amory Lovins

The energy future will not be like the energy past. It entails a difficult transition away from reliance on oil and gas. But the nature of the transition depends on how we define the problem we're trying to solve. If we try simply to expand domestic supplies to meet projected total demands, we will continue our "hard" energy path—a policy of Strength Through Exhaustion that converts ever scarcer fossil and nuclear fuels to premium forms (fluids and electricity) in ever larger, more complex, more centralized plants.

But the costs of the hard path are intolerably high—in money, risk, even freedom—for it is inevitably centrist, autarchic, vulnerable, technocratic. It produces a world not of free enterprise and pluralistic choice but of subsidies, $100 billion bail-outs, oligopolies, regulation, nationalization, corporate statism—and perhaps Bertram Gross's "friendly fascism."

Suppose, instead, that we start by asking what tasks we want the energy for, and how we can do each task by supplying a minimum of energy (and other resources) in the way that is most effective for that task. We then find that we need new supplies of heat (58 percent of present United States needs for delivered energy) and liquid fuels (34 percent), not electricity (only 8 percent—far less than our current generating capacity). More power stations of any kind are not a rational response to this problem: They take too long to build, are far too costly, and provide a higher-quality form of energy than we can use economicallly.

Smooth Transition

We can construct a smooth transition, over 50 years, to a virtually complete reliance on renewable energy sources by doing three things, starting now: using far more efficiently the energy we have; relying increasingly on "soft technologies"—diverse renewable sources (such as solar space and process heat, conversion of farm and forestry wastes, wind, and microhydroelectricity) that supply energy at the scale and of the quality we need—and meanwhile using fossil fuels briefly, cleanly, and sparingly in special "transitional technologies."

Such a "soft energy path" has its own political problems, but they are far more tractable than those of the hard path, and the soft path is also cheaper, quicker, surer, and safer—virtually anywhere in the world—assuming only presently available soft technologies and present life styles and social organization.

Since outlining this thesis in *Foreign Affairs* (October 1976) and in *Soft Energy Paths: Toward a Durable Peace* (Friends of the Earth/Ballinger, May 1977) I have responded to over 30 critiques (United States Senate, Small Business and Interior Committees, *Alternative Long-Range Energy Strategies*, 2 vols., 1977/8, and *The Energy Controversy*, Friends of the Earth, 1979), and had discussions with many people in the dozen-odd countries where soft-energy-path studies are under way. While much of the controversy had been technical ("Soft Energy Technologies, "*Annual Review of Energy 3*, 1978), a persistent political theme has also emerged: How can a free society implement a soft path without economic or institutional changes for which Americans may not be ready?

Inequitable Access

One important way of financing the transition to soft energy technologies will be outlined here in the broader context of energy prices and equity. Of course finance, while necessary, is not enough: we must also reform building codes, restrictive utility practices, conflicting incentives for landlords and tenants or for builders and buyers, and a long, messy list of other "institutional barriers." But inequitable access to capital may be the most fundamental obstacle to a smooth transition. The way we can overcome it illustrates how slight alterations in existing institutions can take us in new directions, turning conflict into cooperation and disparate problems into mutual advantages.

Many people who otherwise could and would use efficiency-improving devices and soft technologies lack the money to do so. At the same time, attempts to build centralized, hard-technology energy-supply systems are driving electric and gas utilities toward bankruptcy because those investments require too much capital and repay it too slowly. A logical approach to both problems is to transfer capital by loans from the second group to the first. This could make energy efficiency and soft technologies equitably available to all while making utilities financially healthy, thus directly benefiting both consumers and utilities. Capital transfers would simultaneously help to increase employment, clean up the environment, decrease inflation and interest rates, rapidly replace oil and gas, strengthen the dollar, and diminish nuclear proliferation.

Some utilities already loan money to consumers for insulating their homes (see *Business Week*, July 18, 1977) because insulation is a cheaper heat source than new power stations or new gas fields. Several states, such as Oregon (H.B. 2157, 1977), are mandating such loans. I too would have utilities—competing with heating-oil distributors, banks, insurance companies, the Federal Housing Administration, the Veterans' Administration, the Department of Housing and Urban Development, farm loan organization, and other institutions—loan money to householders (and to others ranked according to how difficult it is for them to get cheap capital now) for fuel-saving investments.

THE RELEASE of atom power has changed everything except our way of thinking. . . . The solution of this problem lies in the heart of humankind.

Albert Einstein

Equal Access

But two conditions should be added. First, the utilities should loan the money at the same rate of interest at which they would otherwise loan themselves money to build, say, a new power station. Second, borrowers should repay the loan (through their utility bills) at or below the rate at which the fuel-saving investment is expected to save them money. (The saving could be computed against the energy price the consumer would have paid if the utility had met his or her needs by building a new plant instead.) The first condition is meant to ensure that hard and soft technologies enjoy equal access to capital; the second, that loan repayments do not increase consumers' utility bills.

The utility would only loan the money. It should neither execute nor control the project, either directly or indirectly (for instance by setting equipment standards). The loan would not be added into the utility's rate base (its total investment on which it earns a regulated return); People who choose not to take part in capital transfers should not have to pay for those who do. The utility's profit, at the normally regulated rate, would be from interest on the principal loaned and would equal the return that the utility would otherwise have earned from a new plant. The utility's normal operations would continue—as would needed efforts at utility rate and structural reform.

The loan would have the same legal status and remedies for default as any other. It could be taken over by a new owner or tenant just like a utility hookup or a mortgage, and could be repaid prematurely without penalty and for an interest credit. Preferably the loan should be unsecured, since many who need it most have no collateral. Disconnection after due notice and hearing might be a last resort in case of brazen default.

Consumer Benefits
Capital transfers under this system would benefit both consumers and utilities. Consumers could heat their houses more cheaply than if they had not installed heat-saving or solar devices, yet without having to pay extra for improvement. Second, insulation and solar heat would largely protect consumers from future rate hikes. Third, the fuel-saving investment would make the utility's cash flow more attractive (see below), would make the very costly new plants unnecessary, and would save the utility money and fuels by using present capacity more efficiently; these things all help to avoid rate hikes in the first place. (Solar heating in an energy-efficient building should have enough storage to need no back-up and hence should not make the utility's peak-load problem worse.)

Further, the lower capital requirements of soft versus hard technologies would mean lower interest rates and slower inflation. If utilities had to heat houses by building power plants and synthetic-gas plants to replace oil and gas, they would need so much capital that they would starve other sectors of the economy—leading to a net loss, directly and indirectly, of about 4,000 jobs per thousand-megawatt power station built. In contrast, conservation and soft technologies make more jobs per dollar invested, and leave more dollars available to create jobs elsewhere in the economy.

Utilities, while continuing to supply present lighting and appliance needs and perhaps eventually evolving into a distribution system similar to the telephone company (based largely on dispersed renewable sources), would avoid astronomical *new* investments to electrify space and water heating. Adding a completely solar heating system to a heat-conserving house requires about half as much capital as building a nuclear and heat-pump system to heat the same house, and one-fourth as much capital as building a nuclear system with resistance heaters (the kind now commonly used). Building solar heating for a whole neighborhood rather that for a single house would roughly double the capital saving. Heat conservation requires approximately one-sixth to one-thirtieth as much investment as a nuclear-powered heat-pump system; in new buildings, it can even *reduce* total construction costs.

Enemy Co-opted

While a power station often takes 10 years to build and then 30 years more to repay its cost, conservation and solar investments take days or weeks to build and pay for themselves in about one to 10 years. If utilities invested in the latter systems rather than in the former, they could turn over their money faster and improve their effective rate of return, which they are sentimental about. Thus the transitional process, which they once saw as a threat, would become an opportunity—a better business to be in than building power stations—and a former enemy of soft technologies co-opted as a merchant banker for them. (Already, utilities in New Jersey and California that fought industrial cogeneration for years are scrambling to finance it because they can find neither money nor sites for conventional power stations that would be worse investments anyway.)

A healthier cash flow would improve utilities' bond ratings, reduce the rate of return they need to maintain those ratings, make their equity worth more, avoid dilution of existing stockholders' equity by new issues, and eliminate the rate hikes now commonly needed to make both debt and equity more attractive. Those rate hikes—a desperate measure by many utilities now at or near their legal limits on interest coverage, and borrowing in short-term paper just to pay dividends—might even be reversed.

Indeed, continuing to tie up huge blocks of capital for long construction periods would make utility cash flows fundamentally unstable. It takes so long to build a plant that by the time it is finished, the interim rate hikes needed to finance its construction (both directly and by keeping debt and equity marketable) may keep people from buying as much electricity as they were expected to buy. Revenues would then be too small to pay the fixed charges on the plant, requiring still higher prices, further reducing demand, and so on into the "spiral of impossibility" familiar from United States railroad finance. Diverting new investment into another business with short lead times and fast pay back—solar and conservation—would remove this instability.

Keep Utilities Solvent

Thus capital transfers, which look like a Robin Hood act to consumers, don't hurt utilities. On the contrary, they keep utilities solvent without a bailout, and thus help to keep taxes down. (Your taxes now pay about 20 percent of the cost of every new power station; Senator Long wants to increase the nuclear subsidy to about 70 percent.) The roughly two-thirds of typical rate hikes now needed to finance new plants would become superfluous. Rates would no longer zoom out of control and could even come down. And poor people would be as able as anyone else to afford insulation and solar heat.

Gus Speth, now a member of the President's Council on Environmental Quality, once proposed a refinement that could in practice help to substitute for pricing fuels at the cost of replacing them in the long run. He suggested that utilities should not get their Certificate of Public Necessity and Convenience to build a plant until they prove that they have exhausted the potential for energy efficiency improvements, peak-load management, and soft technologies that (1) would do the same jobs for consumers as the proposed plant, (2) compete with it economically, and (3) could have been financed by transfers of the capital allocated to build the plant. Only if these conditions were met would the plant economically and efficiently meet its customers' energy needs. Further, to encourage realistic cost estimates and careful cost control, the amount the utility could add to its rate base, if it did build the plant, could be limited to the real plant cost it assumed in making the above comparison. This would keep utilities from simply passing on their un-controlled cost over-runs to consumers. It is a simple con-trol mechanism that could make investments more socially responsible without requiring a stifling bureaucracy.

Larger Pattern

Capital transfers, whether or not linked with the utility certification test, are part of a larger pattern of efforts to meet people's energy needs fairly and at a reasonable cost. Yet economically efficient ways of allocating energy—or food or water or shelter—are always inequitable because some people start off rich and some poor, and rich people can always buy things that poor people cannot afford. A society worth living in will ensure that even its poorest members can afford the energy (and other things) needed for a decent life. But should we do this by fighting poverty or by subsidizing the innumerable things poor people need but cannot afford?

The latter approach means making energy (for exam-ple) artifically cheap—several times cheaper than what it costs us to replace it. But while this puts some energy in reach of the poor, it also means giving cheap energy to rich people. And if we want to use energy prices as an instru-ment of distributional equity, why not do the same for food, housing, education, travel, and everything else?

An alternative approach is to price energy (and other things) at levels reflecting actual costs and simultaneously to make poor people less poor by other means. Redistributing wealth or income, though it requires some political nerve, is a more direct, honest, and effective way to achieve social justice than tampering with prices in a futile attempt to make everything seem cheap enough to be afforded by people whom we haven't the compassion—or political will—to help directly.

Kidding ourselves, even in the name of fairness, into thinking energy is cheaper than it really is—long the cor-nerstone of United States energy policy—does not in fact yield cheap energy for anyone. It costs us dearly, if not immediately, then after the next election. Some of the cost is direct—the tens of billions of dollars in taxpayers subsidies that we pour into the energy system every year—but even greater costs arise from subtle inefficiencies and distortions throughout our society.

Suppose, for example, that we continue to pretend oil is very cheap, We will then probably continue to waste it and thus import more and more—bad news for our own independence and for other industrial countries more oil-dependent than we, and disastrous news for the third world. Then we must earn the money to pay for the oil. We do this mainly in three ways. We run down domestic stocks of commodities, which is inflationary. We export weapons, which is inflationary, destabilizing, and immoral. We export crops like wheat and soybeans, which inflates Midwestern land prices, raises our food prices, and makes us mine ground water in west Kansas (a cost that will soon catch up with us). We sell the wheat to the Soviets, enabling them to divert investment from agriculture into military activities. We must then raise our own military budget, which is inflationary—and which we must raise anyway to defend the sea lanes for oil tankers and to defend the Israelis from the arms we sold to the Arabs. (The easiest form of Middle Eastern arms control might be American roof insulation.)

NOWADAYS we can see as never before that the peril which threatens all of us comes not from nature, but from man, from the psyches of the individual and the mass.

Jung

Because the wheat and the soybeans are becoming more important to our oil balance of trade, we turn increasingly to more energy- and water- and capital-intensive chemical agribusiness. This damages the natural life-support systems, so we need more energy- and capital-intensive technical fixes like desalination and artificial fertilizers, and so on in a vicious circle. Meanwhile, back in the cities, we substitute "cheap" energy disproportionately for people, replacing human skills with energy-intensive machines. (This increases "labor productivity"—of people still working—and makes us call for more such machines to fuel the economic growth deemed necessary to employ the people disemployed by this very process.) This "structural" unemployment increases proverty and inequity, which increase alienation and crime (not to mention calls for cheaper energy). We then are hard-pressed to find money for crime control and health care since most of the money has already been spent on the energy sector, which is contributing to the unemployment and illness at which those social investments are aimed.

Garrison State

At home we drift toward a garrison state, trying to protect the vulnerable energy systems from strikes, sabotage, and dissent. Abroad we ignore rational development goals, strengthen oil and uranium cartels, and vie in the competitive export of weapons, inflation, and reactors to the third world. These things encourage international distrust and domestic dissent, both entailing further suspicion and repression. As we burn the "cheap" fuels, we add to the air substance's that could change climate and jeopardize world agriculture, especially in the thrid world monsoon belt and in the Midwestern bread-basket on which the third world increasingly depends for exported food. Our nuclear exports spread bombs all over. The world becomes more inequitable, hungry, anarchic, and tense.

These examples suggest that energy that *looks* cheap may actually be very expensive everywhere else in the economy—especially for poor people. Sooner or later, too, the high cost of replacing historically cheap fuels will come home to roost. In fact, we are *already* paying these costs: newly ordered nuclear electricity will cost, in heat equivalent, about seven times today's OPEC oil price.

Renewable sources now available are much cheaper than nuclear or synthetic-fuel systems for the same jobs—though many cost somewhat more than today's oil and gas.

Thus whether we use soft technologies or not, energy prices will rise because the fuels on which we have long relied are becoming scarcer and harder to get. The question is not *whether* prices will rise, but how fast, how predictably, how controllably, and who will get the money.

Two Inducements

There seem to be only two noncoercive ways to induce investors to save money by building soft technologies in time to replace the oil and gas but before the artificially cheapened average energy prices would make them profitable. The first way is to subsidize soft technologies so they can immediately "compete" with those average prices. But this subsidy to supply perpetuates an illusion of cheap energy (with all the indirect costs that implies) and merely transfers costs from our energy bills to our already swollen taxes.

The second method—which is much better economics—is to charge ourselves realistic prices, reflecting true replacement costs, for those no-longer-cheap fuels we are rapidly burning up. But how can we get our prices right? An across-the-board energy tax would be unfair and ineffective: We want only to raise the price of *depletable fuels* toward that of their long-term sustainable substitutes, the soft technologies. Further, an abruptly imposed fuel tax could be as disruptive as the sudden 1973-74 rise in OPEC oil price. Any tax should be introduced gradually, perhaps over a decade or more: It need only outpace rises in real wages and interest rates. But people must be able to anticipate future energy prices in today's investment decisions, so the tax should be phased in on an anticipatory schedule, avoiding the unpredictability and possible abruptness of deregulation. Such taxation does not raise prices simply to satisfy some masochistic prejudice that high prices are desirable. Rather, it anticipates and softens the inevitable, encouraging us to substitute soft technologies for oil in good time to minimize long-term energy prices—and ensuring that the money will be used in ways that remain under political control.

Severance Royalty

Many kinds of taxes on depletable fuels might serve this purpose. We now tend to use excise taxes on final fuels, such as gasoline; these require rebates for equity, so they have high administrative costs and lead to a swamp of intricate rules and exceptions. A much simpler approach would be a *severance royalty*—a uniform federal tax on all depletable fuels, charged according to their energy content, and levied as they come out of the ground or into the country.

This tax would automatically become embodied in all goods and services according to their total direct and indirect energy content. Administration would be relatively easy because the machinery is already in place—the severance royalty is like a depletion allowance backwards—and because the royalty is simple and universal.

End-use excises hit the poor hardest, because poor people spend the largest fraction of income on direct energy purchases. But a tax imposed on primary fuels would not be significantly redistributive, because the fraction of income that Americans spend directly *and indirectly* on energy does not vary significantly with income (with a minor exception in the highest income bracket): Higher-income people simply spend a larger fraction of their energy budget on indirect energy embodied in goods and services, and the royalty would affect direct and indirect energy purchases equally. Further, revenues from a severance royalty could be rebated promptly to poor people or to especially hard-hit regions or groups, or used to finance efficiency improvements or soft technologies for those who need them most.

Nor would a severance royalty lead to the unbalancing side effects of more selective, special case fuel taxes, because it applies as much to uranium as to oil, gas, coal, oil shale, etc.: All are depletable fuels. It would not disturb the present cost disadvantage of nuclear power. Rather than the reverse, it would highlight the economic advantages of soft over hard technologies. Depletable fuel prices need not be made higher than soft-technology energy prices—at which virtually all hard technologies would still be very *un*competitive (to say nothing of their nasty side effects). We would then have achieved indefinitely stable energy prices lower than if we had done nothing. And while we might want some subsidies meanwhile to help conservation and soft technologies compete with the more heavily subsidized hard technologies, it is better economics not to subsidize *any* energy investments. Conservation and soft technologies can look after themselves on their inherent economic merits; only hard technologies cannot survive true competition.

Capital transfers are not a subsidy; they correct an imperfection in capital markets. But wider tax reform would also be helpful. For example, we should reform the policy that lets businessmen write off fuel as a business expense but forbids them from similarly deducting the capital costs of renewable systems; or reconsider the outmoded practice of taxing labor and subsidizing capital; or encourage durability by making excise taxes on consumer ephemerals (such as cars) inversely proportional to the length of the warranty. And while there is no natural monopoly on solar energy, abuses of market power are just as possible there as in agriculture, minerals, and industry generally, so vigorous antitrust enforcement and control of antisocial gigantism are important parts of a sound energy policy.

Where I differ in the end from the doctrinaire views that pervade the energy debate—views ranging from Marxist to pure Keynesian—is that I neither regard free markets as real and perfect nor object to the principle of rewarding people who can sell something better and cheaper. While there is much talk of planning the solar transition, it is a salutary warning to would-be central planners that the Energy Research and Development Administration solar heating and cooling program was far outdistanced by a motley crew of individual entrepreneurs who did more in a year than ERDA thought its massed (if misdirected) resources could do in five years. This country is simply too big and too diverse for central management to be more a part of the energy solution than part of the problem.

Indeed, among the greatest strengths of soft technologies is the fact that one person can understand them and make a basic contribution. There is, so far as we know, nothing in the universe quite so powerful as four billion minds wrapping around a problem. This is now beginning to happen, with extraordinary results. The distaste that some people profess for individual incentive should not make us reject the astonishing advances that human diversity and imaginativeness are already starting to offer. Nobody is wise enough to decide what will be the best solar technologies or how they should fit together: They may not even have been thought of yet, so fast is the field advancing. Thus, while the abuses of pure merchantilism are many, and must be checked by the more consistent use of the laws we are evolving for that purpose, socialism does not seem likely to solve, or even to help to solve, our energy problem. Whether we can respond to the energy challenge goes far deeper than our debates on socialism versus capitalism, or even Jeffersonianism versus Hamiltonianism: It depends rather on our values toward the earth and toward each other, not necessarily on the outward form of our political institutions. Profit and private enterprise can be fair; planning and nationalization can be inequitable—not to mention inefficient.

Much though we need innumerable social reforms, oil depletion will not wait for them. If we make the resolution of our ideological disputes—capitalism versus socialism, price versus regulation, the future of the oil companies and indeed of our whole society—a prerequisite to addressing the energy problem, hell will freeze over first.

But a soft energy path can cut across these increasingly sterile arguments. If, for example, you are an economic traditionalist, you can build a solar collector because it is cheaper than competing sources; if you are a worker, you can build a solar collector because it gives more and better jobs than power plants; if a conservationist, because it is autonomous. Yet it is still the same collector, and you need not agree, in advance or afterwards, about why you built it.

If we can use all the kinds of energy husbandry and renewable sources that people agree about, these will be enough. We can then dispense with the hard technologies that people don't agree about, because those will be superfluous.

Our tendency at times to focus the energy debate more and more on less and less reminds me of a woman who, while living in India, once called in a carpenter to fix a window frame. He followed her sketch too literally and botched the job. When she asked why he had not simply used his common sense, he drew himself up and replied with great dignity, "But common sense, Madam, is a gift of God. I have technical knowledge only."

"Technical knowledge only": perhaps a good epitaph for a civilization. But I think a tolerant common sense is alive, and living with the people, and will not be denied.

The Whistle

by Sigurd Olson

There was no sound, no lapping of the waves against the rocks, no rustling of leaves or moaning of wind through the trees, one of those times when all seems in suspension and even the birds are hushed. While I sat there on the end of the point, my senses all but fused with the enveloping silence, I gradually became conscious of a soft undercurrent of sound like the coming of a wind from far away or something long remembered. But as I looked around me there was no roughening of the water or even the slightest swaying of tree tops and the quiet was as intense as before.

In spite of the fact I saw no change, the undercurrent persisted. Then suddenly I knew, as the long-drawn wail of a steam locomotive drifted over the hills and valleys from the south. Until that moment I had forgotten that just a few miles away was a railroad and a paralleling highway as well. On other days, with a wind and the sounds of the forest to screen it from my hearing, it had not been perceptible.

As the train whistled again and again with the muffled roar of cars growing more and more distinct, I wondered for the first time since coming to the point if I had chosen well, if the railroad and the highway might not destroy the very essence of the sanctuary I had found. Another whistle farther away, plaintive and dying now, and the sound of the train was gone. There was only the cushioned humming of traffic from the road.

Once long ago on another point far to the north and after weeks of wilderness travel I had heard the same sound, but then it seemed entirely different. We were camped that night within a few miles of the steel, as we called the railroad back in the bush. Our maps told us where we were, but it was hard to realize we had come so close, for until then it had seemed almost unattainable. For a long time we had heard only the sounds of animals and birds, the wind in the trees, the thunder of rapids, and the crashing of waves. We had talked about coming out to the steel as though it were the most wonderful thing in the world, which in truth it was to a bush-weary crew. We knew we would reach it if we

154

kept on packing down the portages and following the
waterways, but the goal was always far away, and the longer
we were gone the more unreal it actually became.

Then one night after supper came the whistle of a
train, the same long-drawn musical notes I had just heard off
the point, a sound so foreign to the life we had known and so
filled with meaning that sleep was forgotten. Never before,
it seemed, had we listened to a harmony that meant so many
things—friends and loved ones, towns and cities and all
they denoted. We sat there and none of us said a word, each
man occupied with his own thoughts and dreams. How we
strained to catch those last haunting notes, and how excited
we were at the realization that at last we were going outside.
The final note was like a call of a loon, the mournful wail of a
lone bird with the darkness settling down, but this time there
was no sadness in the sound. In it was a note of finality, for
it wrote the finish to our cruise and all we had experienced
together.

Until then we had gone about the ordinary routine of
wilderness travel taking everything for granted, making the
best of discomforts, spending our evenings and stormy days
busying ourselves with the endless details necessary to keep
an outfit in traveling order, but now all of this was unimpor-
tant. The shaping of the new paddle could wait, the rip in
one of the tents, the broken tumpline, the ax that needed
sharpening. Suddenly impatient at the seemingly senseless
delay of nightfall, we were counting the hours until dawn.
To a man, we would have packed up and traveled in the dark
if our leader had said a word. All that counted now was
getting in, though we knew that in a short time we would be
ready to hit the trails again.

And now on another point of rock I had listened to the
same music, remembering all the mixed-up feelings of my
youth, emotions and hopes that in the light of years and a
maturer perspective seemed quite different from what they
were then. That night of long ago, after the fire had died and
camp was asleep, I had lain awake thinking of many things.
Quietly I had crawled out of my bag and tiptoed down to the
overturned canoes near the shore. I remembered the moment clearly, how the Big Dipper hung and the sliver of a
new moon over the spruces. I went around and looked at the
old battle-scarred canoes, the one that was heavy on the
portages, the one with the cracked ribs that we had almost

lost in a rapids, one whose gunwale the porkies had chewed. Sometime during the coming day we would leave them and scatter to the four winds, and the life that meant so much to us, the companionship we had known, the banter, the fun and hardships, would be ended. It was sad to think of these things, for in the wilds you become welded not only to the outfit itself but in a strange way to those you live with. But, even so, this moment was the one we had worked for, this the reward for long days on the trail.

While I thought of that night long ago, the dark had come to Listening Point and the Big Dipper hung exactly the way it had then. Nothing had really changed at all, for there was the lake with its star shine, there the massed outline of the far shore. The only difference was the fact that, instead of being happy and thrilled, I was now vaguely disturbed. I had chosen the point fully aware of its closeness to civilization. All I had actually wanted there was a window through which I might glimpse at times the wilderness I had known and recapture perhaps some of the feel of the country I had traveled almost to the Arctic. I had accepted my road, motor boats and near-by cabins, and the realization that many times the silence would be shattered. I knew that, while the point was relatively unchanged and like ten thousand such points far to the north, it still was not the wilderness, did not have the element of isolation that only great distances could provide. Then why, I asked myself, was I troubled at hearing the sound of a train?

The leaves of an aspen began to whisper in a sudden breeze and the soft humming from the south was gone. A loon called wildly from the open lake, and miraculously everything seemed as it was before. The point was still part of the wilds, but I could not forget the whistle and sat there in the dusk wondering if it could ever be quite the same.

A few months before I had met a party of Cree Indians along the far reaches of the Athabasca over a thousand miles to the northwest. They too were camped on a stark and lonely point, as much a part of the beauty and silence of their land as the caribou themselves. How would they have reacted to the whistle? Could they understand its real meaning as I did? Could they possibly comprehend Thoreau's famous dictum that "In wildness is the preservation of the world"? I wondered as I sat there, knowing full well if those Crees were taken from their land and transplanted to some city, something within them would die and, while they could not explain their dependence, the ancient need was there. Only through my own personal contact with civilization had I learned to value the advantages of solitude. Without that experience they could not realize how man in an industrial age might need the very background of the life that was theirs. Nor did I know this truth thirty years before when I first heard that train whistle after a long time in the bush.

While I sat there thinking of the Crees and my own early reactions I seemed to hear the whistle again, but now it had assumed a somewhat different note and in the sound I heard something that had not been there before: a deeper meaning than the train itself, one that encompassed man's inventive genius and all the realms of his exploring mind, a sound that was responsible for my own background and everything I knew and felt. And then the realization dawned on me that only because of its connotations and the contrasts that had been mine could I really appreciate the wilds and their importance to mankind.

A motor boat roared down the middle of the lake, its throttle wide open, headlight knifing through the dark. It headed into the west, slapping smartly over the waves, made a wide careening turn near the first islands, and came directly toward me. Fascinated, I watched as it sped by and disappeared. Its roar grew less and less and at last was swallowed by the north channel. Then came the wash, long rollers whispering and chuckling along the shore. Longer and longer became the intervals between them, and at last, like an inaudible sigh, the quiet returned. Again I was disturbed, and again I remembered. This too had the same meaning as the whistle itself.

But there would be many times in the months to come when the lake would be completely undisturbed. I remembered skiing with streamers of snow writhing and twisting and turning red and violet in the slanting rays of the setting sun, days when even the most ardent ice fisherman would

---

What I love is near at hand,
Always, in earth and air.

Theodore Roethke

not venture forth, the time I explored the river when the little cabin at its outlet was sealed and cold and timber wolves had run across the smooth hard drifts of the clearing.

I thought of the fierce storms of late October and November just before the freezeup, with the ducks heading south, snow drifting quietly down, and no one left in the whole country to take away the feeling of the wild; the time before the spring breakup with its black treacherous ice, and the insulation that all harsh weather gives the north. Knowing this, I was ashamed of my resentment at intrusions no matter what they might be. I should be able to listen to all of them with equanimity, attune my mind and thoughts so I would hear them as they should be heard.

Some other day when the wind was right or the quiet as breathless as this afternoon, I would hear the train again and the steady humming of traffic from the highway. I would remember the time I heard the whistle after that long expedition of years ago and the joy it brought me then. No longer would I be disturbed, for I would listen now with understanding, knowing what it really meant. Without that long lonesome wail and the culture that had produced it, many things would not be mine—recordings of the world's finest music, books holding the philosophy, the dreams and hopes of all mankind, a car that took me swiftly to the point whenever I felt the need. All these things and countless others civilization had given me, and I must never again forget that because of the wonders it had brought this richness now was mine.

The next time I heard the whistle I would think of all these things. The very presence of the railroad and highway over the ridges to the south gave new significance to wilderness, to solitude and the entire concept of Listening Point.

Minimum Impact Backpacking

by Aubrey Wallace and Garrett De Bell

You're hiking though the mountains, picking flowers as you go, when over a rise you see a perfect campsite. You hurry down the slope, too excited to follow the meandering switchbacks. After pitching your tent in the meadow near the lake shore, you quickly gather rocks for a fire-ring and get plenty of firewood. For kindling you snap off a lot of small, dead twigs from the trees. A prepared camper brings a shovel, and you use yours to dig a latrine, and a small trench around your tent in case of rain. After you've gathered a pile of pine needles to cushion your bed there's time for a bath. So you jump in the lake, using your biodegradable soap to avoid polluting the water, and lather up. The sun is starting to set as you dry off in front of the large fire that's cooking your dinner. Before dark you put all your food in your pack, and hang it in the trees.

If you don't find a dozen things wrong with that paragraph you're not yet perfect at *minimum impact backpacking*.

Minimum impact has become increasingly important in the last few years. The Park Service sometimes defines it by saying "take only memories, leave only footprints." It means hiking through the mountains (or desert, or shore) without destroying them. Wilderness use has increased dramatically in the past few years, so it is imperative that every user practice the best possible techniques to protect and preserve the wilderness.

Many people don't realize that approved practices have changed with increasing knowledge of wilderness ecology. In some cases the approved practice has been reversed. Groups used to be told to take shovels and dig latrines. Now they are advised never to dig latrines.

But "minimum impact" isn't a firmly established set of rules. It's an attitude and an ethic. Techniques keep changing, as better methods are devised and discovered. You will have to use your own judgment in many cases, and always take into consideration the habitat. Remember the idea is to leave the area looking as if you had never been there.

Most wilderness areas are fragile. The high mountains have a very short growing season. Desert plants grow very slowly. Along the shore plants are important in erosion control. In some areas, like alpine meadows, just walking through is a major impact. In other areas, like hard-packed forest floors, a group could camp for days and not have much effect.

Some ways to minimize your impact follow. It's impossible to cover every particular, but these are the major areas where care is needed.

Please don't eat the columbine. There's been a lot of interest in recent years in edible plants. But the National Park Service asks that you enjoy the knowledge rather than the taste. If you dig up a Mariposa lily to eat the bulb, you have destroyed the plant not for only this year, but for next year, and forever. If you eat a fruit, nut or berry however, the plant continues to live and reproduce. Confine your non-emergency eating to this category. Don't dig up bulbs, or roots, or pick flowers (to eat or collect), or leaves. This comes as a blow to pennyroyal tea lovers, but you can purchase seeds from catalogs and grow it at home.

Travel lightly. When you travel through the wilderness try to stay on the trails, especially if you're with a large group. Avoid walking through fragile meadows. The damp soil of the meadows is easily torn up, and it takes many years to correct itself. When you're hiking on a steep trail, don't cut across the switchbacks. Cutting the trail like this increases the likelihood you will injure yourself or someone below you by dislodging rocks. Many animals live under and around the rocks, and they prefer to be left undisturbed. Cutting the trail also creates a water channel that increases erosion.

If you decide to travel cross country, meaning off the trail, be sure you have a map and compass and know how to use them. It is advised that only small and experienced groups attempt cross country travel because of the increased impact and increased risk to the party.

Choose a nice soft rock. To pick a place for sleeping with the least possible impact, you would choose a large rock. Next best is a smooth flat area under a tree that doesn't have much growth to trample. The meadow may look soft and inviting, but not only will you make a lasting impression on it, you'll probably find it very damp at night.

You want a campsite near fresh water, but keep your camp at least 100 feet away from the lake or stream to avoid contaminating it and to protect the fragile bank. For your own enjoyment, you'll probably want to camp at least 100 feet from the trail too. Choose an area that requires as little rearrangement as possible. You'll almost always have to move a few rocks and twigs, but try to replace them when you leave. Don't gather up pine needles or boughs for a bed, even if John Muir did. You need to do better than he did because there are many more people in the backcountry now.

Don't dig a trench around your sleeping place "in case of rain." A trench is a serious disruption of the ground surface. Modern tents have waterproof bottoms and sides. For your own safety, always take some kind of rain protection.

Remember that most people come to the wilderness for solitude. Don't be so rude as to "park" right next to someone unless invited.

Fire? The use of wood for fire is being discouraged in most areas; there simply isn't enough wood for everyone to build a fire. In any area fire-rings are an intrusion. If you plan to build a fire, camp only at a designated firesite and use only existing fire-rings. Keep the fire small, to use as little wood as possible. There's a saying that you can build a small fire to keep warm by standing close to it, or build a large fire and keep warm by running for more wood. Use only dead and down wood. Standing trees, alive or dead, are an important part of the forest. Small dead branches still on the tree aren't legal for fires.

A gas stove is more convenient and dependable than wood fires, especially if the weather is wet or windy. Stoves don't leave ugly fire stains, don't damage plant life, and can be turned off so you don't have to worry about embers.

There are basically two different types of stove available. One type runs on butane or propane that comes in a large disposable cartridge. It isn't very dependable in cold weather, and creates a lot of waste (throwing away all the empty cartridges). The other kind of stove is run on white gas that you carry in a refillable fuel bottle. There are several models available, like the SVEA 123 or the slightly larger Optimus 111B. The initial investment is a little more than the cartridge stoves, but the fuel is both lighter and cheaper.

White gas, not to be confused with unleaded gas, is available in gallon containers in mountaineering stores, and some grocery stores. Or you can get it from a pump at gas stations in most mountain areas. The gas station version costs about half as much, but you need to bring your own can. The simplest and cheapest way to get an empty gallon can is to buy your first gallon of gas from the store. When that can is empty you can refill if from the gas station pump.

I PASSED through the messianic period, battling the implacable devourers and mutilators of wilderness, and gradually I entered a more philosophic – humanistic stage where I was able, in some small way, to separate personal euphoria from impersonal appraisals of the rights of man to participate in the bounties of his environment. The fact that he has fouled his nest and seems certain to continue with his destruction seems now more of an illness than an expression of evil intent. The problem is not *whether* we must save the natural scene, but *how* we may accomplish it.

Ansel Adams

Fuel bottles to carry in your pack are sold where you buy your stove. They come with a plastic top, and optional pour spout. If you don't get the pour spout, you'll need a small plastic funnel.

Before you go on a trip and your dinner depends on it, practice filling and lighting your stove. Be sure to go outside to a fire-safe place. Do not attempt this in your fireplace. Lighting a white gas stove may seem a little complicated at first, but it will soon become automatic. It involves five simple steps, each of which is essential. These directions are for the SVEA 123. Other models light similarly.

• Fill the stove. Pour gas from the fuel bottle into the stove tank until there's a little air space left at the top.

• Screw the cap tightly back onto the stove fuel tank, or you'll start a larger fire than you had intended.

• Turn the valve with its key to be sure it's off, for the same reason.

• Prime the stove. This is necessary to create pressure so the gas will vaporize. If you prime poorly, especially at high altitudes, the fuel will sputter along with a yellow flame, or might refuse to start at all.

If it doesn't start you have to wait for the whole thing to cool down again before starting over. Overpriming only risks wasting a little fuel, and immediately gives a hot blue flame. Place the stove in a fire-safe place. Pour enough gas to fill the cup at the bottom of the stem, usually about two tablespoons. Don't worry if you spill over a little too much.

• Replace the top to the fuel bottle. Put the bottle away from you. Stand back a foot or two and toss a match on the stove. As soon as the flame quits turn on the valve and light the burner as you would any other stove. A full tank will burn for about 45 minutes.

Protecting your water. If you want to be able to drink the water where you hike, then it's up to you to keep it fresh. Ivory or other biodegradable soap is great for the sake of the soil, but no soap should be used in the lakes, streams, or rivers. Water for washing your dishes, your sox, or yourself should be carried in a plastic basin or bucket at least 100 feet from any water source. Dirty water should be thrown in a wide arc to sprinkle a large area rather than drench a small area. It is best to throw it uphill on dry ground, not on rocks, and not on damp or marshy areas.

To keep clean free running water available, each of us has to treat is as the precious resource it is. Don't wash in it, don't spit toothpaste in it, don't clean fish in it, and don't urinate in it.

Protecting your food. There are two reasons to protect your food. First because if a bear makes off with your week's supply, that's the end of your trip, at least until you get more. But also because the animals of the wilderness should eat natural food to maintain healthy stable populations.

Bears are the most difficult animals to foil. They seem to have come to believe there's a new kind of fruit growing

in the conifers: Backpacker's-food-fruit. They have learned
to associate the rope with the fruit.

Here is the latest "bear-proof" rig: First, take all your
food out of your pack. If you hang your pack in the tree and
the bear gets it, you're out a pack. If you put the food in a
stuff sack, and the bear gets it, you're only out a stuff sack.
Put all the food and garbage in the stuff sack. Bears have
ripped open packs for a packet of salt, a tea bag, or even a
vitamin pill that was accidentally left out of the stuff sack.
They have punctured cans of beer and flasks of whisky.
Young ones sometimes take off with toothpaste.

Tie a rope (500 pound test is best) to your stuff sack.
Hang the sack over a stout limb about twenty feet off the
ground. The sack should hang down five feet from the limb,
fifteen feet from the ground, and ten feet from the tree
trunk. This pretty much guarantees the bear can't reach the
sack from the limb, the ground, or the trunk (even grown
bears can climb trees). The ropes should be tied to a tall
skinny tree, too slender for the bear to climb, but too strong
for the bear to bend over. Tie the rope as high as you can
reach.

Remember that hanging your food in the tree doesn't
guarantee its safety. Some people recommend tying a
couple of metal cups to the bag so if the bear starts shaking it
you'll wake up. But on a windy night you'll create quite a bit
of noise. It's better to sleep with your ears open to the sound
of twigs cracking under heavy bear paws. If you surprise a
bear before it has your food you can probably chase it away.
Once it has your food, give up. Never try to take food away
from a bear (or other animals).

Before you go to sleep, check around the camp. Be
sure you don't leave any dirty pans or cups around. Make
sure you haven't forgotten to hang any food or garbage. If
you find any, take it far away from your sleeping place, and
away from anyone else's too. A good place to put it is in the
top of a tall but skinny tree (not the one you've used to tie
your food rope!). Even candy bars sometimes survive the
night this way. But don't sleep with any food.

It's important to unzip all the pockets of your pack.
Bears will paw through them, even when there's no food
inside (the smell lingers). If the pocket is zipped the bear will
rip it open. Prop the pack against a rock or tree near your
sleeping place, but about five feet away. Keep a flashlight

handy. The light and loud yelling will sometimes chase away a bear. Unless there isn't anyone else camped around you, please reserve banging on metal cups for emergencies. And when you chase the bear away, try to head it back into the woods, not over to the other camp.

If worse comes to worst and you wake up in the morning with your food gone, what do you do? First, even before you start fishing for breakfast, you look for the mess the bear has made of your provisions. It won't be too far away. Now that the bear has finished with it, the responsibility reverts to you. Gather it up and burn it if you're in the fire designated area. If not, pack it out.

How do you go to the bathroom? Latrines used to be the way. But it has been learned that a large latrine which concentrates wastes is more difficult for the environment to decompose. The biologically active layer of the soil, the layer that decomposes things, is usually only about ten inches deep. So groups should choose individual bathrooms, each well away from the water source. The ground around the base of trees is usually loose and easy to dig with the heel of your boot. Make a small hole, about six inches deep and ten inches across. When you've finished cover the hole with soil and pack it tightly. Do not attempt to bury tampons, sanitary napkins or disposable diapers. They require years to decompose. They will burn in a very hot fire. Otherwise you'll need to pack them out in a plastic bag.

Litter. The litter problem has improved in recent years as people have become more aware. Only continued conscientiousness will keep the wilderness clean. Never bury garbage, even organic waste like orange peels. They require too long to decompose. Always pack garbage back out with you. Try to keep that in mind when you plan your food. Smoked oysters, for instance, might taste delicious, but the can makes a mess to have to carry very far. If you are in a fire-designated area, some cans can be put in a hot fire to burn out the food traces. Cardboard boxes and paper wrappings can be burned too. But the burned out cans and any tin foil remnants in the fire must be carried out (after they've cooled).

Permits. Most wilderness areas now require a permit. This is usually a simple process, but the system varies from place to place. It's a good idea to write or call ahead for information.

Go back to the beginning. Can you find the dozen errors now? If so, you're well on the way to being a good backpacker.

Answers. You're hiking through the mountains, picking flowers (1) as you go, when over a rise you see a perfect campsite. You hurry down the slope, too excited to follow the meandering switchbacks (2). After pitching your tent in the meadow (3) near the lake shore (4), you quickly gather rocks for a fire-ring (5) and get plenty of firewood. For kindling you snap off a lot of small, dead twigs from the trees. (6). A prepared camper brings a shovel, and you use yours to dig a latrine (7), and a small trench (8) around your tent in case of rain. After you've gathered a pile of pine needles to cushion your bed (9) there's time for a bath. So you jump in the lake, using your biodegradable soap to avoid polluting the water, and lather up (10). The sun is starting to set as you dry off in front of the large fire (11) that's cooking your dinner. Before dark you put all your food in your pack (12), and hang it in the tree.

The Cirque of the Unclimbables

by Galen Rowell

In the summer of 1972, my friend Jim McCarthy and I flew in his small plane toward Jim's favorite spot on earth—the Cirque of the Unclimbables, an isolated group of granite peaks in the Logan Mountains of Canada's Northwest Territories. Located in a completely roadless area larger than California, the cirque is so remote that at the time of our visit fewer than twenty-five people had ever set foot there, although it is more spectacularly beautiful than any place I have seen in the national parks of North America.

Jim and I had just returned from an unsuccessful attempt on the Moose's Tooth in Alaska, and he assured me that the Logan Mountains, although at the same latitude, had far better weather than the Alaska Range. He had first visited the area a few years earlier, making the first ascent of Lotus Flower Tower in several warm, twenty-hour days. After a wretched spell of Alaskan rain and snow, we were ready for such a sunny paradise.

Our flight in Jim's Cessna over the vast, unpopulated reaches of the North provided a classic contrast between timeless nature and timebound man. The little plane was fully equipped for instrument flying. Often we slipped into the translucent void of a cloud bank, and I would watch Jim scan the panel and recreate in his mind the dynamic perspective of his craft moving across the landscape. Gradually I began to realize the limits of the various devices. When a call to an airport gave us a new barometer reading, Jim dialed it into the altimeter. The needle moved up. The plane did not. It was theoretically possible to read 2000 feet of ground clearance on a gauge a split second before slamming into the side of a mountain. The magnetic compass wigged and wagged as we passed near ore bodies. Nothing was absolute, I thought to myself, except time. Every thirty-six seconds, a new digit snapped into the hundredth's place on the gauge that registered hours.

But how absolute is the human conception of time? As

we flew north across Canada, the dwindling number of set-
tlements below us made it seem as if we were returning to a
time long past in the United States. Calgary, a potential
Canadian Los Angeles, quickly sprawled into a checker-
board of farms. The fields were dotted with small patches of
forest, the only remnants of what was once an unbroken
expanse of woodlands and lakes. Gradually the farms grew
fewer until they became islands in a sea of lakes and forest,
and in the Yukon, signs of man became still less frequent.
Regardless of the regular ratcheting of the hour gauge, we
were traveling backward, not forward, in time.

We landed the plane on the dirt airstrip of a small
mining town. On a hillside above a long valley was the open
pit. Ten-ton Euclid trucks howled back and forth on the
Z-shaped road from the pit to the groaning and clanking
processing mill in town. Pipes gushed black water into silta-
tion ponds. Abandoned cars, empty oil drums, bits of
lumber and sewage formed a wreath around the town;
tungsten and people were the only things carried out. A
portly woman in her forties came riding down the hill on a
motorcycle. We met her later in the mess hall and learned
that she was the cook for the single men living in the dor-
mitories. She offered us food and coffee, and I commented
on both the quality and quantity. "The boys get lots of good
food and high pay," she replied. "They have to. A person
needs that and more up here or else he'll go crazy. In the
winter it sometimes goes seventy below, and the days are
only four hours long. Most everyone has snowmobiles. In
the summer people play baseball, go hiking, swimming—I
ride a motorcycle, you know. A person has to have something else besides working. Why one fellow, he worked lots
of overtime and did nothing but work, eat, and sleep. We
warned him, but he wouldn't listen. They carried him out of
here in a straightjacket."

An hour later we were in a jet helicopter, crossing
icefields and snowy ridges on our way to the heart of the
mountain range. Blue lakes lay below peaks in glacier-
carved bowls. Far below the hanging alpine valleys were the
trenches of the main rivers. The long hours of summer sun
had melted the surface of the permafrost, changing level
valley floors into impassable brush-tangled bogs that formed
moats around the granite cathedrals in the center of the
range.

The helicopter deposited us and our pile of gear in an alpine meadow and flew off. We planned a multi-day ascent of nearby Parrot Beak Peak and brought food for five days; the helicopter was to return on the fifth. Granite towers thousands of feet high loomed over the small meadow where we pitched our tent.

That evening I took a long walk into the next valley. From the air the vegetation had appeared uniformly green, but on closer inspection, the verdant grasses and mosses proved to be merely the dominant color in a melange of hues. The north sides of the rocks were splotched with colorful lichens; the south sides carpeted with thick mats of yellow moss. Streams were gray, not blue, because they were laden with glacial silt. Wildflowers grew in profusion on the meadowed benches. Rivulets snaked through the meadows and dipped off into the distance. I felt like an intruder as my footsteps squashed down the living mat.

I walked through a meadow decorated with tremendous squared boulders. One gigantic rock was split in three parts and through a narrow crack I could watch clouds swirling around the tops of towers. It gave me the unmistakable impression of being in a natural Stonehenge. Timberline was at only 4000 feet, and this meadow was far above the last trees. I saw marmot, finches, ptarmigans, and plenty of signs of mountain goats. I was surprised to find a dwarfed spruce growing behind a boulder in less than two inches of caribou moss. Although it had more than twenty sets of limbs, it was no more than eight inches tall. I would have taken for granted the most stately spruce, but this lone, small tree caught my attention and made me wonder how long it could last.

Morning dawned gray and cloudy. Jim and I agreed to delay our multi-day ascent and instead chose to climb a shorter but fine-looking buttress on the highest peak in the region, Mount Sir James McBrien. After three hours of unroped scrambling, we reached the beginning of technical climbing. A few hundred feet higher we came to a steep head-wall. It was my turn to lead. Climbing here required a more cautious attitude than in a more accessible region; in case of injury or sickness, one might wait a long time to be evacuated. My feet began to twitch involuntarily, and I placed three pitons within arm's reach to protect one move over a difficult 5.10 ceiling.

Reaching the summit early in the evening, we saw a storm advancing from the other side of the peak. The complex descent on the easiest side of the peak involved traversing narrow ledges and kicking steps down snow-filled couloirs. Lower down we found fresh goat tracks and followed them onto a well-worn trail across grassy ledges. As we rounded a corner, I spotted a family of five goats ascending a nearby ridge. It was ten o'clock that night before we reached our tent in the rain.

It was still raining the next morning, and it continued for three more days without stopping. Around noon on the third day, Jim discovered that our beautiful meadow was fast becoming a lake. Although we had chosen the highest piece of ground, it was only six inches above the overall level; the water was rising fast and we were already on an island. Within five minutes we were furiously digging trenches with ice axes, defending our little portable environment against an onslaught of silt-laden water—the same waters which had created the meadow from a trap basin in the glacial moraine. It didn't work; the water was coming from every direction, faster than we could drain it with our crude tools. We paused to take stock of the situation and then spotted the main source of the water—a large stream pouring down the hillside just above the meadow. We concentrated our efforts there, building dams and trenching until we had altered the course of the stream to avoid the meadow completely.

It would be nice to be able to say that we considered all the alternatives and chose one that was both practical and environmentally sound. However, I can't recall either of us suggesting that we simply move up onto the rocks and huddle under a tarp. How ironic that we who talked of preserving this place were busy trenching and damming at the first threat of getting wet. We even felt proud of our efforts. I finally understood how Floyd Dominy must have felt when he dedicated Glen Canyon Dam. All the same, I was horrified at my thoughts. Just a week earlier, flying over endless mles of woodland, I had experienced similar feelings when I found myself thinking, "Why are they cutting all that beautiful timber in California when they could be logging up here and nobody would miss it?" I quenched the thought immediately but recognized that for a moment I had experienced the frontier ethic of the North.

There was nothing to do now but wait in the tent. I teased Jim about his weather prophecy. He said the rain would quit soon, but I noticed him toying with his dismantled survival rifle and began to consider the serious possiblity that we might be trapped here long enough to need it. When we awoke the next morning it was snowing. The clouds parted for a brief glimpse of the cliffs, and the scene was wild beyond description. Towers plastered in white loomed somberly out of the mist. A foot of snow lay on our meadow, and the goat paths on the mossy ledges were buried. Falling snowflakes dampened the acoustics of the cirque; except for the roar of an occasional avalanche, all was still.

The sixth day passed. Our food supply was very low, and we talked about what we could do if the helicopter never came. It might take us weeks to hike the fifty miles of brush and marshes between our cirque and the mine town. Suddenly I was no longer in a comfortable living room thumbing through a picture book of wilderness images. Here, in trouble, the value of civilization came clear. The embarrassing pride we felt over damming the stream, my flash of faulty logic about logging the North, and our present helplessness all began to fit together. I needed the tools of civilization. What did I have that I could do without? My mountain boots? My food? My sleeping bag? Without the umbilical cord to civilization that these things represented, I would be in bad shape. Back home, I had been lulled into false confidence in my own survival abilities by the nearness of civilization. I could reach habitation in two days of hiking from the most remote area in California.

In strict terms, much of what passes for a "wilderness experience" is counterfeit. Once in a while someone really does make a break for a short time—often it is accidental, termed "exposure," and results in a visit to a hospital. The "ruggedness" of a wilderness experience is not merely the physical effort involved, but the chance that the conditions of nature will exceed the capabilities of the equipment we bring with us. In other words, we risk being thrown into a true wilderness situation, one that modern people carefully avoid by special equipment, clothing, and rations.

Jim and I had brought an element of the technological world into the backcountry. Mountain tents do considerably less damage than many other kinds of portable environments, such as recreational vehicles, but even the most adaptable self-contained travelers, wilderness backpackers, leave their marks. Footsteps gradually wear footpaths; campfires gradually develop into permanent campsites, and the pursuit of the unknown sooner or later becomes a section in a guidebook. Even though backpackers are equipped to deal with a far wider set of circumstances than are recreational vehicles, when the limits of their adaptability are exceeded they must either suffer or change the land to suit their needs, as we had chosen to do by trenching and damming.

In the natural world, an animal must adapt to its environment or perish. Civilization implies adapting the environment to human needs; much of the appeal of wilderness is that it can return people to the primeval situation to which humans are adapted. Keeping equipment down to a few simple items is one step toward this goal, but many people become more concerned with the means than the ends. Equipment is counted and compared like batting averages. The differences between various brands of equipment are far down the list of things that the modern, urban person needs to know in order to understand and enjoy the wilderness.

I peered outside the tent into a mist-shrouded dreamland of meadows, streams, and granite towers. A heavy rain was washing the snow from the meadow, but it was still snowing on the summits. The scene was magnificent, but I longed to be back in the mining town, though a week earlier I had scoffed at its prefabs, snowmobiles, and life styles. Once again the ethic of the North had caught up with me; it is hard to consider the intrinsic value of wilderness while it is a real adversary. In the United States, we are beginning to realize that our wildlands are finite, but in the Northwest Territories, an earlier spirit prevails. The people of the North are not wrong, any more than Americans were wrong to drive cars without smog devices in 1935, or to shoot buffalo when there were millions of them. Modern pioneers are living in a different age. Their daydreams are still of the future, and their frontier heroes have modern equipment. Today's Abraham Lincoln lives in a log cabin with central heating and a freezer full of moose. Today's Snowshoe Thompson has treads and makes rather more noise. And today's Davy Crockett—I met him in person, in Alaska—

dynamites coyotes from his airplane. "Thirty-dollar bounty and you get to keep the pelt, you know."

My mental ramblings might not solve the problems of the developing North; but I did gain an increased awareness of how thoroughly we are trapped in our own time—I in mine, and the pioneers of this land in theirs. They must live through the same mistakes made by earlier pioneers before they can realize what they have lost. As for me, I still had to think in terms of basic survival. There was a helicopter buzzing in the back of my consciousness, and I hoped it would soon appear in reality.

GOING to the mountains is like going home.

John Muir

The eighth morning dawned gray. Rain was intermittent, and fog hung low in the distant river valleys. Clouds still veiled the summits of the peaks. I put on my wet boots and stepped outside. Every watercourse was full. I grabbed my pack and a camera and announced that I was going for a walk. I'd gone only a hundred yards when the humming of the water was drowned out by a gradually increasing noise; I barely beat the helicopter to the tent. Suddenly time was of the highest value. Minutes ticked by at hundreds of dollars per hour as the helicopter waited for us to dismantle our camp. Darting around the meadow, we must have resembled the frantic, choppy characters in an early silent film. The pilot seemed puzzled that we took the time to bag up garbage and tie it into the baskets.

As we rose into the air, we had a view of the lower meadow completely submerged in water. We were witnessing the forces of its creation still at work today. But the silt-laden water was prevented by our earthworks from reaching the meadow where we had camped. We had been thoroughly conditioned to pick up garbage, even at great cost; but we had not thought of tearing down the dams during our expensive rush to return to civilization. Unconsciously, we had placed a dollar value on nature's chosen course for a mountain stream. I looked back at the sheer 2000-foot face of Proboscis, as impressive as Yosemite's Half Dome, following the clean granite with my eyes until it abruptly merged with jumbled red rock. A contact-metamorphic zone: what every prospector seeks when hunting copper, lead, and gold. The list could continue—tungsten, molybdenum, silver, zinc—but the meaning was the same. Call it progress, manifest destiny, the ethic of the North—time could all too easily catch up to these mountains.

When I returned home I wrote about our visit without using a single place name. I wanted to emphasize the nature of the experience rather than the place itself, and I feared that the area might be damaged by overuse if my article attracted too many visitors. Through word of mouth and mountaineering journals, the Cirque has since become well known to climbers all over the world, and the experience is no longer the same. There is garbage in the meadows and the solitude is gone. What I choose to remember is the feeling of moving backward through time, back to the kind of experience enjoyed by the early explorers of the Grand Canyon, of Yellowstone, the Grand Tetons, or Yosemite; back to the time before these scenic wonders became islands of wild country surrounded by cities, roads, and farms. Finding this experience in North America in the 1970s was the journey's greatest reward.

The New Resource Management

Restoring Fire to National Park Wilderness

by Bruce M. Kilgore

It was early October in Yosemite National Park. Flames crept slowly through the pine needles until they reached a pile of dry twigs and branches. Then they exploded, racing up through the inter-laced branches of a 15-foot red fir, killing it before moving slowly up the slope.

This fire, touched off when lightning struck a snag in the vicinity of Mount Starr King just south of Yosemite Valley, had been burning for two months at an elevation of 8,000 feet. Before it was put out by early winter snow, it had spread across nearly 4,000 acres of Yosemite's red fir-lodgepole-Jeffrey pine forest.

For the first two months, the National Park Service made no effort to suppress the flames, although Dick Riegelhuth, Chief of Resources Management at Yosemite, and Dr. Jan van Wagtendonk, the Park's Research Scientist, watched closely to see that it stayed within a designated zone where natural fires are allowed to burn. As the flames neared the edge of the natural fire zone, Yosemite Superintendent Les Arnberger and Riegelhuth decided to establish a small fire line along the side to keep the fire inside the zone boundary.

Meanwhile, in Grand Teton National Park, Wyoming, a similar fire was attracting national attention from the news media. Also started by lightning in July, it covered nearly 3,700 acres of forest land before it was put out by late autumn snows.

Because the slow-burning Grand Teton fire was highly visible across Jackson Lake and smoke at times obscured the view of the mountains, public controversy erupted. Some permanent residents, visitors, and elements of the tourist industry accused the Park Service of a "scorched earth" policy and complained of air pollution from smoke.

Superintendent Gary Everhardt feels such public reaction is understandable, conditioned as it was by years of believing that all forest fires are bad and should be put out immediately. But what people were witnessing was a rather spectacular example of a new policy, begun modestly in 1968, under which National Park rangers and scientists, working with Mother Nature, are restoring natural fires and sometimes "prescribed" fires to their historic role in National Park ecosystems.

It should be emphasized that in size at least, The Grand Teton and Yosemite fires were not typical. More than 90 percent of these natural burning fires are less than one-quarter acre in size.

They do, however, represent a basic shift in the National Park Service attitude toward fire. From the founding of the Service in 1916 until the mid-1960's, the "no burn" policy—personified by Smokey the Bear—was rarely challenged. National Park Service policy called for prompt suppression of all fires on park lands, whether natural or man-caused, often at great cost in both money and environmental impacts. Over the past decade, the NPS has spent an average of $1.3 million per year on emergency fire suppression. And although much of this would have been essential under any policy, it is hoped in the future to save a good share of this expense by learning to work with fire to reduce the inevitable buildup of wildland fuels.

Beginning in the 1950s, some scientists began taking a closer look at what unnatural suppression of all fires was doing to the ecosystems of certain national park forests and grasslands. And they didn't like what they found.

At Everglades National Park in Florida, Research Scientist Dr. William Robertson, Jr. discovered that fire plays an important role in controlling tropical hardwoods which in absence of fire replace pines, natural to these areas. Other scientists also found that fire was essential to maintaining the stability of saw grass glades.

Cautiously, the scientists and rangers at Everglades began helping Nature by deliberately substituting a few fires of their own in carefully selected locations and under the right conditions. This policy of scientifically setting fires, for ecological reasons, is called "prescribed burning," the first such program in the Park Service.

Meanwhile, in the Sierra Nevada of California, scientists like Dr. Richard Hartesveldt and colleagues from California State University, San Jose, and Dr. Harold Biswell and associates at the University of California, Berkeley, as well as the author and other Park Service scientists, conducted experimental studies involving prescribed burning in the Sequoia mixed-conifer forests of Sequoia and Kings Canyon National Parks.

This work, together with field and laboratory studies by U.S. Forest Service scientists at Missoula, Montana, and Riverside, California, led to the conclusion that fire plays several essential roles in the ecology of the sequoia mixed-conifer forests, and that sequoia forests literally can't survive wthout it.

The role of the fire in these forests is as follows:

1. Fire prepares a seedbed in which sequoia seeds sprout and flourish. It does so by changing the thick litter and duff into soft, friable, ashy soil on which the lightweight sequoia seeds fall and are buried. It also kills pathogens such as damping-off fungi which kill seedlings. And by reducing litter and duff and killing some trees, more water reaches the soil and is available to sequoia, an important factor in summer survival of seedlings.

2. Fire efficiently recycles nutrients back into the soil by releasing minerals formerly tied up in dead plant materials. While hot fires volatilize some nutrients, lighter burns often increase available nitrogen, phosphorous, potassium, calcium, and magnesium and generally improve soils chemically.

3. Recurring light fires adjust the successional pattern by favoring sunloving and fire-tolerant species (such as sequoia and pine) over shade-tolerant and fire-susceptible species (like white fir). They do so by periodically killing understory young fir and producing sunny openings in the forest where sequoia seedlings grow well.

4. Fire in sequoia-mixed conifer forests provides conditions which favor wildlife by stimulating germination or sprouting of palatable shrubs, herbaceous plants, and trees useful to birds and mammals for food and cover. It also makes openings in forest understory and canopy which improve habitat for many species of wild animals.

5. Fire contributes to the development of a mosaic of age classes and vegetation types because species differ in their tolerance to fire and because Sierra forests burn in a highly variable pattern. It may burn hot enough to kill fir and even young pine where surface fuels or larger pine are present but not in openings left by previous hot burns. Thus, when fire creates openings by burning hot enough to kill all

fir and pine in a given area, the new young pines and sequoia will survive the next fire.

6. Fire changes the numbers of trees susceptible to attack by insects and disease. While insects are attracted to fire-damaged trees, fire also apparently has a sanitizing effect by thinning stands and improving vigor of trees, making them more resistant to insect attack. It also eliminates old trees before insects and disease have overtaken them, and smoke plays a role in inhibiting disease organisms.

IN NATURE there are no rewards or punishments; there are consequences.

Horace Annesley Vachel

---

7. Lighter burns reduce the likelihood of extremely hot crown fires by removing the ladder of understory trees and brush and reducing accumulations of dead surface fuels.

Armed with this information, and bolstered by a recommendation from the prestigious panel of scientists known as the "Leopold Committee," (named after its Chairman, Dr. A. Starker Leopold, of the University of California, Berkeley) the National Park Service in 1968 updated its traditional policy of total fire suppression, and adopted instead a three-part program of fire management. The new policy seeks to restore and maintain natural environmental conditions in the parks; to do so, the Service must restore natural processes—including fire—or simulate the results of fire. This nation-wide policy was first implemented at Sequoia-Kings Canyon.

The new program: (1) establishes a policy of letting some natural fires burn when they do not threaten human life or developed properties; (2) recognizes prescribed burning as a proper tool of forest management; and (3) continues total fire suppression in lower elevations and around developed areas.

Today, two or more segments of this three-part program are in effect in eleven national parks, namely Everglades, Sequoia and Kings Canyon, Yosemite, Grand Teton, Yellowstone, Rocky Mountain, Wind Cave, Carlsbad Caverns, and North Cascades National Parks and Saguaro National Monument.

More than 3,000,000 acres within these parks are being managed so that fires play a more natural role in the ecosystems. Lightning-caused fires in these "natural fire"zones are kept under close observation but are not automatically suppressed. Provided the fires can achieve desired vegetation or wildlife management objectives such as preparing a seedbed for fire-dependent species, making openings for wildlife habitat, or reducing hazardous fuels, they are allowed to burn. As noted earlier, most natural fires in the Sierra and Rocky Mountain parks are small and go out before they reach one-quarter acre in size.

A wide variety of vegetation types are found in the natural fire zones of these areas, reflecting considerable differences in burning conditions and the frequency, intensity, and hence, the role of fire. Vegetation ranges from the pineland, saw grass glade, and coastal prairie communities of Everglades to the basket grass, cactus, and yucca of Guadalupe Mountains; from the ponderosa pine forests of Saguaro National Monument, to the red fir, lodgepole pine and mixed-conifer forests of the Sierra Nevada; and the lodgepole pine, spruce, Douglas-fir, and aspen of the Rocky Mountain parks.

This program has expanded considerably since 1968 from the relatively small program at Sequoia-Kings Canyon to 74 fires covering more than 15,000 acres in 1974. Over the seven-year period, 1968 to 1974, a total of 274 natural fires covered almost 30,000 acres.

During the same period, 267 "prescribed burns" took place, covering some 37,000 acres in six parks—Everglades, Sequoia and Kings Canyon, Yosemite, Grand Teton, and Wind Cave. In Everglades, Resource Manager Larry Bancroft points out that such burns simulate the role of natural fire in favoring pine over hardwoods, reducing fuels, and controlling exotic plants. While dealing with different vegetation, the programs in the Sierra parks, at Grand Teton, and Wind Cave have similar objectives, with strong emphasis on reducing the adverse impacts of past fire suppression—particularly buildup of understory thickets and the accumulation of abnormal quantities of surface fuels. All such burns are only carried out under specifically prescribed conditions of temperature, humidity, wind and fuel moisture.

Fire suppression, the traditional part of the new NPS

program, will continue as the primary action in developed areas and zones with high cultural resource value. Man-caused fires are still suppressed, except in some cases at Everglades. Suppression also will be applied to natural fire zones when the fire threatens areas outside the zones or is not achieving the desired purpose.

There is also the problem of wood smoke and air pollution. As noted earlier, the Grand Teton fire gave rise to cries of "air pollution." The Park Service is deeply interested in studies of wood smoke now being made by the Forest Service, the University of California and other universities. We try to take advantage of the best possible weather conditions for burning to minimize negative effects. But we feel it is important to draw a distinction between the quality and quantity of materials released in wood smoke and those found in industrial pollutants or automotive exhaust.

Wood smoke is primarily composed of particulate matter, carbon dioxide, and condensed water vapor. Automotive exhausts and industrial discharges, in contrast, contain much larger percentages of poisonous sulfur and nitrogen oxides and lead. The differences are profound and they are environmentally important. The desire to avoid smoke resulting from prescribed burns must be tempered by the need to control smoke and intense resource damage that inevitably would result otherwise from future wildfires of a major nature.

The Service is aware, however, that it is one thing to accept the role of fire intellectually, and quite another to support it when smoke from a natural fire has persisted in an area for many days. While the long-term best interest of the forest resources may be helped by such a fire, the day-to-day gut reaction to smoke may still be negative—thus creating substantial public relations problems for this program.

While many changes have occurred in recent years in NPS fire management efforts, even greater changes can be expected in the next decade. Fire research is essential to gain new information and monitor results in the eleven national parks with on-going management programs. In addition to such management-oriented fire research at Sequoia-Kings Canyon, Yosemite, Grand Teton, Yellowstone, and Everglades, similar studies at Grand Canyon, Glacier, Lava Beds, Isle Royale, and Point Reyes can serve as a basis for intelligent fire management programs which may be implemented in the near future in these parks.

Further, the Service must continue to work closely with researchers of the Forest Service and universities to gain the new information required to constantly improve our fire management programs. Among the things we need to know are: (1) How often should an area be burned? (2) What prescription is appropriate, i.e., what temperature, humidity, wind, and fuel moisture conditions should be used to bring about a given intensity of fire? (3) How much fuel accumulation indicates the need to prescribe another burn? and (4) What management actions can best simulate "naturalness" and at the same time minimize smoke contribution to adjacent communities?

Answers to these questions must be sought by carefully controlled laboratory and field studies. But information also must be gathered by monitoring actual experimental burns and wildfires. As conclusions are reached, managers must apply them under field conditions to determine their validity in actual management programs.

All National Park managers face four basic choices in fire management. They can (1) suppress all man-caused and natural fires at all times; (2) prescribe burn in certain zones at certain times; (3) allow natural fires to burn in certain zones under certain conditions; or (4) allow all man-caused and natural fires to burn at all times.

The fourth alternative, of course, is unrealistic because of many adverse impacts on biological, social, and economic values that would occur. Equally important, it would be unacceptable to the public. Most managers, however, will be able to utilize the first three as appropriate alternatives.

In wilderness areas, allowing natural fires to burn may be most desirable whenever experience and conditions of adjacent landowners permit. In developed zones, on the other hand, total suppression combined with manual removal of the fuel is appropriate.

In the middle or gray zone, perhaps where unnatural fuel accumulation needs to be reduced and where scientists have developed "prescriptions" for a particular fuel type, prescribed burning may be the answer. The exact mix for a given park will be determined partly by research and partly by experience.

We can no longer afford to follow the seemingly secure policy of total fire suppression. We must face up to the needs of the real, ever-changing world of forest and grass-land ecosystems, wherein fire has played a role in the past and will continue to do so in the future, either through wildfires, natural fires, or prescribed fires.

We must determine the most logical and responsible policies for managing these dynamic ecosystems and estab-lish integrated programs of prescribed burning, suppression, and allowing natural fires to burn in selected zones.

For despite efforts by the most effective fire fighters in the world, coniferous forests, chaparral, and similar vegeta-tion will burn periodically. It behooves us, therefore, as scientists, laymen and environmentally concerned citizens to learn all we can about the natural role of fire in our wild-lands and to support intelligent management decisions based on this knowledge. This is particularly true of our national parks and wilderness areas, where natural processes should be allowed to run their course, as closely as possible.

Finally, we must recognize the public relations prob-lem we face with a generation of Americans who have been conditioned by the "all fires are bad" syndrome. But we also know that an informed public is a supportive public. The challenge in getting our message across is obvious.

The answer is not to force Smokey the Bear into re-tirement, because his precepts remain essential and valid for vast areas of forest lands. But we must go beyond simple fire suppression.

The National Park Service is committed to maintain-ing (and in some cases, restoring) the integrity of our natural areas down through the long future. This objective can only be accomplished when the natural processes that developed and maintained these ecosystems—including fire—are al-lowed to operate as closely to their natural role as possible.

We must approach the assignment of restoring or maintaining natural environmental conditions with humility and great ecological sensitivity. Our goal must be to provide not the "safest" management over the short run, but the best possible *long-range* management of America's wildland resources.

The Ruination of the Tomato

by Mark Kramer

It wasn't a conspiracy, it was just good business sense—but why did modern agriculture have to take the taste away?

Sagebrush and lizards rattle and whisper behind me. I stand in the moonlight, the hot desert at my back. It's tomato harvest time, 3 A.M. The moon is almost full and near to setting. Before me stretches the first lush tomato field to be taken this morning. The field is farmed by a company called Tejon Agricultural Partners, and lies three hours northeast of Los Angeles in the middle of the bleak silvery drylands of California's San Joaquin Valley. Seven hundred sixty-six acres, more than a mile square of tomatoes—a shaggy, vegetable-green rug dappled with murky red dots, 105,708,000 ripe tomatoes lurking in the night. The field is large and absolutely level. It would take an hour and a half to walk around it. Yet, when I raise my eyes past the field to the much vaster valley floor, and to the mountains that loom farther out, the enormous crop is lost in a big flat world.

This harvest happens nearly without people. A hundred million tomatoes grown, irrigated, fed, sprayed, now taken, soon to be cooled, squashed, boiled, barreled, and held at the ready, then canned, shipped, sold, bought, and after being sold and bought a few more times, uncanned and dumped on pizza. And such is the magnitude of the vista, and the dearth of human presence, that it is easy to look elsewhere and put this routine thing out of mind. But that quality—of blandness overlaying a wondrous integration of technology, finances, personnel, and business systems—seems to be what the "future" has in store.

Three large tractors steam up the road toward me, headlights glaring, towing three thin-latticed towers which support floodlights. The tractors drag the towers into place around an assembly field, then hydraulic arms raise them to vertical. They illuminate a large, sandy work yard where equipment is gathering—fuel trucks, repair trucks, concession trucks, harvesters, tractor-trailers towing big open hoppers. Now small crews of Mexicans, their sunburns tinted light blue in the glare of the three searchlights, climb aboard the harvesters; shadowy drivers mount tractors and trucks. The night fills with the scent of diesel fumes and with the sound of large engines running evenly.

The six harvesting machines drift across the gray-green tomato-leaf sea. After a time, the distant ones come to look like steamboats afloat across a wide bay. The engine sounds are dispersed. A company foreman dashes past, tally sheets in hand. He stops nearby only long enough to deliver a one-liner. "We're knocking them out like Johnny-be-good," he says, punching the air slowly with his right fist. Then he runs off, laughing.

The nearest harvester draws steadily closer, moving in at about the speed of a slow amble, roaring as it comes. Up close, it looks like the aftermath of a collision between a grandstand and a San Francisco tram car. It's two stories high, rolls on wheels that don't seem large enough, astraddle a wide row of jumbled and unstaked tomato vines. It is not streamlined. Gangways, catwalks, gates, conveyors, roofs, and ladders are fastened all over the lumbering rig. As it closes in, its front end snuffles up whole tomato plants as surely as a hungry pig loose in a farmer's garden. Its hind end excretes a steady stream of stems and rejects. Between the ingestion and the elimination, fourteen laborers face each other on long benches. They sit on either side of a conveyor that moves the new harvest rapidly past them. Their hands dart out and back as they sort through the red stream in front of them.

Watching them is like peering into the dining car of a passing train. The folks aboard, though, are not dining but working hard for low wages, culling what is not quite fit for pizza sauce—the "greens," "molds," "mechanicals," and the odd tomato-sized clod of dirt which has gotten past the shakers and screens that tug tomato from vine and dump the harvest onto the conveyor.

The absorbing nature of the work is according to plan. The workers aboard this tiny outpost of a tomato sauce factory are attempting to accomplish a chore at which they cannot possibly succeed, one designed in the near past by some anonymous practitioner of the new craft of *management*. As per cannery contract, each truckload of tomatoes must contain no more than 4 percent green tomatoes, 3 percent tomatoes suffering mechanical damage from the harvester, one percent tomatoes that have begun to mold, and .5 percent clods of dirt.

"The whole idea of this thing," a farm executive had explained earlier in the day, "is to get as many tons as you can per hour. Now, the people culling on the machines strive to sort everything that's defective. But to us, that's as bad as them picking out too little. We're getting $40 to $47 a ton for tomatoes—a bad price this year—and each truckload is 50,000 pounds, 25 tons, 1100 bucks a load. If we're allowed 7 or 8 percent defective tomatoes in the load and we don't have 7 or 8 percent defective tomatoes in a load, we're giving away money. And what's worse, we're paying these guys to make the load too good. It's a double loss. Still, you can't say to your guys, 'Hey, leave 4 percent greens and one percent molds when you sort the tomatoes on the belt.' It's impossible. On most jobs you strive for perfection. They do. But you want to stop them just at the right amount short of perfection—because the cannery will penalize you if your load goes over spec. So what you do is run the belt too fast, and sample the percentages in the output from each machine. If the load is too poor, we add another worker. If it's too good, we send someone home."

The workers converse as they ride the machine toward the edge of the desert. Their lips move in an exaggerated manner, but they don't shout. The few workers still needed at harvest time have learned not to fight the machine. They speak under, rather than over, the din of the harvest. They chat, and their hands stay constantly in fast motion.

Until a few years ago, it took a crowd of perhaps 600 laborers to harvest a crop this size. The six machines want about a hundred workers tonight—a hundred workers for 100 million tomatoes, a million tomatoes per worker in the course of the month it will take to clear the field. The trucks come and go. The harvesters sweep back and forth across the field slowly. Now one stands still in midfield. A big service truck of the sort that tends jet planes drives across the field toward it, dome light flashing. It seems that whatever breaks can be fixed here.

After the first survey, there is nothing new to see. It will be this way for the entire month. Like so many scenes in the new agriculture, the essence of this technological miracle is its productivity, and that is reflected in the very uneventfulness of the event. The miracle is permeated with the air of everyday-ness. Each detail must have persons behind it—the inventions and techniques signal insights into systems, corporate decisions, labor meetings, contracts, phone calls, handshakes, hidden skills, management guidelines. Yet the operation is smooth-skinned. Almost nothing anyone does here requires manual skills or craft beyond the ability to drive and follow orders. And everyone—top to bottom—has his orders.

The workday mood leaves the gentleman standing next to me in good humor. We'll call him Johnny Riley, and at this harvest time he is still a well placed offical at this farm. He is fiftyish and has a neatly trimmed black beard. His eyebrows and eyelashes match the beard, and his whole face, round, ruddy, and boyish, beams behind heavy, black-framed glasses. He's a glad-hander, a toucher, with double-knit everything, a winning smile that demands acknowledgement, and praise to give out. It is enjoyable to talk with him.

"There are too many people out here on the job with their meters running. We can't afford trouble with tomato prices so low. If something hasn't been planned right, and it costs us extra money to get it straightened out, it's my ass," he says.

The tomato harvester that has been closing for some time, bearing down on our outpost by the edge of the field, is now dangerously near. Behind the monster stretches a mile-and-a-quarter-long row of uprooted stubble, shredded leaves, piles of dirt, and smashed tomatoes. Still Johnny Riley holds his ground. He has to raise his voice to make himself heard.

"I don't like to blow my own horn," he shouts, "but there are secrets to agriculture you just have to find out for yourselves. Here's one case in point. It may seem small to you at first, but profits come from doing the small things right. And one of the things I've found over the years is that a long row is better. Here's why. When you get to the end of a row, the machine here. . ." Riley gestures up at the harvester, notices our plight, and obligingly leads me to one side. He continues, ". . .the machine here has to turn around before it can go back the other way. And that's when people get off and smoke. Long rows keep them on the job more minutes per hour. You've got less turns with long rows, and the people don't notice this. Especially at night, with lights on, row length is an important tool for people management. Three fourths of the growers don't realize that. I shouldn't tell you so—it sounds like I'm patting myself on the back—but they don't."

And sure enough, as the harvester climbs off the edge of the tomato field and commences its turn on the sandy road, the crew members descend from the catwalk, scramble to the ground, and light up cigarettes. Johnny Riley nods knowingly to me, then nods again as a young fellow in a John Deere cap drives out of the darkness in a yellow pickup to join us in the circle of light the harvester has brought with it. It's as if he arrived to meet the harvester—which, it turns out, is what he did do. He is introduced as Buck Klein. Riley seems avuncular and proud as he talks about him.

"He's the field supervisor. Just a few years ago he was delivering material for a fertilizer company. Soon he was their dispatcher, then took orders. He organized the job. He came here to do pesticides, and we've been moving him up." Buck Klein keeps a neutral face for the length of this history, for which I admire him. He is of average height, sturdily built, sports a brush moustache that matches his short, dark blond hair. He wears a western shirt, a belt with a huge buckle that says "Cotton" on it, and cowboy boots. He has come on business.

"We just got a truck back," he says, "all the way from the cannery at Fullerton—three hundred miles of travel and it's back with an unacceptable load. It's got 12 percent mechanical damages, so something's beating on the tomatoes. And this is the machine that's been doing it."

Johnny Riley appears to think for a moment. "We had three loads like that today. Seven percent, 11 percent, and 17 percent mechanicals. You got to take the truck back, get some workers to take out the center of the load and put in some real good tomatoes before you send it back. It ties up workers, and it ties up a truck."

Buck and I join the crew for one lap of harvesting. Then, while the crew members smoke, Buck and a staff

---

IN SKATING over thin ice our safety is in our speed.

Ralph Waldo Emerson

mechanic go at the machine with wrenches and screwdrivers. Finally, it is fixed. As we drive off in his truck, Buck talks about the nature of corporate farming. "We have budget sheets for every crop. It's what the management spends their time worrying about, instead of how to make the crops better. It's all high finance. It makes sense, if you think about what they have in it. But I'll tell you something. It's expensive to farm here."

Buck points across the darkness, to the lights of the assembly yard. "Just beyond those lights there's a guy owns a piece—a section of land, and he grows tomatoes there, too. A guy who works with the harvesters here, he knows tomatoes pretty well. And he says that guy has a break-even about 18 tons—18 tons of $40 tomatoes pay his costs, and he's watching every row, growing better than 30 tons to the acre. Our breakeven is 24 tons. Why? Because we're so much bigger. They give me more acres than I feel I can watch that closely. The partnership charges 35 bucks an acre management fee, good prices for this and that in the budget. And there is a stack of management people here, where that guy drives his own tractor while he thinks about what to do next. You can't beat him. This is not simple enough here.

"Here, they're so big, and yet they are always looking for a way to cut a dollar out of your budget. Trying to get more and more efficient. It's the workers who they see as the big expense here. They say, okay, management is us, but maybe we can cut out some of those people on the harvesting machines. We can rent these machines from the custom harvester company for $6 a ton bare. We got to pay the workers by the hour even when we're holding up the picking. Twenty workers to a machine some nights and $2.90 a worker is 58 bucks for an hour of down time. You keep moving or send people home.

"Of course this will all be a thing of the past soon. There's a new machine out—Blackwelder makes it—and it's not an experimental model. I mean, it's on the job, at $104,000 and up a shot, and it still pays. It does the same work, only better, with only two workers on it. It's faster, and there's no labor bill. It's an electronic sort. It has a blue belt and little fingers and electric eyes, and when it spots a tomato that isn't right, the little fingers push it out of the way. You just set the amount of greens you want left alone,

and it does that, too. We're going to have two of them
running later in the harvest, soon as they finish another
job."

"What about the workers who have always followed
the tomato harvest?" I ask.

"They're in trouble," says Buck, shaking his head.
"They'll still be needed, but only toward the end of the
harvest. At the beginning, most of what these cullers take
away is greens. The electric eye can do that. But at the end
of the harvest, most of what they take away is spoiled reds,
stuff that gets overripe before we pick it, and they say the
machines don't do that as well. That leaves a lot of workers
on welfare, or whatever they can get, hanging around waiting for the little bit we need them. They get upset about
being sent away. This one guy trying to get his sister on a
machine, he's been coming up to me all evening saying
things about the other workers. I just ignore it, though. It's
all part of the job, I guess."

The trouble in which California farm labor finds itself
is old trouble. And yet, just a few years ago, when harvesting of cannery tomatoes was still done by hand, ten times
the labor was required on the same acreage to handle a
harvest that yielded only a third of what Tejon Agricultural
Partners and other growers expect these days. The transformation of the tomato industry has happened in the course
of about twenty years.

Much has been written recently about this phenomenon, and with good reason. The change has been dramatic,
and is extreme. Tomatoes we remember from the past tasted
rich, delicate, and juicy. Tomatoes hauled home in today's
grocery bag taste bland, tough, and dry. The new taste is the
taste of modern agriculture.

The ruination of the tomato was a complex procedure.
It required cooperation from financial, engineering, marketing, scientific, and agricultural parties that used to go
their separate ways more and cross paths with less intention. Now larger institutions control the money that consumers spend on tomatoes. It is no more possible to isolate a
"cause" for this shift than it is possible to claim that it's the
spark plugs that cause a car to run. However, we can at least
peer at the intricate machinery that has taken away our tasty
tomatoes and given us pale, scientific fruit.

Let us start then, somewhat arbitrarily, with processors of tomatoes, especially with the four canners—Del Monte, Heinz, Campbell, and Libby, McNeill & Libby— that sell 72 percent of the nation's tomato sauce. What has happened to the quality of tomatoes in general follows from developments in the cannery tomato trade.

The increasingly integrated processors have consolidated, shifted, and "reconceptualized" their plants. In the fast world of marketing processed tomatoes, the last thing executives want is to be caught with too many cans of pizza sauce, fancy grade, when the marketplace is starved for commercial catsup. What processors do nowadays is capture the tomatoes and process them until they are clean and dead, but still near enough to the head of the assembly line so they have not yet gone past the squeezer that issues tomato juice or the sluice gate leading to the spaghetti sauce vat, the paste vat, the aspic tank, or the cauldrons of anything in particular. The mashed stuff of tomato products is stored until demand is clear. Then it's processed the rest of the way. The new manufacturing concept is known in the trade as aseptic barreling, and it leads to success by means of procrastination.

The growers supplying the raw materials for these tightly controlled processors have contracted in advance of planting season for the sale of their crops. It's the only way to get in. At the same time, perhaps stimulated by this new guaranteed marketplace—or perhaps stimulating it—these surviving growers of tomatoes have greatly expanded the size of their plantings. The interaction of large growers and large processors has thus crowded many smaller growers out of the marketplace, not because they can't grow tomatoes as cheaply as the big growers (they can) but because they can't provide large enough units of production to attract favorable contracts with any of the few canners in their area.

In turn, the increasing size of tomato growing operations has encouraged and been encouraged by a number of developments in technology. Harvesters (which may have been the "cause" precipitating the other changes in the system) have in large part replaced persons in the fields. But the new machines became practical only after the development of other technological components—especially new varieties of tomato bred for machine harvesting, and new chemicals that make machine harvesting economical.

What is remarkable about the tomato from the grower's point of view is its rapid increase in popularity. In 1920, each American ate 18.1 pounds of tomato. These days we each eat 50.5 pounds of tomato. Half a million acres of cropland grow tomatoes, yielding nearly 9 million tons, worth over $900 million on the market. Today's California tomato acre yields 24 tons, while the same acre in 1960 yielded 17 tons and in 1940, 8 tons.

The increased consumption of tomatoes reflects changing eating habits in general. Most food we eat nowadays is prepared, at least in part, somewhere other than in the home kitchen, and most of the increased demand for tomatoes is for processed products—catsup, sauce, juice, canned tomatoes, and paste for "homemade" sauce. In the 1920s, tomatoes were grown and canned commercially from coast to coast. Small canneries persisted into the 1950s.

Tomatoes were then a labor-intensive crop, requiring planting, transplanting, staking, pruning. And, important in the tale of changing tomato technology, because tomatoes used to ripen a few at a time, each field required three or four forays by harvesting crews to recover successively ripening fruits. The forces that have changed the very nature of tomato-related genetics, farming practices, labor requirements, business configurations, and buying patterns started with the necessity, built so deeply into the structure of our economic system, for the constant perfection of capital utilization.

Some critics sometimes seem to imply that the new mechanization is a conspiracy fostered by fat cats up top to make their own lives softer. But though there are, surely, greedy conspirators mixed in with the regular folks running tomato farms and tomato factories and tomato research facilities, the impulse for change at each stage of the tomato transformation—from the points of view of those effecting the change—is "the system." The system always pressures participants to *meet the competition*.

Even in the 1920s, more tomatoes were grown commercially for processing than for fresh consumption, by a ratio of about two to one. Today the ratio has increased to about seven to one. Fifty years ago, California accounted for about an eighth of all tomatoes grown in America. Today, California grows about 85 percent of tomatoes. Yet as recently as fifteen years ago, California grew only about half

WE MAY FIND in the long run that tinned food is a
deadlier weapon than the machine-gun.

George Orwell

the tomato crop. And fifteen years ago, the mechanical harvester first began to show up in the fields of the larger farms.

Before the harvester came, the average California
planting was about 45 acres. Today, plantings exceed 350
acres. Tomato production in California used to be centered
in family farms around Merced. It has now shifted to the
corporate farms of Kern County, where Tejon Agricultural
Partners operates. Of the state's 4000 or so growers harvesting canning tomatoes in the late sixties, 85 percent have left
the business since the mechanical harvester came around.
Estimates of the number of part-time picking jobs lost go as
high as 35,000.

The introduction of the harvester brought about other
changes too. Processors thought that tomatoes ought to
have more solid material, ought to be less acid, ought to be
smaller. Engineers called for tomatoes that had tougher
skins and were oblong so they wouldn't roll back down
tilted conveyor belts. Larger growers, more able to substitute capital for labor, wanted more tonnage per acre, resistance to cracking from sudden growth spurts that follow
irrigation, leaf shade for the fruit to prevent scalding by the
hot sun, determinate plant varieties that grow only so high
to keep those vines in rows, out of the flood irrigation
ditches.

As geneticists selectively bred for these characteristics, they lost control of others. They bred for thickwalled-
ness, less acidity, more uniform ripening, oblongness, leafi-
ness, and high yield—and they could not also select for
flavor. And while the geneticists worked on tomato characteristics, chemists were perfecting an aid of their own.
Called ethylene, it is in fact also manufactured by tomato
plants themselves. All in good time, it promotes reddening.
Sprayed on a field of tomatoes that has reached a certain
stage of maturity (about 15 percent of the field's tomatoes
must have started to "jell"), the substance causes the plants
to start the enzyme activity that induces redness. About half

of the time a tomato spends between blossom and ripeness is spent at full size, merely growing red. (Tomatoes in the various stages of this ripening are called, in the trade, immature greens, mature greens, breakers, turnings, pinks, light reds, and reds.) Ethylene cuts this reddening time by a week or more and clears the field for its next use. It recovers investment sooner. Still more important, it complements the genetic work, producing plants with a determined and common ripening time so machines can harvest in a single pass. It guarantees precision for the growers. The large-scale manufacturing system that buys the partnership's tomatoes requires predictable results. On schedule, eight or ten or fourteen days after planes spray, the crop will be red and ready. The gas complements the work of the engineers, too, loosening the heretofore stubborn attachment of fruit and stem. It makes it easier for the new machines to shake the tomatoes free of the vines.

The result of this integrated system of tomato seed and tomato chemicals and tomato hardware and tomato knowhow has been, of course, the reformation of tomato business.

According to a publication of the California Agrarian Action Project, a reform-oriented research group located at Davis (some of whose findings are reflected in this article), the effects of an emerging "low-grade oligopoly" in tomato processing are discoverable. Because of labor savings and increased efficiency of machine harvesting, the retail price of canned tomatoes should have dropped in the five years after the machines came into the field. Instead, it climbed 111 percent, and it did so in a period that saw the overall price of processed fruits and vegetables climb only 76 percent.

There are "social costs" to the reorganization of the tomato processing industry as well. The concentration of plants concentrates work opportunities formerly not only more plentiful but more dispersed in rural areas. It concentrates problems of herbicide, pesticide, and salinity pollution.

As the new age of cannery tomato production has overpowered earlier systems of production, a kind of flexibility in tomato growing, which once worked strongly to the consumer's advantage, has been lost. The new high-technology tomato system involves substantial investment "up front" for seed, herbicides and pesticides, machinery, water, labor, and for the "management" of growing, marketing, and financing the crop.

In order to reduce the enormous risks that might, in the old system, have fallen to single parties, today's tomato business calls for "jointing" of the tomatoes. Growers nowadays share the burden of planting, raising, harvesting, and marketing—"farming" together with a "joint contractor." The tomatoes grown by Johnny Riley and Buck Klein on land held by Tejon Agricultural Partners were grown under a joint contract with Basic Vegetable products, Inc., of Vacaville, California. TAP's president at the time, Jack Morgan, was previously executive vice president of Basic Vegetable.

"Jointing" deals are expensive both to set up and to administer. The tomato-growing business situation is becoming so Byzantine that the "per unit cost of production," the cost to a grower of producing a pound of tomatoes, is no longer the sole determinant of who gets to grow America's tomatoes. Once, whoever could sell the most cheaply won the competitive race to market. Today, the cost of doing all business supersedes, for large-scale operations, simple notions such as growing tomatoes inexpensively. Market muscle, tax advantages, clout with financiers, control of supply, all affect the competitve position of TAP as much as does the expense of growing tomatoes.

The consequence of joint contracting for the consumer is a higher-priced tomato. Risks that until recently were undertaken by growers and processors and distributors separately, because they were adversaries, are passed on to consumers now by participants that have allied. Growers are more certain they will recover the cost of production.

Howard Leach, who was president of TAP's parent company, Tejon Ranch, at the time of the tomato harvest, understood very well the economic implications for consumers of joint contracting.

"Productivity lessens," Leach explained to me. "Risk to the producer lessens, which is why we do it. The consumer gets more cost because the processor who puts money in will try to lower supply until it matches the anticipated demand. If you're Hunt-Wesson, you gear up to supply what you forecast that sales will be. You want an assured crop, so you contract for an agreed price. You're locked in, and so is the farming organization. But they are locked into a price they are assured of, and they are big enough to affect the supply."

Under this sort of business condition, the marketplace is fully occupied by giants. It is no place for the little guy with a truckload or two of tomatoes—even if his price is right. Farmers who once planted twenty or thirty acres of cannery tomatoes as a speculative complement to other farming endeavors are for the most part out of the picture, with no place to market their crops and no place to finance their operating expenses. As John Wood, a family farmer turned corporate manager, who currently runs TAP, puts it, "The key thing today is the ability to muscle into the marketplace. These days, it's a vicious fight to do so." And Ray Peterson, the economist and former vice president of Tejon Ranch, sums up the importance of the business side of farming now that the new technology has increased the risk and scale of each venture. "Today," he says, "vegetable farming is more marketing than farming."

The "jointing" of vegetable crops integrates the farming operation with the marketing, processing, and vending operations so closely that it takes teams of lawyers to describe just where one leaves off and another begins. And joint contracting is only one of several sorts of financial and managerial integration with suppliers and marketers that occur in the new tomato scene. Today chemical companies consult as technical experts with farming organizations. Equipment companies consult with farming organizations about what machines will do the jobs that need doing. Operations lease equipment from leasing companies run by banks that also lend them funds to operate. Financial organizations that lend growers vast sums of capital for both development and operations receive in return not merely interest but negotiated rights to oversee some decision-making processes. Agricultural academics sit on agribusiness corporate boards.

Today the cannery tomato farmer has all but ceased to exist as a discrete and identifiable being. The organizations and structures that do what farmers once did operate as part and parcel of an economy functioning at a nearly incomprehensible level of integration. So much for the tasty tomato.

Pest Control Strategies

by Richard Garcia and Donald L. Dahlsten

The majority of our food and fiber production is conducted with a minimum of pesticides. Of those used in agriculture, about two-thirds are committed to crops such as cotton, tobacco, fruits, corn and vegetables. Pesticides are also used in rangelands, forests, and in urban areas for a number of different reasons. Historically, before the advent of modern synthetic pesticides shortly after World War II, there were ways of producing large quantities of food and fiber without the use of pesticides. Then specialization, mechanization, and new crop varieties, in addition to growing and shipping of products the year round from warmer areas, forced some of the reliable older methods out of existence and ushered in the heavy reliance on pesticides. Many of these past ways of controlling pests are being re-examined because of the myriad of real and potential problems posed by the use of modern pesticides. Many of the older methods fit well into the basic framework of what we call integrated pest management (IPM)—at least under its original intention. The original IPM was an ecological approach to pest management with the following basic attributes:

1) know the biology and ecology of the particular species and assess the problem carefully;

2) use economic or action levels previously determined through accumulated information and knowledge;

3) use the least disruptive control procedure when an action becomes necessary; and

4) consider the impact of your actions on the entire ecosystem.

The backbone of the system consists of natural enemies, cultural practices and resistant plant varieties. Tactics or methods such as augmentation with natural enemies, genetic manipulation, selective pesticides and others may be utilized if necessary.

Since the 1970s we have been in the age of IPM. This approach—and it is an approach, as opposed to a technique—is also referred to as integrated pest control or simply as integrated control. Unfortunately, many who use the term IPM either never fully understand the basic concept or care not to understand it and simply apply the term to their own ideas or interests in pest control. If you review the agrichemical trade journals you see IPM used essentially synonymously with chemical-based control—the rationale being that since there are no non-chemical techniques available for integration you must rely on methods which are at hand, namely chemical pesticides.

The term IPM has been abused and misused to such an extent that we feel it would be much more appropriate to call the original IPM as discussed above "Ecological Pest Management" (EPM). This would better reflect the basic concept of the approach. However, we will continue to use the term IPM and ecological pest management as one and the same for the purposes of this article.

Agriculture

Some good progress has been made in developing IPM for a number of crops, but for most crops, in most regions, pesticides remain the technology of choice. Some examples of the striking reductions in pesticide use or control costs providing equal or better control than previous programs are listed in Table I. Since cotton and apples alone use more than 50% of the agricultural pesticides applied, any appreciable reductions of pesticide use on these crops would have major importance in reducing pesticide risks to people and pollution in the environment.

Another area of crop production which is gaining more interest and revived attention is organic farming. Practised for many years, this form of agriculture requires an intensive understanding of the plant requirements and cultural practices to avoid pest problems. Organic products are gaining wide appeal among the public but market costs remain somewhat higher than those of products produced by other means. Reasons for the increased demand for organic products are undoubtedly related to the public's awareness and concern over the hazards of pesticide residues in food.

Forestry

Pest control in forestry is essentially only giving lip service to integrated pest management because forestry may be heading in the same direction as modern mechanized agriculture. The current trend is toward intensive forest management the goal of which is to maximize fiber production. There are trends to complete-tree (all but roots) and entire-tree (roots included) logging, and planting genetically selected stocks in managed single-species stands, much the same as an orchard or alfalfa field in agriculture. The agricultural approach to forestry means greater investment and therefore greater desire and need to control pests. Even in natural stands the trend is to use more and more insecticides sprayed by aircraft over large acreages. This rather extensive use of insecticides in forests has been alarming and is due primarily to the gypsy moth, Douglas-fir tussock moth and the spruce and western budworms (See Table II). Note in Table II that acreage has been steadily increasing, since Earth Day, 1970. It is ironic that there is some evidence appearing in studies that these defoliators (moths and worms) are closely linked to primary productivity in the forest and are actually *increasing* wood production.

The forest community lends itself readily to an ecological approach to management since the forester can control the density, species composition and age structure. Insects and pathogens often assume this role in the absence of humans. A silvicultural approach supplemented by biological control procedures would be well within our reach for most problems in the forest this decade. Unfortunately, the desire for efficiency in logging and increased profits creates an undesirable atmosphere for the conscientious pest manager, making the future for sound pest management here rather bleak.

The Home and Surroundings

There are many available habitats for organisms in and around the home. People have unknowingly created numerous places and conditions for organisms to flourish and become pests. There are many well known and publicized pests within the home—roaches, flies, fleas, termites, ants, etc.

Some of the most flagrant misuses and overuses of chemicals occur in the urban-suburban environment. In most cases, if the city dwellers and urban pest control operators were to follow basic priniciples of integrated pest management, pesticides seldom would be used.

The most useful IPM programs in urban environments are educational ones such as those developed through the

John Muir Institute, Northern California Committee for Environmental Education, and others. These programs offer non-chemical alternatives to the use of pesticides and demonstrate to people that in many cases the organisms that concern them are not a threat to their plants, pets, stored products or their own well-being. By promoting common sense and not pesticides, the urban environment can be a much safer and wholesome place to live.

Public Health

Genetic pesticide resistance is probably nowhere more striking and important than in this group of organisms. Failures to control such important vectors and pests as mosquitoes, flies, lice, and others, dramatically underline the need for much broader ecologically based programs for their control. The failure of a chemically based strategy was emphasized dramatically in California during the late 1960s when resistance developed to such an extent among two of the state's most important mosquitoes that essentially all registered public health pesticides were found non-effective. This failure, more than anything else, forced a reappraisal of control programs in California. More emphasis was placed on non-chemical methods such as source reduction, biological control agents and the use of safer and more selective chemicals. During the last 10 or so years the mosquito abatement districts in the State have reduced pesticide use (other than oils) by more than 60%. Much work still needs to be done, however, along with the preservation and maintenance of many of the current programs through adequate financial support, if long-term effective mosquito control is to continue and progress.

The major concept, re-emphasized during the last couple of decades, is that programs based on sound ecologi-

---

THERE IS no reason whatever to believe that the order of nature has any greater bias in favor of man than it had in favor of the icthyosaur or the pterodactyl.

H.G. Wells

cal principles offer the most promise for long-term continuous control. The approach should always be to carefully examine the source of the problem first and then apply the appropriate procedures which will alter or change the conditions to the disadvantage of the vector or pest population. In the case of animals like rats, mice and flies, they can be effectively controlled through proper sanitary procedures which eliminate their food and shelter. With mosquitoes, it may be the elimination of unwanted water clogged in drains or it may require a more sophisticated approach such as in a salt marsh where the biology of the entire system must be well understood in order to eliminate the mosquito source, while retaining the integrity and resources of the marsh.

The role of chemical pesticides in the public health arsenal should lie in the prevention of disease outbreaks arising from unforeseen or otherwise unpredictable circumstances, and not as the method for prolonged control.

Pesticide Appeal

The strong sales and advertisement pressure exerted by the chemical industries, the dramatic and effective killing power of pesticides, their convenience, availability and their applicability to modern mechanized agriculture either as individual or combined attributes provide an appeal that is compelling and difficult to resist by the user. Furthermore, in providing a protective umbrella against crop damage in agriculture, pesticides provide insurance and allow the grower flexibility in crop selection, planting and harvesting.

In agriculture, where some cost-benefit estimates have been made, the use of pesticides has been estimated to return about 3 to 5 dollars for every dollar invested. However these estimates, in general, include only direct costs and benefits to the producer of the crop and do not include the social and environmental costs such as the effect on the public's health and impact on environmental quality. When some of these external costs are included, estimates reduce the ratio to about $2.50 returned for each dollar invested. General economic analyses of this latter sort are useful in exposing the importance of external costs, but the real issue is who in society actually bears the brunt of these costs both now and for the future. Let us look briefly at the widespread contamination of ground water in California due to the use of the pesticide DBCP to kill nematodes in citrus and other

Pesticide Policy

We should be looking toward solutions that work with nature rather than for magic cure-alls. We must shift from chemical-intensive, pesticide-dependent agriculture to ecologically sensitive pest control, the current focus of which is integrated pest management. IPM requires more intelligence and selection and analysis for each pest-control situation and fewer of the big-bang solutions our government/educational/industrial complex keeps coming up with.

Pesticides are widely used simply to reduce labor costs, not for any other purpose. To create a firebreak to keep weeds a safe distance back from roads, road departments spray herbicides rather than hoe. Energy is consumed in manufacturing and spraying the petroleum-based herbicides and serious risks of birth defects are created, all to put a few guys out of work and, often, onto government relief.

The kind of work that discovers how to use ladybugs to fight aphids is the kind we need to encourage, and the use of synthetic pesticides(petroleum-based) needs to be more drastically limited. This will require consumer acceptance of cosmetic flaws on produce that tastes like produce rather than like cardboard. You can be part of this effort. Around your own home, use environmentally sound pest control along the lines described in *Organic Gardening and Farming*.

GDB

crops. The presence of this chemical has created much anxiety and fear among the population using that ground water, and immediate and long-term health effects are a distinct possiblity. Despite a government ban on the widespread use of the chemical which prevents further contaminations, the residues from previous use still remain in the water at relatively high levels. How long the chemical will stay, no one is sure. Just who will pay the costs if widespread health effects are recognized? It is not likely that the manufacturer or the users will pay the cost. It would probably be society in general, with the people directly exposed paying the highest price. Obviously the only way to handle this kind of problem is through prevention by alternative methods and a strict regulatory program.

From the chemical industries' standpoint pesticides are crucial to our agricultural system. Actually the role they play is a small part of the large technological package which forms today's modern mechanized agricultural and distribution system. However, the technology which produces this wealth of food fiber is vulnerable at its base, for its production system is to a large degree dependent on massive inputs of non-renewable fossil fuels. The great agricultural abundance we see is produced through a waste of non-renewable energies, and petroleum-based pesticides are just one of them. Perhaps the rise in pesticide costs and other constraints related to energy supplies in the future will play an important role in how we produce our food and fiber and consequently how chemicals are used. But for now the cost of energy still remains only a minor influence on production practices.

Regulatory Programs

It is well known that many of the chemicals currently employed, some for a very long time, pose both a continuous and potential long-term hazard. It is true that certain governmental regulations have curtailed or banned the use of chemicals such as DDT, 2,4,5-T, DBCP and a few others, but only after dramatic public appeal and compelling evidence to do so. The magazine *Science,* in its News and Comments, states the following on toxic substances:

"Despite a panoply of laws intended to protect society from hazardous chemicals the regulatory road from discovery of a hazard to its control remains rough. Bureaucratic inertia and delay are permanent features of the process; pressure from affected industries is constantly applied; and statutes are often unworkable from the start. As a result, prompt regulatory action is virtually nonexistent, and when action does occur, it is usually at the prodding of outside citizens groups."

Government regulatory agencies, in and by themselves, do not seem to be the answer for the protection of society and the environment from chemical hazards. There is an important role for concerned citizens to play here and that is to organize and take an active part in demanding that the numerous laws and regulations that are on the books, be actually implemented and enforced.

Technological Problems of Pesticide Use

Of all the pesticides, insecticides offer the clearest and best documented cases of problems created through their use. Most of the difficulties are biological reactions resulting from the killing power of these chemicals and can be generally described as follows: most insecticides kill a wide variety of animals when applied to a particular field situation. From the chemical industry standpoint, this broad killing power is frequently beneficial since the more organisms a chemical can kill the more potential it has for greater sales. However, from a biological and ecological standpoint, this wide spectrum of death can be disastrous. When these kinds of materials are applied to a crop, they can create what is called a "biotic vacuum" due to the destruction of much of the faunal complex residing in the crop. Thus, not only is the target species destroyed but so are the innocuous residents as well as the pest's natural enemies and the other beneficial organisms. The surviving or re-invading pests can explode in numbers quickly without the regulating influence of their natural enemies which require more time to re-establish their populations. During this time, other insect and mite populations previously considered innocuous or of only minor importance rise to serious pest status as a result of the destruction of their natural enemies. These are called secondary or pesticide-induced outbreaks and are frequently the aftermath of a pesticide program aimed at one or two primary peets. Sometimes the induced pest becomes a greater problem than the original pest.

Resurgence and secondary pest outbreaks result in more frequent applications of pesticides. This drenching of the fields with chemicals leads to a basic breakdown in the technology itself with induced pesticide resistance in the target populations. Once this occurs, the pesticide is useless, and a substitute, if available, must be found. In the cotton industry, resistance combined with resurgence and secondary pest outbreaks has led to rising production costs and declining yields. Dramatic examples of this were documented in Cañete Valley in Peru in the 1950s and in

Northern Mexico in the late 1960s. In the latter case, over 1
million acres of cotton were lost, leading to disastrous social
and economic dislocations in the area.

The importance of these problems is reflected in a
California study which found that of 25 important pests each
responsible for a million or more dollars in losses and costs
to agriculture, 24 are either resistant, insecticide-aggravated
and/or their chemical control is involved in induced outbreaks of other species. Pesticide resistance has now been
reported in over 400 species and is not only increasing in
numbers of species but is intensifying within the geographic
ranges of the resistant pests and vectors. Genetic resistance
to pesticides probably stands as the major obstacle in the
use of these chemicals for pest control rather than the externalities such as impacts on human health and the quality of
the environment.

Human Health Effects

There are approximately 130 million pounds of insecticides produced annually in the United States which are
termed Class I poisons and must be marked with the "skull
and crossbones" to indicate their extreme toxicity to humans. Of the 26 most commonly employed insecticides in
the United States, more than one-half fall into this category.
Human poisoning with these chemicals is unfortunately
rather a common occurrence especially among farm workers and others who handle these poisons in the process of
their labors. It has been estimated that some 45,000 poisonings occur yearly in this country alone. In 1977 there were
about 1500 reported poisonings in California of which more
than one-half were among farm workers. Health officials,
however, believe that these figures are grossly underreported because various economic and social pressures prevent the workers from seeking assistance and there are difficulties in associating such ubiquitous symptoms as
diarrhea, headaches, vomiting and rash with pesticide
poisoning. However, even with this underreporting, Cali-

IT'S INTERESTING to live when you are angry.

Yevgeny Yevtushenko

fornia agriculture has a higher rate of injury from toxic chemicals than any other occupation in the state.

On a worldwide basis, it has been estimated that pesticides cause some one-half million accidental poisonings annually with a fatality rate of 1% (5000) among 19 countries surveyed. Other estimates have placed fatal poisonings at over 20,000 annually; however, it is probable that these figures are grossly underestimated. Just how extensive and underreported poisonings may be in the less developed world can be illustrated by the following episode which was investigated more thoroughly. There have been several outbreaks of poisoning in the third world from the fungicide methyl mercury. Seeds coated with this poison intended originally for planting were instead used as food by local populations. In Iraq in 1972, a team of investigators found that of 6350 people hospitalized for this poisoning, 459 died while in the hospital. It was estimated that some 100,000 people were actually involved with about 6000 deaths and many survivors crippled for life.

There has been more concern recently among governmental agencies regarding the hazards to foreign recipients of exported pesticides banned in the United States. Although this comes as a welcome change to the *let the consumer beware* attitude that was prevalent before, it should be understood that banned pesticides are only part of the problem. The United States exports some 600 million pounds of pesticides annually, a portion of which ends up in the third world countries. Other industrialized countries such as Switzerland and West Germany are also very active in exporting these chemicals and it is not known how much the Communist bloc countries contribute. Thus, large quantities of very toxic chemicals end up in the less developed world. As an example, cotton production alone in Central America used over 60 million pounds of pesticide in 1975, much of which was highly toxic. El Salvador, the heaviest user, applied over 60 pounds for every acre of cotton; much of it was the highly toxic organophosphate, parathion. Consequently, legally registered pesticides such as the parathions are responsible for many of the poisonings and deaths that occur in the cotton-growing regions of Central America. Thus, while it is laudable and necessary to take action against banned pesticides, it would only partially reduce the hazards. Clearly, the problem lies in the shipment of highly toxic poisons without the appropriate technology of safe handling and use. Appropriate government regulations should be developed to curb the irresponsible practice of exporting these extremely hazardous materials to third world countries. Expertise on ecologically sound pest management should be the message we send.

Carcinogenesis

Perhaps one of the most alarming repercussions surrounding the use of pesticides is the fact that some are known to be (and others are suspected of being) carcinogenic. The Environmental Protection Agency estimates that among 1500 active ingredients in registered pesticides, probably one-fourth are carcinogenic. Residues of these materials exist in our food and water and pose a serious immediate and future health threat. It is unfortunate that of the relatively large number of pesticides suspected, only minor action to remove them has been taken by the regulatory agencies. It would seem prudent for the regulatory agencies to move quickly in this area; however, this will probably not come to pass unless there is strong public pressure to do so.

Environmental Quality

Environmental quality remains a major focussing point for all people who are concerned with what is happening to our environment. The application of billions of pounds of pesticides throughout the world over the last three decades, some so persistent that they last for decades, has left its mark in every nook and corner of the globe. Biomagnification, reproductive failures in animals, massive fish and bird kills are all the legacies of the pesticide syndrome. We believe that the most important way of reducing these hazards and the load of pesticides on the environment is through sound ecological pest management.

Pest Control in the 80s

We hope the ecological pest management approach will survive and flourish, and the public will increase their awareness in this form of pest control as well as give their much-needed support—support for the research necessary for field implementation and application to show that it can be effective.

In the decade to come the public will need to put more and more pressure on the regulatory agencies to accomplish what they were established to do, namely, protect society and the environment from unnecessary pesticide abuses.

Greater funding should be generated for the development and implementation of non-chemical methods in the area of biological and ecological controls. Weed and insect control are of special importance since they constitute about 50% and 40% of the pesticide market, respectively.

As a final note, we should not be exporting our pesticide pollution and health dangers to the poorer countries of the world. Instead, we should send our knowledge and expertise on appropriate ecological control methods to help solve problems in pest and vector control.

Table I.   Reduction in Cost or Pesticide Loads on Crops Protected by Integrated Pest Management Systems

Crop	Locality	Reduction
Apple	Washington	> 50 % cost
Pear	Sacramento, California	~ 85 % worm control costs
Pear	Lake City, California	~ 50 % worm control costs
Cotton	San Joaquin Valley, California	~ 50 % insecticides
Cotton	Arkansas	> 80 % insecticides
Cotton	Trans Pecos, Texas	pesticides virtually eliminated
Citrus	California	~ 50 % insecticides
Tomato	California	~ 50 % insecticides

~ = approximately.

Adapted from **The Pesticide Conspiracy**, by R. van den Bosch, 1978.

Table II. Acres of Forests Sprayed in the United States with Chemical
Insecticides for Selected Years from 1945 through 1976.

Year	Thousands of Acres	Comments
1945	16	
1950	1,548	
1954	1,733	
1955	3,653	
1956	2,306	
1957	4,902	Peak year
1958	1,775	
1959	305	
1960	446	
1961	259	
1962	1,623	**Silent Spring**
1963	2,243	by Rachel Carson
1964-1969	891 to 134	Steady decline
1970	456	Earth Day
1972	690	
1973	732	
1974	1,077	
1975	2,333	
1976	3,594	

Adapted from **Forest Pest Control**, National Academy of Sciences, 1975,
and unpublished U.S. Forest Service data.

Bibliography

Anon. 1977. New Frontiers in Pest Management. Conference Proceedings. Senate Office of Research, State of California, Sacramento.

Anon. 1979. Toxic Substances: EPA and OSHA are Reluctant Regulators—News and Comment. Science 203: 28–30.

Epstein, S. 1978. The Politics of Cancer. Sierra Club Books. San Francisco.

Metcalf, R.L. 1980. Changing role of insecticides in crop protection. Ann. Rev. Entomol. 25: 219–256.

Pimentel, D., J. Krummel, D. Gallahan, J. Hough, A. Merrill, I. Schreiner, P. Vittum, F. Koziol, E. Back, D. Yen and S. Fiance. 1978. Benefits and costs of pesticide use in U. S. food production. BioScience 28(12): 772–783.

Pimentel, D., and J. H. Perkins, Editors. 1980. Pest Control: Cultural and Environmental Aspects. AAAS Selected Symposium #43. Boulder, Colorado. West View Press.

Smith, R. J. 1979. U. S. beginning to act on banned pesticides. Science 204: 1391–1392.

Van den Bosch, R. 1978. The Pesticide Conspiracy. Doubleday & Co., Garden City, N. Y.

From Nausea to a 'Cold'

A Building Can Make You Ill

by Harold Gilliam

THE BUILDING where you live or work might be making you sick. Probably not as sick as the legionnaires who were poisoned by that hotel in Philadelphia. Maybe not as sick as Clare Booth Luce when she was ambassador to Italy and poisoned by the paint on her ceiling. Perhaps not as sick as the current residents of the Amberwood Apartments in Daly City, California, who have developed nausea, eye irritation, sore throats, flaky skin, head pressures and chest tension. Maybe your own building just gives you a mild headache, a cough or "cold," watery eyes or feelings of chronic fatigue.

Allergists and environmental health specialists are learning that many people have bad physical reactions to certain substances commonly used nowadays in building construction and furnishings. With this knowledge, architects in the future should be able to design buildings that make us feel better. Just as the present push in architecture is for energy-efficient buildings, the next step in architecture is likely to be the design of buildings that are health efficient. The trouble is that most architects don't yet seem to be aware that many of the materials they use can make people sick. The Amberwood Apartment complex in Daly City is about a year old. Resident managers Irving and Carol Funk had lived there only a few months when they began to suspect that the building was responsible for their eye and throat irritation, nausea and feelings of depression. The symptoms disappeared when they left the building for any length of time and reappeared after they returned.

They compared notes with other residents, who said they had been feeling the same way. Radio news reports of the "mysterious illness" were heard by William Radley, an architectural consultant based in the East Bay town of San Ramon, Ca. He recognized the complaints. They were the common symptoms of ureaformaldehyde poisoning. That chemical is widely used in particleboard and other building materials.

San Mateo County, Ca., health officials investigating the case had to come to the same conclusion. Radley later inspected the building. "The most obvious source of formaldehyde," Radley says, "is the kitchen cabinets, which are made of particleboard. Plywood has less formaldehyde but enough to cause trouble under some circumstances. Heat can bring it out, and I found places where the hot water pipes are right up against the plywood."

What happens with these materials, Radley explains, is "outgassing" or "offgassing." Not only particleboard and plywood but many synthetic materials, including foam rubber, dacron, nylon and insulating materials give off gasses that can set off allergies. In time the outgassing tapers off; it is particularly strong when the materials are new.

"Most new buildings have similar effects," Radley says, "but the symptoms are not so pronounced, and the residents don't realize that the building is the source of their low-grade headaches or eye irritation or lethargy. At Amberwood the rooms are very small; there is no adequate ventilation; and most of the residents are older people who are more likely to feel the effects."

The building was constructed with federal aid as low-cost housing for senior citizens. Electric wall heaters supply warmth but no air circulation to dissipate the gasses.

John Hoffmire of American Developers, the nationwide company that is the operating owner of Amberwood, believes that the problem has been overblown: "Amberwood has standard materials that have been used in thousands of units we've built. The manager's wife has an allergy, and when other residents hear about it, the power of suggestion is pretty strong. They are elderly people who have some of these ailments anyhow, and it's easy to blame them on the building."

Hoffmire's plans are to seal off the particle board kitchen cabinets by spraying them with Varathane to prevent the formaldehyde from escaping. But Radley is convinced that a sealant won't do the job. He recommends that samples be taken of the floor and wall materials for formaldehyde content, that each unit be equipped with a window ventilator that brings air from outside, warms it up and circulates it inside. And he believes that ionizers in each unit would further purify the air. One of the nation's top authorities on toxic building materials is Francis Silver of Martinsburg, West Virginia, who was trained in gas engineering at Johns Hopkins and became "chemically sensitized" when he received an overdose of tar fumes from the roof of an aircraft plant where he was working in Seattle. Air-system intakes on the roof spread the fumes into the working area. As a result, Silver is abnormally sensitive to many environmental toxins. "When I travel," he says, "I carry a sheet of aluminum foil to sit on or lean against as a protection from outgassing by the vinyl seat materials."

But Silver has put his sensitivity to work. "I can put my hands on a surface," he says, "and usually tell whether it's outgassing, unless it's too hot or too cold." Silver works with allergists; he goes into their patients' homes and work-

---

How to Get Rid of Pesticides in Your House

Now that you have decided not to use toxic pesticides in and around your home, what can you do with the supplies you might already have on hand? The fact that we have to ask the question at all gives you an idea of the state of hazardous waste disposal in the country as a whole.

For the time being the solution is probably to leave them in a closed cabinet in the garage, or on the top shelf in the basement, or in a locked trunk in the attic—until a more acceptable option comes along. If you can't do this don't just throw them in the garbage. Many pesticides and other chemicals become more dangerous in combination with another. And rain seeps through the garbage dump then moves on to wells and reservoirs used by people. For the same reason, don't bury them. (This has been recommended by some well-intentioned but misguided environmental groups.) Either of these practices is the same sort of hit or miss action that has resulted in catastrophes at Love Canal in New York and Aerojet General near Sacramento where long-buried toxic wastes have re-entered the environment.

Alternate possibilities, which are only marginally acceptable, include returning the pesticide to the store, on the theory that if someone is going to use it anyway at least by returning it there might be a slight decrease in production; or, on the same theory, giving it to someone who is going to use it anyway.

GDB

places to pinpoint the causes of allergic reactions. Among the common causes, he says, are organic mercury fungicides found in latex paints and wallpaper pastes.

Peter Breysse of the Department of Environmental Health at the University of Washington is an industrial hygiene engineer who is also in great demand to find the source of toxins in homes and public buildings. "The problem is made worse," he says, "by the efforts to save energy. The tighter the building, the less ventilation there is. Good air circulation is the only thing that will dissipate the gasses."

Hal Levin, a University of California specialist in "Building Ecology" (the title of his forthcoming book) and a member of the California Board of Architectural Examiners, says that European building designers, unlike U.S. architects, have been aware of the problem for many years. "In Denmark, for example, they remove much of the gas in manufacturing by subjecting the material to high temperatures and high moisture. In the U.S. there has never even been an article in the professional journals until just recently." Levin says that nowadays it is fashionable to attribute many physical symptoms to emotional disorders. "The fact is that in many cases the trouble is not within ourselves but in the environment, and we can do things to change the environment."

●

Chemist Craig Hollowell of US's Lawrence Berkeley Laboratory, heading a project on indoor air pollution, recommends some specifics: "One thing that can be done is better quality control in manufacturing to reduce the outgassing. There is talk about reducing the permitted occupational exposure to formaldehyde from 3 parts per million to 1 ppm. Some European countries have standards as low as ten per cent of that. Outgassing can also be controlled to some degree by heat exchangers in rooms. They take in air from the outside, circulate it and exhaust it near the intake so some of the heat is recirculated."

The Amberwood Apartment complex is not the only Bay Area building with indoor pollution problems. The new Social Services building on Otis street in San Francisco has been the subject of complaints by employees with running eyes and nose-throat irritation. The Environmental Protection Agency office on Fremont Street has an environment that is evidently not very well protected. It is in an old building that was recently modernized, with synthetic materials and sealed windows. Employees there, too, have complained about respiratory problems.

Dr. Phyllis Saifer of Berkeley is a member of the Society for Clinical Ecology, a group of professionals in many fields in various parts of the country who share information about environmental diseases. She says: "I've had to move dozens of people out of their work places to get them away from environmental chemicals that were poisoning them. Some are students in these new schools that are full of synthetic carpeting and plastic building materials. One young girl had serious behavior disorders. A high school senior was flunking out. In old buildings with wood and steel materials they have no problem."

If the clinical ecologists are successful, we can look forward to an era when architects will design buildings for health as well as efficiency and beauty. Some scholars now believe that the ancient Romans were done in by lead poisoning from the flagons they used for wine. If our architects are able to eliminate the poisoning many of us are receiving from our buildings—who knows?—we may yet avoid the fate of Rome.

How to Stay Healthy in an Unhealthy Environment

by Eleanor Smith and Harry Dennis

According to the U.S. surgeon general Americans are healthier than they were ten years ago. Death rates from heart disease have dropped 17 per cent since 1970 and life expectancy for the general population has risen to 73.2 years, up from 70.9 at the beginning of the decade.

Most cancer researchers now believe that 75 to 90 percent of all cancers are environmentally induced. This is actually good news — it means you can learn what you are doing to affect your health and then cut out the unhealthy habits, activities, or foods.

For instance, if you smoke and have for decades, you are ten times as likely to die from lung cancer as a non-smoker is; if you don't exercise regularly you are much more likely to get arteriosclerosis or heart disease than those who do exercise; if you eat "junk food," bacon, bologna, cured meat or fish, or lots of processed foods with harmful additives (read the labels), your chances of contracting various forms of cancer are increased; if you eat a lot of animal fats, it's more likely you'll develop some form of cancer or arteriosclerosis than a vegetarian would; if you live in a city, particularly in northern New Jersey, you're much more liable to get cancer than someone in rural Wyoming.

An experimental program being conducted at the Center for Disease Control in Atlanta is aimed at thwarting such statistical probabilities. More than 1,400 employees have provided intimate details about their lives and medical histories to a computer. The computer has then informed them of their chances of dying during the next decade if they continue on the same path and how much greater their chances of survival might be if they changed their habits. They are offered programs to stop smoking, lose weight, change their driving habits, free themselves from stress, take up exercise, and the like. The results have far exceeded expectations; most participants are enthusiastic in their efforts at reform and follow-ups have indicated that after 18 months the changed lifestyles persist.

So you don't have to give in to the dastardly statistics; you don't even have to move out of the city. You should, however, really kick that smoking habit, cut down the drinking and drugs, get out and exercise regularly (that means more than once a week), find effective and reliable ways to relax every day (this could include massages, yoga, meditation, racquetball, swimming, hot baths, an hour of quiet music or reading—whatever fits your lifestyle and makes you relax). Developing a more detached attitude about life's ups and downs can reduce your anxiety level too, without the aid of tranquilizers or barbituates.

In addition, educate yourself about the hazards from food additives, consumer products, x-rays, prescription drugs, and the particular risks you and your family face at work, and what to do to avoid them. Everything doesn't cause cancer and heart disease but apathy and ignorance contribute to their pervasiveness.

Water

Pollution from industrial wastes, sewage, agricultural chemicals and the like makes its way into our drinking water supplies more than we'd like to think. At least 10,000 Americans a year suffer from infectious diseases transmitted through tap water; the number increases when you add the regular influenza epidemics, not always recognized as carried by water. In addition; studies have shown that the nation's 50,000 water supplies contain many potentially harmful substances including asbestos, pesticides, heavy metals such as lead and cadmium, arsenic, nitrates, sodium, viruses and organic chemicals.

The process of chlorination used to purify drinking water also contributes to the creation of carcinogens from otherwise harmless substances. The chlorine can combine with other pollutants to form such carcinogens as carbon tetrachloride, bischloroethane, and chemicals called trihalomethanes, such as chloroform. Environmental Protection Agency (EPA) surveys of drinking water supplies around the country have found chlorinated organic chemicals in significant amounts in virtually every municipality. Most of these have not been tested for their carcinogenicity. EPA has fallen short of its enforcement of water quality standards required by the Clean Water Act. Municipal water treatment plants are doing a poor job of cleaning up the nation's drinking water and none use granular activated carbon (the best water purifier) to reduce the level of organic contaminants. Carbon is used for taste and odor control, however, in about 40 plants. Although toxic and carcinogenic chemicals are often present in minute amounts, the average person consumes one and a half or more quarts of water every day. Chronic exposure to small amounts of carcinogens, as numerous tests have shown, represents a significant health hazard.

You may want to buy bottled spring water for your home, but before you do you should check with the manufacturer as to the source, type of processing and results of tests of the water's contents and purity. Most nationally sold brands are probably relatively pure. Your best bet is to pick natural spring water from a protected watershed in a non-industrial area.

Or a variety of commercially available water purification systems can be added to your lines. The three basic types are reverse osmosis filters, distillers, and filters using activated charcoal. Contact a water treatment company such as Culligan or Meyers for more information.

You can make an inexpensive filter yourself. Place a paper coffee filter in a funnel, then wash enough granular activated carbon to fill one-quarter of the funnel. To wash the carbon, put it in a jar, fill with water, cover and shake. Let the carbon settle and pour the water off at the top. Repeat until the water poured off is clear. Set the funnel in a large clean jar, add the carbon, slowly pour your tap water through the funnel. Change the carbon every three weeks, or after 20 gallons of water have been filtered through it. Store the filtered water in the refrigerator. To purify your water further, boil it gently for 15 to 20 minutes; this will evaporate many of the carcinogens.

Or, you can build a more complicated, better filtration system. To do so, you'd need: ¼" copper tubing, ¼" tubing tee, 36"x¾" inside-diameter copper or galvanized steel pipe (a shorter column may be used if there are space limitations), ice maker saddle valve, reducing union for ¾" pipe to ¼" tubing, funnel, filter paper, 1 gallon glass bottle, plastic pan, plug of cotton, activated carbon granules. (Granular activated carbon prepared for treating drinking water can be purchased in one-pound bags from Walnut Acres, Penns Creek, Pennsylvania 17862.)

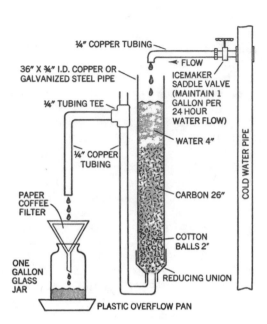

¼" COPPER TUBING

FLOW

36" X ¾" I.D. COPPER OR
GALVANIZED STEEL PIPE

ICEMAKER
SADDLE VALVE
(MAINTAIN 1
GALLON PER
24 HOUR
WATER FLOW)

¼" TUBING TEE

WATER 4"

¼" COPPER
TUBING

COLD WATER PIPE

PAPER
COFFEE
FILTER

CARBON 26"

COTTON
BALLS 2"

ONE
GALLON
GLASS
JAR

REDUCING UNION

PLASTIC OVERFLOW PAN

1. Construct the filter as illustrated.

2. Disinfect the empty column with a 5% solution of laundry bleach by filling the column and letting it stand for a couple of minutes.

3. Rinse the column thoroughly.

4. Put a plug of cotton in the bottom of the column.

5. Fill the column with water and add previously wetted (2 hours) washed carbon to a depth of 26".

6. Maintain the water level above the carbon by placing the ¼" tubing tee above the surface of the carbon as illustrated.

7. Operate the carbon column continuously, 24 hours a day, at a flow rate of 1 gallon per day, using the saddle valve to adjust the flow rate.

8. Pour the water from the filled jar into a pan and bring it to a boil, then reduce the heat and simmer it as slowly as possible for 15 to 20 minutes. Boiling will both sterilize the water and further remove certain volatile organics like chloroform.

9. Store in the refrigerator until used.

10. Change carbon every three weeks, or after 20 gallons of water have been filtered.

Consumer Products

Concerned consumers need to aggressively investigate the hazards of the products they use and decide for themselves how much risk they want to take. A number of cosmetics and personal care products contain dangerous ingredients. The Food and Drug Administration (FDA) is responsible for regulating cosmetics but its power is limited. It cannot require a manufacturer to submit safety data before a product is introduced into the marketplace, nor can the FDA require the manufacturer to provide a product ingredient list. Cosmetics that are proven health risks can generally be banned. Hair dyes are an exception. It they prove to be hazardous, no matter how strong the evidence, the government cannot legally take them off the market. (Dyes based on coal tar dyes are the most likely to cause cancer. Vegetable-based dyes, like henna, are not likely to be dangerous.) Many hair dyes are absorbed through the scalp; if used regularly they are sometimes absorbed in large enough amounts to discolor urine, even if used according to directions. This can only mean that large amounts of the dye have circulated throughout the body with at best unknown and at worst toxic or carcinogenic effects.

Benzene in solvents, pentachlorophenol in wood preservative, estrogens in birth control pills, and products containing chlorinated hydrocarbons are among the compounds best avoided. You can find out about the safety of hair dryers that might contain asbestos and many other consumer products by calling the Consumer Product Safety Commission's toll-free information number, (800) 638-8326.

Microwaves

No one knows for sure how much microwave radiation is harmless to your health. As is the case with ionizing radiation such as medical and dental x-rays and radioactivity from nuclear weapons blasts or nuclear power plant wastes, for instance, no "threshold dose" exists for nonionizing microwave radiation (which is less disruptive to cellular activity than ionizing radiation). This means that no amount of exposure, however small or brief, can be considered completely harmless. So the government's limit of five milliwatts leakage from every microwave oven does not guarantee that this will never adversely affect your health. Until scientists know more and can agree on the results, the

American public will continue to be guinea pigs in experiments on microwaves' threats to health.

Cumulative effects of exposure to low levels of microwave radiation are being studied. A number of air traffic controllers, radar technicians, and a couple of newspaper editors who used Video Display Terminals (VDT) have contracted cataracts, which were linked to their long-term exposure to microwaves. Others regularly exposed to microwave radiation—including bank tellers, airlines reservations agents, librarians, and others who use VDTs regularly in their work—may suffer other microwave-related ailments such as headaches, dizziness, irritability, loss of judgment, fatigue, leukemia, heart trouble, cancer, central nervous system disorders, and possibly genetic damage.

In December 1979, the Food and Drug Administration recalled some 20,000 Whirlpool microwave ovens which malfunctioned, allowing them to leak potentially dangerous amounts of radiation.

In addition to leaking microwave ovens (they all leak to some extent) the public is bombarded by microwave "electronic smog" from television transmitters, burglar alarms, automatic garage-door openers, telephone relay systems, CB radios, and military and civilian radar systems, including police speed traps on roads. The only thing you can do to minimize your exposure is to avoid the source.

Food

Some people cringe at the sight of any unfamilar word on a product label, but sodium caseinate is nothing but the primary protein in milk and is used as a thickener and whitener. Calcium propionate is added to bread, cakes and pies to prevent mold growth, and like sodium caseinate, is considered safe by the very cautious Center for Science in the Public Interest (1755 S Street NW, Washington, DC 20009.)

But our food supply is laced with other additives which preserve, color, fortify and otherwise affect it. The use of additives has increased with the increase of food distribution. If hot dogs are to be distributed nationwide, they must contain nitrates to prevent spoilage during shipping. The food industry's search for new, marketable products also leads it to produce more highly processed, additive-laden foods.

Many food colors, which serve no other purpose than to increase the attractiveness of foods, continue to be used even after studies have indicated that they cause cancer. Red dye #40—known to cause cancer in mice—is widely used in sweets, soda, pet food, and sausage. Citrus red #2 is sometimes used on the skin of Florida oranges in spite of tests indicating it may be carcinogenic.

Not only are there intentional additives, some substances get into foods unintentionally. Residues of pesticides, herbicides, drugs, and industrial chemicals are entering the food chain in ever increasing amounts. They are sprayed on our produce and cattle grazing lands; they are dissolved in our agricultural water; plants may even take them up from polluted air.

It is more important than ever to carefully wash produce before eating it. California grows 30 percent of the nation's vegetables and 40 percent of the nation's fruits and nuts. This food had anywhere from 100 to 400 million pounds of pesticides applied to it in 1978.

Many of the chemicals applied to food crops are systemic—they circulate within the plant—and therefore will not wash out. Even organically grown food may be contaminated by spray drifting from adjacent fields or by impure water.

Additives permeate American beef, too. From 1954 to November 1979, DES (Diethylstilbestrol) was an approved feed additive for cattle, poultry, and hogs. DES, a synthetic estrogen, makes animals gain weight faster and on less feed, thus saving the growers a substantial amount of money. Unfortunately, DES is highly carcinogenic and traces of it can sometimes be found in beef. By the time the U.S. Food and Drug Administration banned its use in animal feed concern about the harmful effects of DES had led many European countries to ban American beef imports.

NOTHING could be more salutary at this stage than a little healthy contempt for a plethora of material blessings.

Aldo Leopold

With the FDA's ban, DES should disappear from American beef. Unfortunately other toxins will continue to contaminate beef. In 1979, the EPA estimated that 13 percent of all American beef was contaminated with dioxin, an especially potent carcinogen. Dioxin is a contaminant of 2,4,5-T, an herbicide that is sprayed on our rangelands to block shrub growth. When the cattle graze on the sprayed grass, the traces of dioxin they ingest accumulate in their fat. If you eat beef, choose lean cuts and trim off the fat.

What Can You Do?

Cutting down on your meat intake, washing your produce carefully, and similar measures will decrease the amount of dietary carcinogens you expose yourself to, but far from eliminate them. Maintenance of your health demands political action. Write your Senators and Representatives of your concern about our increasingly contaminated food supply. Let the EPA Administrator know how you feel. A Department of Agriculature task force has just produced a report endorsing organic farming and Integrated Pest Management as the best way to halt the disastrous erosion that threatens our farmlands. A shift away from chemicals on our farms would also have a beneficial effect on the quality of our food. Let the Secretary of Agriculture know how you feel about the heavy use of chemicals on our food supply. Friends of the Earth is lobbying intensively to strengthen pesticide and herbicide regulation. Contact Erik Jansson at our Washington, D.C., office (530 Seventh St. SE, Washington, D.C. 20003) if you want to get involved.

The Workplace

Many workers are routinely exposed to high concentrations of hazardous substances and reveal acute reactions that may not be seen or would be impossible to identify in the general public.

Asbestos workers suffer debilitating or fatal lung disease often enough that in 1918 American and Canadian insurance companies stopped covering them. In 1957, a new occupational disease named acroosteolysis was reported among plastics workers. Induced by exposure to vinyl chloride—the chemical out of which most plastic is made—the disease causes clubbed fingers and toes, spasmodic

To Your Health

While some people's concern for the environment is rooted in their interest and appreciation for wilderness and wildlife, to many others the primary reason for concern is environmental pollutants that could adversely affect their health.

One level of involvement in this area is self-protection: you can avoid such pollutants as tars and nicotine by quitting your smoking habit and by using no-smoking sections in public places. You can remain alert to news reports of such hazards as asbestos in hair dryers or leaking microwave ovens and check yours and get it repaired or disposed of if it's the dangerous type. Another level of involvement is group action: pushing for adequate regulations and enforcement to reduce environmental pollutants. Finally, to be an environmentally responsible citizen, you also need to cooperate—even if it costs you a little. If you use leaded gas you are adding to the amount of lead polluting the air, particularly near well-travelled roads, and if you use it in a car that *should* use unleaded gas you are contributing further by ruining your car's catalytic muffler.

GDB

blood vessel contractions, painful bone changes, and arthritis of the knuckles. Today, California's agricultural workers suffer a documented 14 thousand pesticide poisonings a year, and many times that number may go unreported.

Over the years, occupational health scientists and industry have developed an "unholy alliance," only recently challenged. For decades, chemical, plastics, and pharmaceutical companies would contract with university or private researchers to study the safety and efficacy of new substances. If the contracting company didn't like the results, it could, and often did, file them away and forget about them.

For example, in 1958 Dr. Charles Hine of the University of California completed a study for Shell Oil that found that Shell's pesticide, DBCP, caused atrophy of the testicles and reduced sperm count in test animals. The report was shelved and forgotten. In 1977, 36 out of 38 workmen at one DBCP production plant were found to be sterile. In the hearings that followed, the report was brought out before the public. The manufacture and use of DBCP was completely banned by the federal government two years later.

Regulatory control of most new substances coming on the market is now more stringent. Safety data must now be made available to the relevant agencies before approval. The agency's decision is then based on the submitted data. Companies can no longer hire university personnel to do their research. However, the people who now conduct the research are generally employed directly by the contracting firm or may receive substantial consulting fees from them, so the test results should still be viewed skeptically.

The public is still being exposed to thousands of chemicals whose approval years ago was based on inadequate testing. The Environmental Protection Agency is attempting to recheck compounds that were assumed safe and to conduct new tests where necessary. But keeping up with the evaluation of the multitude of new compounds already stretches their capabilities, leaving limited resources for rechecking previously approved compounds.

WHEN THE MOVIES came, the entire pattern of American life went on the screen as a nonstop ad. Whatever any actor or actress wore or used or ate was such an ad as had never been dreamed of. The American bathroom, kitchen, and car, like everything else, got the *Arabian Nights* treatment.

Marshall McLuhan

Workers in high risk industries may choose to change jobs, but this is rarely easy and often not at all practical. If your job is hazardous and you want to stay within the industry, you are best off choosing a well-run shop with a strong union. Through the union, you can work to insure the safest possible working conditions. If you feel stuck in a dangerous workplace, you can at least try to learn the nature of the dangers you face and find out what can be done to minimize them.

The first problem faced by workers, especially those in the chemical, drug, or cosmetic industries, is finding out just what it is they are handling. Citing the need for "protection of trade secrets," employers can hide from the employees the identity of the substances they handle. Compounds are often only identified by code number. If the company won't reveal the identity of the compound, various occupational health institutes or public interest groups may be able to provide reasonable hunches or even definite information.

If you determine that you are handling a hazardous substance, learn what you can from independent sources about what you can do to minimize the dangers of exposure. (Don't rely on company information. If its safety procedures are inadequate, company officials are unlikely to admit it.) Work with your union or co-workers to press for better working conditions.

In many cases, changes in personal habits can have a big effect on the amount of risk you face. Cigarette smoking has risks of its own, but when combined with chronic exposure to toxic fumes or particulate matter, it poses an even greater hazard. This can result from the synergistic effect of the chemical mixture within the body, or, the heat from the glowing cigarette may cause vapors in the air to react to make new, possibly more dangerous compounds.

The National Institute for Occupational Safety and Health estimates that 880,000 workers are exposed to the carcinogens recognized and regulated by the Department of Labor's Occupational Health and Safety Administration. Many more are exposed to carcinogens that are not yet regulated. Learn about the potential hazards in the workplace and you may prevent some future grief.

Doctors and Dentists

A routine visit to your family doctor or dentist poses a certain amount of risk to your health. Doctors and dentists rely on x-rays far more than they ever used to for diagnosing problems or "just to check things out." And doctors prescribe a multitude of drugs to treat even the mildest of symptoms (often at the request of the patient) to a degree unprecedented in history.

If x-rays were as harmless as sticking out your tongue and saying "ah" there would be no cause for concern. But x-rays are a form of ionizing radiation (which can disrupt molecules as it passes though them) and, like radioactive releases from nuclear power plants or weapons blasts, exposure to even low levels of it have been shown to cause cancer and genetic damage.

One might ask, "Aren't the expected health benefits worth the slight risk of an x-ray or two?" Often, they are. But doctors and dentists order many x-rays when they are not *medically* called for; that is, when they are used for potential legal defense ("documentation") in case of a malpractice suit. This is called "defensive medicine" and three out of four doctors surveyed by the American Medical Association in 1977 said they practiced it regularly.

To add to the x-ray dilemma, a recent study by the General Accounting Office (GAO) discovered that more than a third of dental x-ray machines and almost half of the breast x-ray machines surveyed by the federal Food and Drug Administration emitted dangerous levels of radiation. GAO concluded that federal and state programs to regulate sources of radiation were inadequate.

If you are told to get an x-ray, ask your doctor or dentist if it is really necessary for a diagnosis and if there are less risky alternatives. Use your own judgment or get another opinion if you're not sure about it. If you have a chronic problem, learn about the regular practices and what you can do to help yourself. Also ask the x-ray technicians when the machines were last checked for leakage and what the results were. Ask them if they are aware of the controversy over health effects of low-level radiation (chances are they are if they run behind the door when the machine is on). Discuss your concerns about radiation with them and with your doctor and dentist. If they are not sympathetic or understanding, change your doctor or dentist. There are many who are. Another potential health hazard you may be subjected to on a visit to the doctor's office is one or more of the hundreds of harmful prescription drugs, many of which have yet to be thoroughly tested for adverse side-effects. Antibiotics can have serious effects; penicillin alone causes some 300 deaths a year in the US. Sulfa drugs, a type of antibiotic, given for certain kinds of bacterial infections, including common bladder infections, can cause thyroid enlargement and can injure the kidneys. Cortisone, given to reduce inflammation, can cause liver damage and sterility; antihistamines, taken for allergies, can affect the nervous system, the heart, and the digestive tract; and tranquilizers, prescribed for anxiety and tension, can cause cataracts and hepatitis after extended use.

Among the most controversial prescription drugs with known harmful side-effects are female hormones, birth control pills, and estrogen supplements to relieve the discomforts of menopause. About 13 million women in the US routinely use estrogens, usually for a period of several years. Studies conducted over the past few years have proven that women who take oral contraceptives or use hormones to get through menopause are increasing their risk of cancer. Women who took menopausal estrogen supplements for more than a year risked uterine cancer five to ten times more than women who never used them.

Hormones do have valid medical uses, however: for birth control for women not in the high risk cancer category and to control osteoporosis (loss of bony tissue after menopause). But many scientists today believe that estrogen drugs are ineffective in treating menopause nervousness, depression, or in maintaining a youthful appearance, and are likely to promote cancer.

The alternatives to estrogens are not unattractive; more benign methods of birth control, like condoms, foam, and the diaphragm are effective, if not as convenient as the pill.

Many women can reduce the disruptions of menopause with diet and exercise that increase their ability to take flushes and flashes in stride. They should cut back (ideally, cut out!) nervous stimulants like caffeine and tobacco, and cut back on refined sugar and honey which contribute to hypoglycemia that adds more irritability, trembling, tension and anxiety. To further counteract bouncing blood hormonal levels and nerve impulses, get plenty of regular exercise. Get *physically* tired every day.

Suggested Reading

How to live in our Polluted World, May Bethel; Pyramid Books, New York, 1970.

Does Everything Cause Cancer?, Center for Science in the Public Interest; Washington, DC, 1979.

Malignant Neglect, The Environmental Defense Fund and Robert Boyle; Alfred A. Knopf, New York, 1979.

The Politics of Cancer, Samuel Epstein, MD; Anchor Press/Doubleday, New York, 1979.

The Zapping of America, Paul Brodeur; W. W. Norton and Company. New York, 1977.

The New, Improved Ecopornography

by Tom Turner

Companies, particularly big companies, worry about what the public thinks about them. For the little guys, it's a question of whether you'll buy their widget instead of their competitor's; for the Fortune 500 it's a bit different. Sure, Exxon wants you to buy its gas instead of Shell's, but that's not the main worry—someone's going to buy all the gas available. No, Exxon is worried about more strict regulation of its drilling operations, more stringent controls on its refineries, a potential oil field being declared wilderness, a bigger tax bite being taken out of profits—particularly the windfall profits resulting from events in the Middle East that are in no way due to Exxon's contribution. So Exxon, and dozens of other giant companies in and out of the oil industry, spend their advertising dollars on what is often called "image" advertising; too often it deserves another sobriquet: "ecopornography."

In the past ten years especially, they have gone from advertising ecologically unsound products, like snowmobiles, to advertising ecologically unsound—and wide-sweeping—policies.

Quicker Life Through Chemistry

This has to be the least subtle ad headline of 1979: "Natural Farming is perfectly all right, as long as you believe in natural famine." The advertiser is a company you've probably never heard of: Penwalt corporation. But Penwalt has been around since 1850, making all sorts of things, including agricultural chemicals. The ad itself isn't quite dishonest, but it tells a terribly one-sided story of the interaction between crops and bugs: "Every year American farmers plant over a billion acres of crops, but every year over 40%—almost 500 million acres—is destroyed by pests. Even in the face of this tragic waste it has become fashionable, in some circles, to criticize the use of chemical pesticides and fertilizers. The facts are really quite simple. Without the intelligent use of agricultural chemicals it's unlikely that the United States could produce enough food for its own current consumption and certainly not enough for those countries that look to us for food."

There are so many things wrong with that ad that it would take books to unravel them all, but here is an outline (and note how Penwalt doesn't *lie*, exactly, but indulges rather in what a friend calls imitation honesty): Crop losses have stayed more less constant over a long period of time in spite of all the millions of tons of pesticides sprayed over all the millions of acres. Bugs are just too quick. As soon as a new pesticide is invented a new substrain of bug appears that can resist it. As a result, the amount of pesticides applied to farmland has increased many times over without making much of a dent on the bug problem. Now it's true that if the use of pesticides were stopped overnight we would suffer huge crop losses—but no responsible people advocate that. What is advocated instead is a shift, with all deliberate speed, to a system or combination of systems that relies very much less on synthetic chemicals. (The complaint against pesticides isn't only because they don't work very well and are very expensive in money and energy—it is also because they kill lots of things besides bugs, including birds and other creatures, but that's another story.) Even the US Department of Agriculture has given its blessing to a system known as Integrated Pest Management, which relies far less on the chemicals Penwalt wants to keep selling.

In fact, Penwalt is right: "Without the *intelligent* use of agricultural chemicals. . . ." It just depends on who decides what intelligent use is.

Regulation, the New Shibboleth

The energy industry seems to do most of the image advertising, often through its trade associations like the Edison Electric Institute and the Atomic Industrial Forum, and it's hard to pick out only one or two contributions to our list of dubious achievers, but we'll try.

The National Rural Electric Cooperative Association, which calls itself a group of "the nation's consumer-owned nonprofit electric cooperatives and power districts," is not one of your giant bad guys, but it recently parroted the new theme that government regulation is the problem—rather than the solution—as regards the environment. Again we

have the unsubtle headline: "If you like the gasoline shortages of the 70's, you'll love the electric power shortages of
the 80's and 90's." All who like the gasoline shortages of the
70's will please stand up and cheer.

"We're not joking." the ad continues solemnly, power
shortages loom unless "a ball of red tape we call the regulatory process is cut down to size—immediately." Nice
touch, that, but where do you start cutting a ball? "Our
nation's present generating capacity is 540,000,000
kilowatts. Conservative forecasts show that by 1990 we
must be able to produce 300,000,000 kilowatts more; by the
year 2000, we'll need 200,000,000 kw on top of that." Now
just a minute. First of all, forecasts don't *show* anything
except the forecaster's biases. What they do is make educated guesses about what may come to pass in a situation
afflicted with hundreds of variables. Intelligent forecasters,
like intelligent people in any profession, can disagree, and
often do.

Also, note the tricky words: "*Conservative* forecasts. . ." Conservative my foot. Predicting a doubling of
electricity supply capacity by the end of the century is
wildly radical, not to say reckless, unnecessary, and a lousy
idea. A truly conservative forecast, and some very compelling ones have been made, suggests that electricity supply
could remain where it is now or even decline by the end of
the century, without unhappy consequences on anything
like the scale we would suffer under the ad's scenario.

But we strayed from the subject. It's very easy to
complain about red tape, about regulatory agencies, about
meddlesome bureaucrats, especially in these days of Howard Jarvis and that great anti-government President, J. Carter. It's harder to remember just how beneficial those regulations and agencies have been on the whole. One of the
reasons it's hard is that benefits are sometimes hard to measure and take a long time to appear. There is no doubt, for
example, that the Clean Air Act has saved money that
would have been spent on doctor bills by people who didn't
get sick because the air was cleaner than it would have been
without the act. Likewise, fewer work days have been lost
to illness for the same reason, but a firm number is impossible to calculate.

Obviously, after a decade of implementing sweeping
new laws and regulations to protect the environment and

health there are considerable examples of duplication between different levels of government, multiple inspections of the same thing, unnecessary paperwork and so forth. We agree with the business community that these should be streamlined and made more efficient but let's be careful not to throw out the baby with the bathwater. Just because the Department of Energy required every business in the country to calculate the square feet of every building affected by emergency thermostat setback requirements—a calculation for which they had no need or use—is no reason to cancel the setbacks. But the unnecessary paperwork required by the government *should* be eliminated.

Remember the environmental movement is mainly interested in changing priorities; industry is trying to divert attention to the details. When a company gripes about regulations and red tape, it's a good bet that it has its own interests in mind, and if they conflict with yours, too bad.

The Let's Be Reasonable Ploy

Boise Cascade, one of the big timber and paper companies, has always been a prolific advertiser, no doubt because the private timber companies need the trees on the national forests and therefore need to keep the public on their side. Some of BC's colleague companies take a hard line, but in 1979 BC was all sweetness, if not all light.

"Trees. Cash crop or natural monument? If you're like most of us, the question splits your mind." The ad goes on to proclaim BC an outfit that's for all the good things—jobs, wood fiber, and living trees—in the right kind of balance, of course. It also speaks grandly of its tree-farming activities: "Farming trees is no different than [sic] farming wheat."

This one is a good deal more subtle than the electric cooperative's or the chemical company's. What Boise doesn't say is that this year (1979) and next, the fate of millions of acres of national forest lands will be decided by Congress: some will be set aside as wilderness, some will be set aside for other uses (including logging, but a kind known as sustained-yield, not the wheat-field variety Boise likes). BC and its peers are in there fighting for the smallest possible wilderness declaration, for their own purposes, but you'd never guess from this ad. The ad also neglects to describe the considerable dangers associated with tree-

farming schemes. The main problem is that when a forest
consists of trees that are all the same age and are more or
less genetically identical, it is terribly vulnerable to the unexpected disease. Remember, these trees will be born in test
tubes. Native trees have evolved with native pests and they
are resilient. They also are varied in their genetic make-up.
Pests and blights can harm multi-age, multi-species forests,
but they're unlikely to wipe them out. A wheat field full of
pinus superosa is another matter: one virulent bug could
clean out the whole works.

The Perspective Problem

This is a relatively old ad, and most advertisers and
their agencies have stopped such flagrant misrepresenta-
tion—either through a new surge of honesty or out of fear of
being caught. The ad pictured a father and son at Fish Pond
Lake in Appalachia. The advertiser, a big coal company,
bragged that its reclamation program had been so good that
one could now catch fish where only yesterday there was a
hideous strip mine. It all looked great until a photographer
tracked down Fish Pond Lake and took a picture of it from
the air: it was a tiny oasis in a huge moonscape, carefully
manicured for the ad but no legitimate example of successful
reclamation. One other oldie-but-goodie from the ecoporn
hall of fame fits this category: an ad from the Potlatch Corporation that purported to show what good guys Potlatch
were by showing a magnificent stretch of Idaho river and
extolling the virtues of their water-pollution clean-up system. The only problem was that the picture was taken fifty
miles upstream from the nearest Potlatch plant.

The Egg On Your Face Department

Every once in a while events will take a turn that
makes an old advertisement a delicious joke. It may also
give a clue about what to look for in similar, contemporary
ads.

Exhibit A appeared in the *Wall Street Journal* in 1975.
"Three Mile Island Unit 1: Performance to Be Proud of."
Need we go on? The ad bragged about how smoothly TMI
had been running, how reliable it was, and like that. The
unspoken message was, let's get on with building more nuclear power plants. Notice, for example, how they're inclined to call a reactor Three Mile Island *I*, so we'll get used
to the idea of there being a TMI II, or TMI III.

IT TAKES TWO to speak the truth – one to speak
and another to hear.

Henry David Thoreau

Well, they went ahead and built a TMI II; in the spring
of 1979 it came within a whisker of melting down and causing untellable physical damage to the people and landscape
of eastern Pennsylvania. It has already caused incalculable
damage to the prospects of the nuclear power industry.
Some have even called Three Mile Island the end of the
nuclear age.

The Publisher's Dilemma
All right, it's a free country, we've got the First
Amendment, and slanted advertising is nothing new. But
what about the magazines, the newspapers, the television
and radio networks that depend on the advertisers' fees? Do
they knuckle under to the advertisers' political needs? It's
hard to say. No periodical is likely to admit to yielding to
such pressure, but sometimes the circumstantial evidence is
compelling. *Time*'s persistent and shrill defenses of nuclear
power in what are supposed to be news stories come to
mind.

But what of another problem, the problem of what ads
to accept for your righteous magazine? In the late '70s the
National Audubon Society lost members when its magnificent magazine, *Audubon*, published several outrageous
examples of ecoporn. The worst was from Potlatch, and it
infuriated lots of Society members, particularly those in the
Northwest. The ad pictured a backpacker out in the woods;
he says, "I just spent three weeks in the back country and
didn't see another soul. We've got plenty of wilderness. We
don't need more wilderness."

Potlatch, don't forget, isn't doing this to stamp out
loneliness, it's in it for the trees on all that land we don't
need as wilderness. Members wrote angry letters to *Audubon*'s editor, Les Line, reprimanding him for accepting such
offensive tripe. "Why give those guys such a respectable
podium?" was the gist of the milder letters.

Line's response is interesting and not to be dismissed

lightly. He maintains that *Audubon*'s readers are quite sophisticated enough to see through the blatant misrepresentations in the ads, that his editorial policy has not been affected one whit (which is demonstrably true); put another way, if *Audubon* isn't doing a good enough job of educating its readers to see through ads like Potlatch's, then *Audubon* isn't doing its job. Still, the argument rages.

There are hundreds more examples. You can't pick up a popular magazine without finding a gem of ecoporn. The only defense—unless the ad contains outright falsehood—is a healthy skepticism: who is running this ad, and why? What is the rest of the story the ad doesn't reveal? What's the color of the wool they're trying to pull over my eyes?

Remember the other side of the story is being told by small citizens' groups, environmental organizations, and volunteers who don't have budgets for four-color national ads. Your membership in one or more of these groups at least allows you to hear the other side.

What Have Teachers Learned?

by Mark Terry

In 1970 we knew we had to initiate a decade of intensive environmental education and in 1980 we look back on an abundance of attempts, a sharper focus of study, a wealth of classroom experience, and more definitions than anyone can use. But it has only been accomplished in this and that fragment, in scattered schools and districts, and nowhere has it been pulled together for a significant number of students throughout their school years—due to a combination of ignorance and economics. Lack of adequate school funding will continue to plague creative educators in the decade ahead and praise is due those who make things happen despite its suffocating hold. Its ultimate resolution may depend, as do many environmental problems as well, on development of regional self-sufficiency and a restructuring of regional government—but that's another article.

Exemplary programs today can guide us into the 80's with an assurance of effective education. Nothing like the following examples was available as we entered the 70's, so they represent a true case of progress as if survival mattered. They have been selected out of one educator's experience to show the variety of productive avenues open to us: a single teacher's elective course, a state level teacher's education program, a corporate curriculum package (!), two district-wide programs, and an entire independent secondary school.

A teacher in a small independent high school in the San Fernando Valley of California has created an elective course that is attracting national attention. The course, offered for science credit to students prepared in biology, is a year long study of occupational health. It represents the best sort of environmental education for several reasons:

1. It *builds* on a basic science background: students survey, through individual projects, each of the body's systems and the occupational hazards and diseases that affect each one.
2. It connects politics, economics, biology and ecology: stu-

dents explore outwardly—the industry, working conditions and larger environmental effects—and inwardly to the chemistry and physiology of diseases.

3. It brings into high focus real local problems and the people entangled in them: students visit several types of work environments and talk with those directly involved.

4. It stresses individual responsibility: students find many opportunities to connect their actions in the marketplace with the perpetuation or elimination of serious environmental and health problems, and in the process learn the politics of purchasing power.

5. It provides serious avenues for action: students are enabled not only to chart their own consumer choices and careers, they actually aid in studying workplace problems and lobby for change at various levels of government.

The impact of the course is such that several students have already gone on to college and graduate careers dedicated to the improvement of worker health. It demonstrates the usefulness of a precise focus and the ability of high school age students to become engaged in concern for their fellow man. Most important, it demonstrates the impact possible for a single dedicated and creative teacher. The course has gotten the attention of occupational health professionals and students have prepared a slide narrative and presented it in person to national occupational health conventions.

To learn more about this course, contact: Paul Witt, Science Department, Oakwood School, 11600 Magnolia Boulevard, North Hollywood, California 91601.

A remarkable individual from a liberal arts background *outside* the education establishment, and an equally remarkable state education offical have teamed up in the Puget Sound region to produce one of the most significant environmental education efforts in the nation—in terms of both content and impact. Over several years these two have transformed well deserved federal funding from the Office of Environmental Education, plus local funds and in-kind support, into a challenging, changing and accessible teacher education program that involves:

1. Evening seminars for teachers carrying through the full school year, offered for credit through local teacher training institutions, mixing presentations of challenging content by local and

national experts with hands-on involvement and design of activities tailored for classroom use.

2. Summer workshops in which teachers who have gone through the program have produced *exceptional* curriculum guides for elementary and secondary levels.

3. A focus on understanding energy as a link between ecology, food and society and as an appropriate topic for study by students at any grade level in a multitude of disciplines.

4. A habit of meeting controversial issues head-on, always with a humane and inquisitive approach, but not shying from the challenge of bringing difficult local questions into the classroom.

5. Establishment of an accessible and potent resource library.

6. Establishment of a supportive and communicative cadre of teachers at all grade levels, all committed to better environmental education and to implementation in their own lives of the principles they teach

The program is the best example of making *something* work with whatever funds are available. Recently funds have shifted from environmental sources to health-related sources—so the program has retained its format but shifted to a study of the environment/nutrition connection. The result is that an ever broadening group of teachers is coming under its influence.

To learn more about this program, contact: Chris Peterson and Tony Angell, "Energy, Food and You," Shoreline District Offices, N.E. 158th and 20th N.E., Seattle, Washington 98155.

Although corporate-sponsored programs are biased and should be examined carefully (a point I'll expand on later in this piece), I *am* going to recommend a Tenneco program. Actually a collaboration between Tenneco and the American Association of School Administrators, the program goal is energy conservation, pure and simple, which makes it safe for everyone. In this instance the money poured in has produced impressive results. The program, known as S.E.E.D. (Schoolhouse Energy Efficiency Demonstration) has involved:

1. Development of techniques for school energy audits—right down to the appropriate instrumentation—by actually performing such audits in cooperation with some twenty schools in the eastern United States.

2. Development of techniques for engaging the school popula-

tion in the process—from custodian to administration to kids—thereby enhancing the educational experience for everyone.

3. Development of techniques to bring parent organizations and school boards in to support the plans developed for conservation based on surveys and audits.

4. Publication of all this in a comprehensive, readable volume, containing sample results from schools, supportive classroom activities, and a technical manual for the audit itself.

The program's validity is well established through the experience of the twenty schools involved. The fundamental insight of using the institution as a teaching tool is well understood and presented in an appropriately understated way. The focus, energy conservation, is at once narrow *and* all encompassing, requiring careful study of all aspects of school life and fostering thereby a more general environmental consciousness.

To learn more about this program, contact: George Gravley, Public Affairs Director, S.E.E.D., Tenneco, Inc., Tenneco Building, P.O.Box 2511, Houston, Texas 77001.

WHEN I was a boy I was told that anybody could become President; I'm beginning to believe it.

Clarence Darrow

In a similar vein, but originating in the work of two district administrators, are two district-wide energy education programs in Colorado and Arizona. Characteristic of these programs are:

1. Study and action components for students at all grade levels involving energy auditing and conservation in individual buildings throughout the district.

2. Actual dollar savings to the districts involved, and efforts to make these savings visible by using them to make noteworthy purchases or donations.

3. An ability to run comparison tests on innovations and conservation measures by coordinating efforts of several schools.

As with the Tenneco program, the narrow focus on

energy belies the wide-ranging environmental concern that results. And a lesson about the *importance* of energy can be taught through these K-12 programs that simply cannot be taught any other way: every year the focus is there—the problem of supplying energy efficiently and equably does not go away.

To learn more about these programs, contact: Calvin E. Anderson, Director of Energy Conservation, Jefferson County Public Schools, 809 Quail Street, Lakewood, Colorado 80215.

Or contact: Henry Dahlberg, Energy Programs, Prescott Unified School District #1, P.O. Box 1231, Prescott, Arizona—86302.

Finally, an entire school is in the process of formation with environmental consciousness built into its very fabric. A group of three experienced educators has set about establishing a secondary school in Seattle that makes sense of a student's total education through a threefold emphasis on arts, humanities and environment. Its environment program, which concerns us here, is notable in part because it is designed to complement, not upstage, the other two. In fact, the most important elements of the program are so much a part of the life of the school as to become second-nature, part of the expected background. These elements are:

1. Faculty/student involvement in all campus maintenance and operation.

2. Use of custodian and cook as masters of their crafts to whom faculty and students are apprenticed.

3. A comprehensive transportation program ensuring that mass transit, bicycles, car pools and feet accomplish *all* school transportation.

4. Student/faculty preparation and serving of a daily meal stressing local agriculture and supplemented from the school's own solar greenhouse.

5. A comprehensive school energy program involving conservation and innovation.

6. Community extension of environmental skills in energy conservation, neighborhood beautification, greenhouse and pea patch agriculture.

7. Establishment of all these programs in a 1905 school building in the heart of a major city.

Filling out the program are environmental emphases in all science and social science courses (including a required science course on the scientific issues of the twentieth century taken concurrently with the twentieth century humanities year), a wilderness expedition program for all students, and a physical education program that recognizes the value of walking, bicycling and wilderness outings. In addition, interdisciplinary programs are established with the school's arts faculty in environmental awareness and with the humanities faculty in the history of man's use of the earth. The guiding philosophy of the program in general is that responsibility is learned through responsible action, and the environmental responsibility is essential to the full development of the individual. Its enactment is made possible because this philosophy is shared by all faculty, board members and parents.

To learn more about this program, contact: Mark Terry, Associate Director, The Northwest School, 1415 Summit, Seattle, Washington 98122.

Due to poor communication and a tendency among educators to revere definitions above all else, many teachers, districts, conferences and authors have never left 1970 and persist in adding definitions of environmental education to an already overburdened professional literature. Existing excellent programs are apparently unconvincing, and redefinition is preferred to implementation, funneling dollars away from effective action and littering the landscape with reinvented wheels. For those still looking for something like a definition, here is a very serviceable set of goals for environmental education worked out in the office of the Superintendent of Public Instruction for the State of Washington:

Students should be able to derive from their education—

1. an accurate and comprehensive grounding in how the environment works, including man's interaction with the environment.

2. experience in valuing environmental quality, including the aesthetics of both "untouched" and "man-made" environments.

3. experience in how personal choices and actions affect environmental quality, with the aim of identifying and improving the opportunities in their own future.

4. experience in methods of enacting community responsibility, including all aspects of citizen - government - business decision making.

While the best way to proceed is to publicize further and demonstrate what works, it is also worth paying attention to what does not work and what is downright counterproductive. The sheer quantity of environmental education programs and materials produced over the last ten years suggests that there must be some chaff. The following five danger signals may proved useful:

1. *Corporate Sponsorship*. It is hard for individuals to be objective, but it is much harder for corporations, which are so much clearer about what they wish to accomplish in (and with) the world. The beauty of those four-color classroom presentations with handy multi-media components at irresistible prices (if they cost at all) seduces many a bored and harassed teacher. In fact, there is no need to resist the temptation as long as the following protective measure is enforced: *always* allot time to study the sponsoring group itself, its goals and the manner in which the material it has so generously provided might further those goals. This way the classroom can safely be decorated with those marvelous posters, because the corporate logo will no longer be subliminal but will be highlighted as a subject of study itself. Corporate education packages are, after all, advertising, and should always be seen as such.

2. *Ecology as Basic Science*. Many teachers, curriculum supervisors and textbook authors now introduce ecology as the foundation science of the future, guaranteed to lift kids out of boredom and rocket them into a twofold commitment to further science courses and a lifelong environmental ethic. Too often, the newness quickly wears off and such courses rocket kids right back to boredom. Ecology as a beginning science course is awkward because it is not a *beginning* science. Efforts to make it so leave kids confused and ecology misunderstood. Ecology is a synthetic science built from biology, chemistry, physics and others. At least a basic course in biology, which contains some fundamental chemistry and physics, is necessary prior to a real study of ecology. Ecology *does* make a fine science elective after study of the basics, drawing on all the natural sciences to form an exciting synthesis. But it is not the quick and easy solution to the need for environmental education that many still assume it to be.

3. *Cosmetic Activity Programs*. There is much good to be done, many wrongs to be righted. The difficulty lies in the assumption that picking up litter, or turning off lights, or

running a paper drive takes care of environmental education. Each of these is a worthwhile activity in its own right or as part of a much broader range of activities *all* designed to enact environmentally responsible behavior. But if presented as *the* school contribution to "the ecology," as it's so often incorrectly stated, then kids are right to smell a rat and we should worry about those who don't. None of these activities goes to the heart of the matter, each is cosmetic. They are good cosmetics, but should not be promoted as more. The real issues are the *needless production* of litter, the *design* and care of building lighting systems, the *excessive use* of paper and mismanagement of forests. Without accompanying activities and study focused on these issues, the cosmetics are counter-productive, implying that a new age is at hand when really the old one just lumbers on ahead and we're doing a bit better picking up after it.

4. *Heart Throbs and Hand Wringing*. It is downright dangerous to throw at kids sorrowful images of endangered species or third world starvation and depend on the pain to do the work. Firsthand experience of a tragedy or disaster sometimes moves a person to seek understanding and commitment, the Hollywood version seldom does. This is not at all to suggest that such problems should not be studied. They should indeed, but *only* in depth. A brief media-based exposure to tragedy simply doesn't do it—in fact, it generally promotes an outward show of concern and an inward turning away which is much more lasting.

5. *Avoidance of Local Issues*. It is also downright dangerous to avoid, or forget, or remain ignorant of the issues directly affecting the local community. The best possible course on world ecological problems is counterproductive if unaccompanied bz equivalent study of the local issues. We run the risk of teaching that it's best to worry about long distance solutions to other people's problems because no one knows about or can agree on the problems right outside the door. Damage is also done by the systematic avoidance of a true local hot potato. Yes, parents often have strongly held positions on such issues. Air them! Use the issue as an opportunity to practice the vital arts of dialog and compromise.

There is a further lesson in the successful programs described earlier in this article: one or two individuals are at the root of each program's development. These individuals have done their homework and then carried their commitment to environmental education over whatever bureaucratic hurdles stood in their paths. Whatever the district or federal grant guidelines for curriculum development may say, it is some creative and dedicated individual or very small team working closely together that gets new ventures off the ground. So we ought not to look for change to come from any other direction. True change will only come from individual educators who take the initiative themselves, though publishing these programs to a wide audience may spark the imagination and give encouragement sufficient to set another individual on a new course of action.

The broad path for environmental education through the 80's has been well scouted. It remains up to us to set forth on the many individual paths that our students and communities will follow.

What's Ahead in the 1980s?

by Lester David

What lies around the bend as our country enters the 1980s? How about a talking *car*?

Or a choice of *two dozen* TV networks? A telephone that can do practically everything for you except wash your socks?

By 1985 we may have a nine-digit zip code to remember. You didn't think everything was going to be wine and roses, did you?

The next 10 yrs. are likely to bring radical changes in the way Americans live and work. What follows is a forecast of the new world ahead.

For starters, the energy crunch isn't going away. And it looks as if it's going to affect our lives more than any other single factor. Because of relentlessly rising fuel costs, the message of conservation could finally seep through. Americans should be driving less and insulating more.

We don't expect the power crisis to spark a major return-to-the-city movement by suburbanites, but the '80s will almost certainly bring marked changes in housing. Gone like the CB craze is the dream house in the exurbs—country communities that require a long, and expensive, commute to work.

Instead, builders should concentrate on constructing townhouses and other attached housing near city lines, business districts and industrial areas. This means more people will be living in less space.

New homes will be smaller, better insulated and probably will cost less to heat and cool. Prices? By the end of the '80s the average cost of a new home is expected—grit your teeth—to hit $150,000.

Before the end of the decade mass transportation is going up by 50 percent. That's because federal and municipal governments are committed to spending $50 billion to get you and me out of autos and into such mass transit facilities as buses or railroads.

What about those alternative energy sources we've

been hearing so much about? Here's the morning line on the main ones:

Solar energy now provides 6 percent of the nation's power needs and the use of sun power is going to double in 10 yrs. Resistance to solar devices is going to crack as fuel bills soar and buyers begin to snap at the tempting tax breaks being offered to go solar.

Nineteen states now give income tax breaks to solar energy users. California allows homeowners to subtract 55 percent of the cost of installing a system from their taxes. In addition, 25 states let solar users deduct a percentage of their property taxes and 10 also give sales tax breaks.

Shale oil isn't a good bet for the '80s, even though the western U.S. has 16,550 sq. mi. of shale oil deposits. Oil companies are ready to go, but production depends on getting price and production guarantees from the Feds.

Even if these are okayed and the huge problems of preserving the environment are solved, we see only 200,000 barrels a day coming out of the ground. Small potatoes, considering America's daily consumption runs 17 million barrels right now.

The experts give garbage power a fancy name—biomass—but it will grow faster than you think because there's so much available. Currently, a number of cities are generating a good chunk of their electricity by burning solid waste, and more are expected to follow. By mid-decade, a number of states hope to get about 15 percent of their electrical power this way.

In Chicago, thousands are cooking with gas pumped from a plant that converts cow manure to methane, which is about the same as natural gas.

Geothermal energy has some serious geographical limitations that are expected to curtail widespread use in the '80s. Heat trapped in the earth is plentiful in the Southwest and along the West Coast. San Francisco already gets much of its power from wells sunk in the Big Geyser area north of the city. Although geothermal power will probably only be regionally significant in the next 10 yrs., watch it roar ahead in the 1990s.

As for standard energy sources, the name of the game will still be oil but in the next 5 yrs. natural gas will come on stronger than gangbusters. That's because supplies are plentiful and easy to get. Besides, natural gas costs about one-third less than oil, though prices should rise during the decade.

Coal is a question mark. There could be a massive shift to coal-based electric power if the U.S. relaxes its rules governing sulfur dioxide emissions. Even if the rules stand pat, coal use is still expected to increase by about 5 percent every year through the 1980s as the price of oil zooms.

And finally, gasoline. It looks like gas could reach $6 a gal. What does that do to the main user of gas?

Well, cars will be smaller, lighter, less flashy than today's models and should belch fewer pollutants into the air. While the emphasis will be on more miles per gal., manufacturers won't forget style. That's because Detroit knows buyers still want cars to look like cars. But these new cars are expected to talk to you!

You'll be tooling down a stretch of highway, hammer down to the floor, when suddenly the vehicle warns you, "You are exceeding the speed limit!" If you forget to look at the gas tank the car tells you: "Time for a fill-up."

Talkative automobiles can inform you that the parking brake is on or the battery is not charging. The voice comes from a computerized voice synthesizer in the dashboard. It will replace gauges and lights that now give you the same warnings.

Also, look for more plastic inside and out for weight-saving and fuel economy. By 1985, cars are expected to be an average of 700 lbs. lighter than today's models. Plastics may be used in fans, brake fluid reservoirs, oil pans, engine valve covers, carburetor assemblies and even major body parts including hoods and fenders.

And the push is on for an electric car that can travel long distances without a battery recharge. Right now, using the conventional lead-acid battery, electric cars conk out after running between 35 and 50 miles. But scientists are working on new types of power sources and the Department of Energy is financing dozens of projects.

One project utilizes zinc and chlorine, which could store four times as much power as present batteries. Another uses sodium-sulfur and lithium-metal sulfide which can pack six times the punch. These two should be commercially available in about eight years, and will have a 200-mi. range.

During the decade, look for more and different

mopeds, a big upsurge in the use of bikes on city streets and even American versions of Chinese bike-taxis. More and more communities should construct bike lanes and paths.

The years ahead hold an electronic explosion that will change a big part of your lifestyle in everything from home entertainment to the way you shop, phone and get your mail.

Take TV. If Rip Van Viewer had been asleep for 20 yrs. and woke up in the late '80s, he'd never recognize the old box.

For one thing, those video discs you've been hearing about are expected to be a billion-dollar business, even bigger than audio records are now. First of the platters and players are scheduled to hit the shops by the end of 1980. At first, players should run about $400 and the discs between $10 and $17 each, which is cheaper than video cassettes.

If you want to get programs off the air, you'll have your pick of a couple of dozen networks. That's because a whole new crop of communications satellites will be launched. Once these new satellites are strung out in space along the Equator, TV will be a whole new ballgame.

IF ONE ADVANCES confidently in the direction of his dreams, and endeavors to live the life which he has imagined, he will meet with a success unexpected in common hours.

Henry David Thoreau

Film studios, syndicators, advertisers and others will transmit programs to satellites which, in turn, will beam them to local studios or the many cable companies now springing up. Either way, a vast variety of shows will be available.

You'll be able to view all these shows on new kinds of sets, too. TV picture tubes should get larger but less bulky. This means screens will get bigger but the set won't stick out into the room as far as it does now. Toward the end of the decade the TV set should become just a flat panel that can be hung on a wall like a picture.

And here's something exotic. TV bugs who have an

extra $10,000 to $35,000 to spend might be able to buy their own space antennas. Once these antennas are put in the back yard, viewers whose sets are hooked up to them could bypass TV stations and pick up any transmission they wanted from any part of the world.

Sometime during the decade, your set might be linked to a computer system activated by a home keyboard. Punch a set of numbers and you'll be able to get in touch with a store, say, that sells sporting goods. Ask to be shown fishing rods and the computer flips pages of a catalogue. Then pick one out and order, all by computer.

Thousands of homes in Columbus, Ohio are already hooked into a two-way system for a major test of Warner Communications Co. Qube. Viewers have consoles about the size of a typewriter with buttons that can actually talk to 30 channels.

As the electronics revolution rushes into high gear, Alexander Graham Bell won't recognize the gadget he invented. In the coming decade, your telephone will act as a personal gofer, performing a host of personal services. These will be done through electronic switching systems which will store programmed instructions.

All you do is dial your number, add a code and the programmed instructions will be carried out. These services range from turning on lights and appliances to hotel-like wake-up calls.

And the days of the telephone directory are numbered. During the decade Ma Bell intends to put names, addresses and numbers into computer memory banks. When you punch out someone's name on a push-button phone, an automatic voice response supplies his number.

Electronic mail service, or EMS, is already here and should grow like Jack's beanstalk in the next few years. Using phone lines, all kinds of letters can be transmitted across the country and delivered by the mailman in the usual way. It's like ultra-modern V-mail. By the mid '80s, a major proportion of business mail will go this way.

Right now companies are racing to perfect transmission devices to grab off a chunk of the mail business. One company, Telemail, believes that by the late '80s, many American households will own a typewriter-terminal hooked to a computer. You'll send a letter by typing out a message on your home terminal. The computer sends it through a commercial network anywhere in the world. It's like a personal teletype machine.

And about that nine-digit zip code. Expect it in about three years. Postal officials say it should speed up the mails because every block will have its own number.

Electronics, though, isn't the only area that benefits from the new technology. Medical science, continuing its onward march, should make great strides in cancer research.

With new instruments, doctors can diagnose early cancers much faster. One new device is the CT, or computerized tomography scanner, which gives doctors a cross-section picture of the body and shows up tumors better than X rays. Another diagnostic tool is fiber optics—thin, flexible tubes of light with which doctors can actually see what's happening inside you.

Deaths from heart disease, already down as much as 20 percent since the start of the '70s, will continue to dip as doctors learn more about why arteries clog up and public awareness of the big risk factors grows. Health education campaigns will continue to alert people to the perils of high blood pressure, high cholesterol levels, high-tension living and lack of exercise.

The cost of staying healthy—sorry about this—will continue to skyrocket but some kind of national health insurance will probably come about during the decade.

Working habits should change some too. Flexible working hours should expand but the four-day work week stubbed its toe a while back and isn't recovering. While there will be more leisure time, much of it could be used by many people for moonlighting to keep up with inflation. Some things never change.

Eco-Politics

Seventies Into Eighties

Back to the Grassroots
by Jeffrey Knight

The spring of 1970 felt the last great aftershock of the blockbuster societal-quake of 1968. Cambodia, the wave of student strikes, Kent State, several famous trials of anti-war and black activists, all brought on a paroxysm of rage and anger at the Vietnam War and injustices in our society. The rage never again reached such a frenzied or concentrated form. It rose later in the bright but fleeting candidacy of George McGovern, and then, finally disillusioned by its own leaders as well as by its society, it dissipated and turned inward, to vanish into the vague narcissism of the Nixon Years and the Me Decade.

Opposition to the war provided the fuel that launched the environmental movement as we knew it in the seventies. While many people continued to fight the war, a significant number of politicized activists found new commitments in a conservation movement that had a history going back to the earliest days of our republic. To traditional concerns for wilderness preservation, forestry, soil and water conservation, wildlife and parks, eco-activists brought a concern for the damage being done to the earth by urban and industrial development. Spurred by a concern for saving an earth that was being destroyed by war, an earth revealed from the moon as a fragile shimmering ball in space, they set out to make care and concern for the planet a part of our lives. And since we are a nation of laws, the commitment to the earth was encoded into our legal, social and economic fabric. That process isn't finished yet — but the remarkable thing is how quickly this new social ethic has been instilled in the body politic. Few other new ethics have moved as fast.

The Politics

The movement was well afoot before Earth Day 1970. The National Environmental Policy Act of 1969, which went into effect on the first day of the new decade, not only created an institutional advisor to the President — the Council on Environmental Quality — it changed the way government does business. Buried in its provisions was Section 102-2-c, which required an assessment of the environmental impacts of any major federal decision. The Act didn't say more, but the courts did, and at the urging of environmentalists and others who went to court, the federal judiciary spent the seventies expanding and refining the purpose and scope of that now-familiar planning document, the Environmental Impact Statement. The EIS is now a fixture in the administrative firmament. Under NEPA, hearings may be held for public comment, a public review period of a draft EIS is required before a final one is released, and a final EIS must be released before a project can go ahead. NEPA requires full consideration of alternatives to proposed actions, as well. Whole government programs and legislative proposals, as well as many international activities, come under NEPA's ambit; all federal agencies are subject to it. It has been an important step in making government more open and more rational, and it has been emulated in every state and become an important export of the American political system — environmental assessment as a government function has girdled the globe.

In the wake of NEPA came an armada of laws dealing with specific environmental threats and societal activities. In 1970, Congress passed the Clean Air Act and amended it twice later in the decade.

The water pollution control act passed in 1972, and was later amended. Congress passed a law to protect drinking water, and other laws to regulate the strip mining of coal, coal leasing on federal lands, leasing practices on the outer continental shelf, deep water ports, liquefied natural gas terminals, and gas pipelines. Acts were passed that controlled toxic substances, solid waste recovery, and the use of rodenticides, insecticides, and fungicides. Finally, two laws were passed that made the survival of life forms a national goal of highest priority—the Endangered Species Act and the Marine Mammal Protection Act.

The make-up of institutions changed. An Environmental Protection Agency was created by President Nixon to house the environmental regulatory programs of the federal government under one roof. By the end of the decade EPA had become the largest regulatory agency and the administrator of the largest public works programs in the government, the water pollution control program.

The Forest Service and Bureau of Land Management had the laws governing their very existences rewritten to reflect the changes in our perception of how natural resources should be managed. Protection for federal lands was expanded and enchanced in several ways. New categories of protected lands were created, including the National Wild and Scenic Rivers, the National Wildlife Refuges, the National Recreation Areas, National Marine Sanctuaries, and the National Trails System. Vast new parks and wilderness areas were added to existing systems and whole ecosystems were put up for protection in Alaska. Management of the lands slowly improved, too. Mining was halted in national parks. Predator control practices changed. Use of off road vehicles was limited, and concessionaires—the companies that provide housing, food and services in National Parks—were put on a shorter leash. Major inventories of roadless areas on federal lands were undertaken. The Coastal Zone Management Act paid the states to plan for the use and protection of their coastal lands. A national land use planning law did not pass.

Some agencies were abolished, others transmuted. The Atomic Energy Commission, consecrated to the quest after the once-bright hope of the Peaceful Atom, ran afoul of the dragon of reality and was done away with in 1974. The Federal Power Commission passed on. Two agencies—the Federal Energy Administration and the Energy Research and Development Administration—appeared and vanished almost in a single Congress, only to be replaced by a more intractible, less comprehensible Department of Energy. Few people see any benefits accruing from this consolidation. Creation of the Nuclear Regulatory Commission (from part of the hulk of the AEC), the Occupational Health and Safety Administration, the Mine Health and Safety Commission, the Marine Mammal Commission, the fisheries management commissions around the country reflected the public's new concerns.

Sometimes Congress was persuaded to interfere in the regulatory processes it had set up and decide on certain projects on its own. Congress overrode several laws to let a pipeline be build to carry Alaskan oil to south Alaska for shipment to the West Coast (where it wasn't needed). A gas pipeline route was chosen that comes across Canada from the Alaskan North Slope, reaching the Midwest via the best of three possible routes, a route that was identified and chosen only because of the EIS process. The B-1bomber was cancelled, as the SST had been at the beginning of the decade. (Subsequent history proved the SST choice wise. The taxpayers were saved from spending billions on a supersonic transport that, like the Concorde, would never have been used, and Boeing remained a healthy company.)

The B-1 was one of several military issues in which environmentalists took a role. Others included the Trident submarine, the Project Sanguine communications system, the Amchitka nuclear tests, the placement of plutonium weapons facilities on earthquake faults, and the MX missile, a fight that will extend into the early 80s. The Department of Defense, like other departments, had to consider the environment in its decisions. The Securities and Exchange Commission added environmental reporting to the requirements it placed on the issuers of stock.

Environmental issues became part of foreign policy. Whale protection, trade in endangered species, protection of migratory birds, oil tanker standards, nuclear non-proliferation, transboundary air and water pollution, protection for Antarctica, and the use of the seas, became part of the State Department's work. Thanks to an alliance of environmentalists and fishermen, the US extended its economic zone 200 miles into the sea, to protect our fisheries from over-exploitation.

Environmentalists made alliances on many levels— with Native Americans on energy issues and subsistence culture survival, with labor on a wide range of issues, with consumer groups, women's groups, peace groups, minorities, churches, farmers, unions, and small businessmen. At times, alliances even emerged with big industries on certain issues.

The press became regular observers of the environmental scene. Politicians recognized that the environment could swing elections. If the polls didn't bring that message

home, the work of Environmental Action, with its Dirty
Dozen campaign, and the League of Conservation Voters,
with its voting charts and campaign contributions, made it
clear enough. (Environmentalists have the somewhat dubious distinction of having been the first progressives to support Jimmy Carter over other liberal presidential aspirants
in 1975-6).

But not everything changed. The highway juggernaut
— embodied in the Highway Trust Fund — was bloodied
but unbowed. Some funds were diverted to mass transit, but
most of the money still goes to roads. Major government
subsidies to airlines and truckers still keep railroads at a
disadvantage and our energy costs for transportation higher
than they need be. And the water resources development
pork barrel just keeps getting bigger. Control of a growing
population continues to be a good idea that baffles most
people.

Nuclear power's bright light failed during the 70s. Its
supporters' stubborn failure over twenty years to be honest
and open about its problems and the real scale of its poten-
tials caught up with it in an era of high energy prices and in a
social milieu that was less supportive of slow technological
learning curves.

At the beginning of the seventies the opponents of
nuclear power were few and scattered, but over the course
of the decade their concern was built into a national movement that looked likely to succeed. Their success was
rooted in a dedication to honesty and rigorous thought and
in grassroots organizing. It was aided by the disastrous
economics of nuclear power and the near-disastrous performance of nuclear reactors.

Solar energy and conserving energy — doing more
with less — became the wave of the present and the future.
Much of the environmental movement's work resulted in
victories over what would have been bad energy-supply decisions, actions which permitted forces more benign than
Congressional ignorance and alarm or corporate myopia and
self interest to lead us toward the soft path. (The forces:
common sense and the force of the market.) The Soft
Energy Path was developed by an environmentalist, Amory
Lovins, and changed the way people thought about energy
and planned for it. Planners now think not of homogeneous
supply strategies but of planning according to real needs.

There is much work still ahead of us. NEPA and many of the regulatory laws need to be improved. Alaska's wilds need more permanent protection; so do other wildlands throughout the nation. More dramatic steps must be taken to ensure the survival of wild species by protecting their habitats and to protect ourselves from new environmental threats like acid rain, carbon dioxide build-up, ozone-depletion, toxic waste dumps, overuse of economic poisons, radioactive waste dumps, and genetic experimentation. New threats disguised as progress will certainly emerge and old ones — the foremost of which is nuclear war — will demand more attention and more creative thinking. And they will require planetary, not just national, thinking and cooperation.

Limits to Change

The world lags behind us; we must bring it along. There are limits to growth, limits to resources, limits to ingenuity and to achievement of perfection by an imperfect species. The environmental movement's best contribution is characterized by NEPA itself and by the Soft Energy Path, and by the concept of wilderness, which goes back a long way. These ideas have changed the way people think of the world and how they live in it. Compared with other movements, astonishing progress has been made in so little time. But further change must be forthcoming, if these ideas are to be firmly embedded in the psyche of the planet's inhabitants. Questions of military and national security, economic well-being and growth, and individual freedom still are not sufficiently suffused with ecological thought. Meaningful reform takes a long time — as the history of civil rights or freedom of speech in the U.S. shows.

One comes to another lesson learned in the seventies, that there are limits to change, itself, to what any social change can achieve without people changing their own lives, and that those limits will begin to encroach on our actions unless, through education, the lessons of the ecological decade are brought home and made meaningful at the grassroots.

One of the reasons that there are limits to change is that strategies that were novel, innovative and effective for the environmental movement and other public interest movements in the 1970s have been embraced by our adversaries — the ultimate compliment. Direct mail campaigns, message advertising, nationally-directed pressure campaigns directed at Congress, lobbying in the public interest, all have been incorporated by the Destroyers. And, with their greater financial power, they have forced environmentalists to understand that our gains in the eighties will depend on a renewed and enlarged commitment, to grass roots educating, persuading and organizing. As one veteran activist said: "Since we can't outspend them, we have to out-think and out-organize them. Inspired national lobbying riding on a wave of general public support is no longer enough for success. The era of shortages and high inflation has ended that. We must go to the grass roots for our victories in the 80s."

Back to Grassroots

There is security in returning to the grassroots. It is a return to the earth itself, to the local community, to the social ecosystem — to the cells of the planetary organism. It is decentralized, democratic, and looks first within the horizon before looking beyond. It is secular and spiritual, in the great American tradition of concern first for the land.

For the average citizen, the change is relatively minor, for his arena has always been the local one, whether it is dealing with a problem nearby or a Member of Congress or a legislature far away. For the national organizations, it will require a greater change in focus; it will require, in daily practice, an understanding that grassroots pressure is the locus of influence, and that lobbying and fine arguments alone will not achieve what is possible. There must be new dedication to organizing those already waiting to take up the banner of the environment, as well as educating others so that they will join.

This will, however, cause changes in local strategy, away from simple participation in political campaigning to education, and to action on a wider variety of government levels — city councils, state legislatures, planning boards. These bodies receive some attention — but relatively little of our resources are committed to them. There will also be a further growth of voluntarism, because the economic boom which the seventies were to environmental organizations — a boom which allowed them to increase their professional staffs of lobbyists, lawyers, researchers, writers and organizers — is unlikely to make a repeat run in the eighties.

Environmental initiatives in the eighties will stress local problem solving, using the broad frameworks developed in the seventies to imbue local decisions with an environmental consciousness. And, knowing the broader implications of such actions, the environmentalist of the eighties will exploit the opportunities thus gained to build new coalitions, to educate, to politicize his or her neighbors and bring them into the fray. These processes have already begun in the late seventies, with little aid or attention from national groups. Missing the link-up has hurt the effectiveness of such campaigns as those against pesticide abuse and the spread of economic poisons among the populace. The pathway from one's front door leads to all the roads of the earth. We must not overlook the condition of that little pathway in our concern for the highway, lest we track it up with dirt.

Above all, we must find a way out of the predicament David Brower has described: environmentalists only win chances to lose in the future. We'll have to keep fighting fires, be pragmatists and problem solvers, solving broad policy issues in solutions to particular problems. In so doing, the general tenets of an ecologically sound society are tempered and made stronger than philosophical speculation alone can make them. The challenge of the 80s will require stamina more than adrenalin, and dedication to goals we have developed and shared, with more sophisticated and effective tactics and strategies.

The grassroots will strengthen us. The battles may be less spectacular, but no less important. Every generation gets its vote on what the earth should be like, and ours should preserve that choice for future generations, and as important, leave to them the knowledge and the ability to choose wisely. It is a responsibility and a duty that is too often left to chance in modern society. Future planning involves the next election, the next budget cycle, the next profit report or funding proposal. "Our society has too few institutions for the future," says Brower. We need more, and through environmentalism, and dream for harmony and equity within the limits of planetary resources, some deeper and more fundamental concern for the future can be brought into our everyday lives.

Environmental Bill of Rights

This bill of rights was submitted as a ballot initiative in California in 1980. It's a good example for use in other states. Try submitting the ideas to your legislature or adapt them for an initiative campaign in your state. The initiative process has been successfully used to reduce residential property taxes in California (Prop. 13 a.k.a., Jarvis–Gann).

Section 1. INALIENABLE RIGHTS
(Note: **Bold** words in Section 1 are **additions** to the **existing** "Inalienable Rights" provisions in the State Constitution.)

All people are by nature free and independent and have inalienable rights. Among these are enjoying and defending life and liberty, acquiring, possessing, protecting, **and conserving** property, and pursuing and obtaining safety, happiness, privacy, **and a healthful and productive environment.**

Section 28. RIGHT TO A HEALTHFUL AND PRODUCTIVE ENVIRONMENT
(a) **Rights**

The people have a right to a healthful and productive environment. Such right includes, but is not limited to, the benefits and enjoyment of:

1. Clean air in urban centers, industrial and agricultural work places, and elsewhere throughout the state;
2. Adequate amounts of water, unpolluted by toxic wastes or excessive sediments, in streams, rivers, lakes, underground basins, and coastal areas;
3. Renewable, safe, and non-wasteful energy systems;
4. Freedom from involuntary exposure to chemicals, minerals, radioactive substances and energy forms that are hazardous to health;
5. Livable urban and rural environments, with productive employment, afffordable housing, efficient transportation, and freedom from excessive noise;
6. Accessible parks, recreational areas, and open spaces;
7. Agricultural lands protected from urban or suburban sprawl;
8. Unique and scenic resources, including wilderness and coastal areas, freeflowing rivers, lakes, mountains, deserts, forests, historic structures and archaeological sites;
9. Fish and wildlife populations, rare and endangered flora and fauna, and other native plant and animal life, protected and enhanced where possible;
10. A population level compatible with a good standard of living.

b) **Implementation**

The legislature and all agencies of government, federal, state, regional and local, except where explicitly prohibited from so acting by federal law, shall implement the right guaranteed herein as follows:

(1) **Renewable and Recyclable Resources**—Use and invest in renewable, recyclable, or reclaimable energy, water, timber and mineral resources in preference to virgin or non-renewable resources;
(2) **Resource Conservation**—Manage and value natural resources, including energy, water, timber, and minerals in such a way as to minimize waste and sustain productive natural and economic systems;
(3) **Toxic Substances**—Replace toxic methods or substances with non-toxic or less toxic methods or substances whenever they can reasonably serve the same purpose;

(4) **Planning**—Avoid unnecessary long-range costs through comprehensive land use and other planning which coordinates and harmonizes the efforts of individual agencies;

(5) **Informing the Public**—Compile and make readily available to the public accurate inventories of natural reserves, toxic and hazardous wastes, pollution levels, land use, and other basic resource information;

(6) **Economic Incentives and Government Regulation**—Where feasible, use economic incentives and disincentives, rather than governmental regulation, to achieve a healthful and productive environment. When regulations are required, they shall be concise and simply worded, and shall minimize procedural delay and government intrusion into the lives of the people;

Nothing contained in this subsection shall be construed as exclusive of other laws, regulations, or policies needed to implement the people's right to a healthful and productive environment.

(c) **Prohibition**

No laws shall be enacted, or regulations adopted, which unreasonably impair the right of the people to a healthful and productive environment as defined and implemented herein.

(d) **ENFORCEMENT**

Subject to reasonable limitation and regulation by law, this section shall be enforceable through appropriate legal proceedings on or after January 1, 1982.

A democracy can be no stronger nor more enduring than the extent of its citizens' involvement in public decision making.

The inherent good sense of the general public on the need for social change through the institution of new values almost inevitably runs far ahead of the perceptions of those in government. Significant changes in basic public policy generally work their way *up from* and not *down to* the people. Examples include the movement for civil rights, the development of an environmental ethic, and the phenomenal changes in transportation policy and planning that have occurred since 1970.

—*Senator Henry M. Jackson*

Fighting the Highway

by Bunny Gabel

The question is whether New York should spend over a billion dollars for a new interstate highway of 4.2 miles on Manhattan's West Side—or use the money to rehabilitate its crumbling mass transit system. In New York City, where 87% of the work hour commuters (over three million people) use public transportation and only 2% used the old highway for which Westway is proposed as a replacement, Westway is the worst way.

Manhattan is a small island with a population density ideally suited to maximum mass transit use. Subways are three to twelve times as energy efficient as autos on Manhattan's West Side; rail freight is ten times as energy efficient as trucks in NYC. In other words, Westway would divert people and goods from energy-efficient methods of transportation to energy-wasting-ones—and use public funds to do it.

In addition, New York City has the worst carbon monoxide problem in the country and must reduce traffic and auto emissions if we want to reduce lung and heart diseases.

And the highway's necessary dredge and fill operation in the Hudson River to provide the 200 new acres of Manhattan real estate on which Westway would be built would impair the clean-up of the river and resuspend toxic wastes.

It is possible, through a federal provision called an Interstate Transfer, to get the same amount of federal money for mass transit and a substitute non-interstate road. Fifteen other urban areas have taken advantage of the alternative.

Yet nine years and over $20 million have been spent in planning and promoting the Westway plan. Westway proponents have public funds to spend for technical studies, planning, engineering, prestigious law firms and public relations work. In contrast we — the opponents — have raised less than $100,000, mostly in modest contributions, bake sales, small theater benefits, flea markets, door-to-door solicitation, direct mail appeals. Volunteers have devoted years of their lives to this David and Goliath battle — and they have made the difference, but with politics intervening and with a grandiose kind of gold coast mentality among some powerful men muddying the picture, the outcome is uncertain.

Our first mistake was not to have organized sooner. We had been pacified by the extensive public participation exercises of the planning agency, the West Side Highway Project (WSHP). There had been hundreds of meetings with WSHP staff at community gatherings and in environmental offices. WSHP handed out stacks of preliminary studies on every possible aspect of the project: tables, graphs, charts, sets of alternative highway configurations. Our opinions were solicited and it was all very impressive to us, humble non-experts. It took us too long to realize that public participation doesn't necessarily mean a share in the decision-making process.

When the Draft Environmental Impact Statement (DEIS) was issued it showed us where all the public participation had left us. The glossy, oversized, 311-page book indicated the policy had effectively been decided in 1971, when we weren't even looking. The policy having been set, this information was provided to back it up.

Next there were to be public hearings on the DEIS and so neighbors called neighbors, environmental groups alerted their members, and the word spread. We pored over the DEIS. We wrote testimony. We made signs. We took the subway to the hearing hall and we marched and chanted outside. For many this was our first public demonstration and we felt self-conscious, but Greenwich Villagers met Upper West Siders, block association people met environmental groups. We alternately marched and gathered names, addresses, and phone numbers on index card. We learned not to be terrified at making a statement in a public hearing. We learned again that what we said wasn't heard.

From that initial group of index card signers and speakers came the nucleus of highway fighters, a wide assortment of people almost all with lives, careers, families, and daily cares that had previously had nothing to do with political activism, transportation and environment. We felt, and still feel, underequipped to fight this battle on all the legal, technical, political grounds on which it must be fought. There has been no sugar daddy to buy us help and no magic to even the gross disparity of resources — unless you

262 *The New Environmental Handbook*

count the unselfishness of committed volunteers.

Shortly after the first public hearing we had our first organizing meeting, where we met lawyers we later hired to represent us. We formed a coalition and chose a name. We wrote a statement of purpose and mailed it to groups, urging them to join the effort. For about six months we had weekly meetings. We tried to be very efficient, form committees, assign tasks. We found out it's a good idea to try, because it helps define the needs and give people a sense of direction; — but essentially what gets done gets done because there's a person who will do it, not a committee. It doesn't happen by magic but by painful effort.

We agonized over the content of our first question and answer flier. We worked late at night to get mailings out — after typing them, getting them reproduced, buying stamps, folding, stuffing, sealing, stamping. We learned more than we had ever wanted to know about cheap printing places. We learned to use do-it-yourself type face from the art store to make professional display headings. We scrounged and dug into our pockets to pay bills. We learned to gauge our needs so that about the time we ran out of fliers, the situation had changed and a revision was needed anyway. We grappled with technical jargon, researched, read, thought, talked. And we learned to hold a telephone for hours.

Not dramatic or exciting, those nuts and bolts details. But important all along the way — from the first hearing through the last demonstration. Good ideas will get you nowhere, we found out, if there's nobody to do the work. And it was worth it. Our handout material looked respectable; it was carefully researched; it helped us get donations, influence new volunteers, sway public opinion, inform officials and reporters.

We set up phone chains, with phone captains responsible for calling ten or more people assigned from those index cards, to let them know about public hearings, meetings, letter writing needs. We put up card tables on street corners to collect petition signatures and to sell protransit anti-highway buttons. We visited elected officials, wrote to them, called them, being polite and persistent and informative. We organized a few big rallies. We wrote letters to the editors of newspapers. And we worked to keep informed about different aspects of the issue. All of this continues today.

A young law student provided valuable, carefully researched studies showing more jobs and less energy waste in our transit alternative. Other volunteers helped research legal issues. Others opened their homes for fund raisers, baked brownies for cake sales, organized flea markets (a sure way to raise $1,000–$3,000 we learned). Others spent cold and lonely Saturdays at street corner tables, getting barrages of letters to wavering politicians. Others spoke on the radio or television.

Nobody emerged as "boss." Each of us did what he or she felt equipped to do. There are lawyers who performed heroically despite the lack of pay. There are many unpaid or underpaid men and women with expert knowledge of air or water quality, or traffic issues. There are unsung heroes like the retired printer with an indefatigable urge to inform his politicians on the issue; the artist with a genius for dramatic events and sign making; the man who pushed fund raising efforts; the couple who organized street table activities; the woman who has lent her office for a central clearing house where files are kept and where the press can call for information, and who has provided invaluable written summaries that translate difficult or technical information for us all.

The center shifts as the problems and issues shift; strategies evolve out of phone conversations among the people most interested in the matter at hand. Sometimes it would be easier to have a boss. Consensus is difficult at times, but we've stuck together through the siren songs that might have divided us.

As conditions in the subways worsen, as energy shortages cause more hardships, as more and more people get the message about how trade-in can improve life in New York, the opposition grows. Newspaper and television polls have found that citizens favor mass transit by a two-to-one ratio when presented the choice between Westway and mass transit. More than fifty city, state, and federal elected officials have joined several hundred community and environmental groups in opposing Westway. Some of the real estate developers and business people who supported Westway have recently begun favoring a more expeditious solution. If law, reason, right, and the public will prevailed, Westway would be dead by now. The final decision to build Westway or trade it for the environmentally sound alternative rests with the Governor, who has remained adamant in his support of the project, and with New York City's mayor, who has been influenced by the Governor.

But we're holding our own, and we have hope. We've made mistakes and opportunities have slipped by because the volunteer help simply wasn't on the spot at the critical time. We've learned a lot about fighting an interstate highway, and some of the lessons are these:

- You're right to be suspicious; get organized and get moving quickly.
- Don't be lulled into thinking "public participation" exercises mean your voice will be heeded.
- Don't wait for anybody else to save you, especially politicians. If you build a bandwagon they'll ride with you.
- Search out a good lawyer and figure out how to pay him or her.
- Persevere, dig in your heels, show them you're there to stay.
- Don't be bamboozled by stacks of data and computer studies that highway promoters spew out.
- Don't be intimidated by experts; they're usually expert in just one thing; you have a broader feeling for your community's needs. Search out your own technical resources.
- Don't expect to win just because you're right. Reason, intelligent analysis, and ironclad logic will get you nowhere if you don't have strong citizen support. Only broad public support will attract political support, and this is a political battle.
- Discourage credit-grabbers and ego-trippers who want to use the issue for personal reasons.
- Be wary of compromisers and beware of flank attacks.
- Pitch in and do what comes to hand; nobody is too good to stuff envelopes; if you wait for the perfect job or the perfect time, it'll be too late.
- COMMUNICATE! Let your allies know everything you know, pass the word, tell those wonderful and heart-warming stories, chit-chat about the happenings, keep on that telephone.
- *Discuss it with everybody* — at parties, at family gatherings, at the grocery store, at the office. You never know where the spark might catch.
- Enjoy it! You'll never meet a nicer bunch of people than dedicated volunteers, men and women who put the common good before their personal advancement.

Many Happy Returns

by Ross Pumfrey

During the 1970s, few issues generated as much spending and lobbying as the fierce political battle over returnable beverage containers. Since 1976, $6.4 million has been spent by opposing industries to fight state initiatives which would require refundable beer and soft drink containers. More than that has been spent in state legislative battles and relevant national image-making campaigns.

Efforts to pass such laws have been made in Congress and in almost all fifty states. Five state legislatures have responded favorably. Oregon was first in 1971, and has been joined by Vermont, Iowa, Connecticut, and Delaware (laws in the latter two states are not in effect yet). Some citizens have gone the initiative route, emerging victorious two out of nine times — in Michigan and Maine.

After the Oregon enactment, the state's attorney general commented: "I have never seen as much pressure exerted by so many vested interests against a single bill."

Coalitions favoring deposit laws include farm bureaus, consumer groups, environmental organizations, the League of Women Voters, PTAs, the Urban League, sportsmen's clubs, associations of cities and counties, and labor groups representing bottling company employees, truckers, and retail clerks.

Purveyors of throwaway containers take a jaundiced view of this coalition. The Chairman of the Board of the American Can Company claimed that these efforts were part of a "communist conspiracy."

What are the elements and implications of the container debate which have brought on such a confrontation?

A few years ago, all our soft drinks and beer came in returnable, refillable bottles. But the can industry, which grew up during World War II, supplying well-preserved beer and food to American soldiers around the globe, began looking for new postwar markets. They shifted to the domestic beer market, added soft drinks, and the container revolution began.

During the 1950s, inroads made by cans alarmed the glass bottle manufacturers, and in self defense they introduced the throwaway bottle. Concurrent with this new competition between bottles and cans came the realization that there were much higher profits for those who manufactured throwaway containers than for those who manufactured refillable containers: Why sell one refillable bottle to a bottling company when you could sell 20 throwaway bottles or cans instead?

In one '50s beverage company advertisement, two fishermen were shown enjoying a six-pack in their boat and throwing the cans overboard. Most Americans didn't realize the environmental and economic implications of this prodigious waste. Vance Packard, in this 1960 book, *The Waste Makers,* chronicled the passing of durability as a featured ethic in society and the coming of "voluptuous wastefulness." He pointed out a contemporary television advertisement inwhich a voice chanted, "You use it once and throw it away. . . . You use it once and throw it away." This attitude has been an important element in our economic system for at least a quarter century, which is why it is so politically sensitive.

The advent of frozen foods, for one, brought with it the increased need for packaging, and intensified the problems of municipal solid waste management. Because a package (bottle, can, wrapper, box, etc.) is incidental to the product actually desired and used by the consumer, it becomes waste almost immediately. Soft drinks and beer are probably the most popular grocery item in the U.S. In 1978 alone Americans purchased approximately 100 billion soft drink and beer containers. They threw away on estimated 68 billion of those, after refillable bottles and recycled aluminum cans are taken into account. That's an average of 310 containers for each man, woman, and child in the country.

Most of us would feel embarrassed to throw a can overboard today and even the beverage industry of the '70s—while pushing the "convenience" of no-return containers—would stop short of such brazenness. But that is an aesthetic attitude; mos   eople feel no related sense of responsibility about throwin their bottles and cans in the trash. "Properly disposed of" means out of sight, out of mind.

The past decade, though, has witnessed an increasing awareness of this wastefulness. Recycling has enjoyed en-

IT IS EASIER for a man to be loyal to his club than to his planet; the by-laws are shorter, and he is personally acquainted with the other members.

E.B. White

couraging, albeit uneven, growth. Most of this is due to individual citizens/consumers deciding to act more responsibly. Some has been due to certain industries, such as aluminum companies, foreseeing economic chickens coming home to roost in the form of scarcity, dependence on imports, and higher prices.

But continuing waste exposes two weaknesses in our economic system (and not just ours). One is the difficulty of reflecting "externalities" such as pollution and disposal costs in the pricing system. The other is that scarcity of a finite resource, in an historical sense, is reflected too late in the pricing system to do future generations much good.

Container deposit laws represent the first attempt to make the marketing system for a particular product establish a reverse gear to overcome those weaknesses. Beer and soft drink containers are not an arbitrary choice: bottlers and brewers have shown in the past that they can operate a refillable bottle system, and the cans are made of metals which are easily recycled.

Early in the Oregon debate, a maverick pro-bottle-bill grocer by the name of John Piacentini decided to test the opposition's contention that people would no longer bring the containers back. He offered Oregonians one half cent for each throwaway beer or soft drink container which they returned to one of his stores. (The scrap value of the aluminum just about covered his costs.) Piacentini reports: "In 14 days, Oregonians returned over 3.5 million containers to our stores. . . . This was a message from Oregonians that something had to be done about this senseless littering of containers."

Those pushing the Oregon law used litter as their principal argument. Since then, proponents have analyzed nonreturnable containers in terms of energy, raw materials, waste disposal, consumer costs, and employment. A look at these issues is instructive; the beverage container system furnishes us with insights into the trade-offs involved when we are tempted into "convenience."

Litter

The current market for beverage containers, as stated earlier, is substantial. Of the 100 billion soft drink and beer containers purchased in 1978, 55 billion held soft drinks. Of those, 38 percent were returnable (and refillable) bottles, 29 percent were nonreturnable bottles, and 33 percent were cans.

Of the 45 billion beer containers sold, 12 percent were returnable bottles (mostly for use by bars), 23 percent were nonreturnable bottles, and 65 percent were cans.

Estimates vary as to what percentage of litter is represented by these beverage containers: studies made by several states show a range of between 15 percent and 46 percent. In urban areas, the figure may be slightly lower, and along highways, slightly higher.

Analysts agree that the only larger litter category is paper products. Although certainly not more attractive, most paper products are biodegradeable and are unlikely to cause injuries or damage. On the other hand, an aluminum can takes about 140 years to degrade, a steel can 100 years, and a glass bottle almost forever. Because of injuries and damage, bicyclists are among the groups that feel antipathy toward container litter.

Litter pick-up is not done for free by leprechauns. Taxpayers pay for it. California's department of transportation spends $4 million each year, just picking up highway litter.

A deposit system offers two lines of defense against litter: if the consumer chooses to forego the refund and litter a container, the incentive remains for a passerby to claim it.

Experience indicates that this has a significant effect. Highway studies have been done in several deposit states. In Oregon, three studies offer figures of between 66% and 83% for container litter reduction. In Vermont the reduction was 76%, in Michigan 82%, and in Maine 78%.

Estimates of the reduction in *overall* litter in Oregon range from 11% (based on item counts, in which a cigarette, a paper bag, and a half-quart bottle all count the same) to 47% (on a volume basis). The Michigan and Maine transportation departments report 41% and 32%, respectively.

Vermont highway officials reported a first year savings for taxpayers of $78,000, Maine reported a $146,000 savings, and a Wayne Country (Michigan) parks superintendent, terming the results "fantastic," predicted a $300,000 savings just for this one agency.

Energy

Energy savings are a factor which has drawn increasing attention as a deposit law benefit. Seven studies have been made on the energy implications of an all-returnable system — five by federal agencies, one by the Advanced Center for Computation at the University of Illinois, and one by the Wharton School of Business (commissioned by one of the deposit concept's most active opponents, the United States Brewers Association). All concluded that a deposit law would cause the beverage container system, from extraction of raw materials through distribution and return, to experience a measurable reduction in its use of energy. The most extensive of the studies, by the Federal Energy Administration (now the Department of Energy), predicted a 44 percent reduction in energy use by that system.

A few aspects of the system, such as the returning of containers, require additional expenditures of energy, but the system as a whole results in substantial energy savings. The aluminum companies, for instance, contend that they use 95 percent less energy to make a can out of recycled aluminum than to make it from virgin materials.

"In Oregon, energy conservation through can recycling gets a special boost from the state 'bottle bill'," according to a 1978 article in *The Christian Science Monitor*. Aluminum company officials in the Northwest are now commenting favorably on the return rates in Oregon, because they are concerned about the prices which they will have to pay for energy when their contracts with the Bonneville Power Administration are renegotiated in the near future.

In absolute terms, the energy savings resulting from a national deposit law would be in the neighborhood of 225 trillion BTUs per year, or equivalent to 75,000 barrels of oil per day (the actual savings would be spread among oil, coal, nuclear, natural gas, and hydroelectricity).

Resource Conservation

In 1977, Americans threw away 5.2 million tons of glass, 1.5 million tons of steel, and 500,000 tons of aluminum in the form of beverage containers.

Environmental impact occurs both at the beginning and end of the process. Not only was this material dug up from where it was naturally, but it must be buried somewhere else.

STANDING HERE in the deep, brooding silence all the wilderness seems motionless, as if the work of creation were done. But in the midst of this outer steadfastness we know there is incessant motion and change. Ever and anon, avalanches are falling from yonder peaks. These cliff-bound glaciers, seemingly wedged and immovable, are flowing like water and grinding the rocks beneath them. The lakes are lapping their granite shores and wearing them away, and every one of these rills and young rivers is fretting the air into music, and carrying the mountains to the plains. Here are the roots of all the life of the valleys, and here more simply than elsewhere is the eternal flux of nature manifested. Ice changing to water, lakes to meadows and mountains to plains.

John Muir

We have no imminent worldwide shortage of silica/sand (the principal component of glass bottles), bauxite (four tons of bauxite go into the manufacture of one ton of aluminum), or iron ore (the principal component of steel), but such assurances may no longer be an excuse for dismissing other supply-related problems. Sand is strip-mined, and there are now proposals to dredge sand off the New England coast. The environmental impact of these processes is significant. Nearly 90 percent of our bauxite is imported, placing us at the mercy of foreign nations' pricing and taxing policies. Nearly 30 percent of our steel is currently imported. The Department of the Interior has warned that our heavy dependence on other countries for much of our mineral supplies is creating a serious balance of payments problem.

Oregon consumers are returning more than 94 percent of their bottles and 80 percent of their cans. In Vermont, both bottles and cans are being returned at a rate higher than 90 percent. Nationwide return rates such as these would have a dramatic effect on our need to extract raw materials from the earth. With this in mind, the National Commission on Supplies and Shortages, established under President Ford, recommended that Congress pass a national deposit law.

Water is another resource used in the manufacture of glass, aluminum, steel, and the containers; an all-returnable system would reduce water use in these industries by between 44 percent and 69 percent, according to the President's Resource Recovery Committee.

That committee, with nine cabinet-level representatives, split on recommending a national deposit law, with a plurality of four favoring the concept, two opposed, two calling for further study, and one member abstaining.

Waste Disposal

In 1977, Americans spent a staggering $7.5 billion, through taxes or user fees, disposing of their municipal waste — a municipal service price tag second only to education. Areas suitable for landfills are becoming scarcer every month.

Waste disposal was rated the *most serious* municipal problem — above crime, housing, public transit, and other — in a 1974 poll of mayors and city council members conducted by the National League of Cities. Disposable packaging is the fastest growing component of this waste, with soft drink and beer containers comprising between 5% and 7%.

Economics

We're paying for the extra energy, glass, aluminum, steel and water which go into a disposable container system. More than half the cost of a bottle of beer is just for the bottle if it is non-refillable, according to a study made for *Brewing Industry Review*. Soft drinks cost 30 percent more per ounce in throwaways than in returnable/refillable bottles.

Requiring refunds for all soft drink and beer containers will tend to push the non-refillable bottles out of the market, thus reducing the average price paid by those who prefer bottles. Those who prefer cans will enjoy some long-term protection against the type of inflation caused by the otherwise constant need to dig up more and more bauxite and iron ore (espeically when it is imported) and to process the bauxite into aluminum.

The Federal Energy Administration study predicted that savings to American consumers would total $1.8 billion annually by 1982 under a deposit system.

One of the nation's leading Pepsi-Cola bottlers, Arthur Arundel, recently joined the proponents, stating: "We believe it is in the best interests of the American consumer, and in the long run will be in the best interests of our industry. Once in a while we have to put principle before a buck."

Jobs

Under a mandatory deposit system, new jobs would be created in the bottling company plants, in the distribution segment, and in retail stores. Some jobs would probably be lost in the glass- and bottle-making industries, as fewer bottles are made under a refillable system. The degree of loss would be dependent on how fast other business for botttle makers grows as the soft-drink and beer bottle market declines.

Much debate surrounds the speculations about the impact on metal and can industry employees. Although bottles are simply refilled at the bottling plant, the metal from cans is recycled. This means that the savings in resources and energy are accomplished without any loss in jobs in the metals or can companies, if the volume of beer and soft drinks sold in cans does not decrease.

For several years, the aluminum and steel industries, and can companies, were unanimous in predicting disaster as a result of deposit laws. Their predictions were partly a scare tactic, persuading employees that they were likely to get laid off. Steelworkers have testified against proposals which they believed literally "banned the can." During the 1975 debate over enactment of a container law in Massachusetts, a can company official testified that his company would have to close down if the bill passed. The bill failed, and the company shut down anyway.

Part of the industry's fear was based on what happened in Oregon; the initial reaction to that state's deposit law was an 80 percent drop in the use of cans. Opponents of deposit legislation claimed that consumers wouldn't purchase cans under a deposit system; supporters claimed that the beverage industry itself stopped offering cans (partly because the can manufacturers weren't prepared when a simultaneous ban on "pull-tabs" was implemented). Both sides agreed that a provision of the Oregon law encouraging standardized bottles (by means of a lower deposit) was a factor.

Cans have since made a gradual comeback in Oregon, and opinion is shifting. The Coors Brewing Company contends that it can continue to sell its share of cans under a deposit law if no particular container is favored in the law. Alcoa Aluminum Company made a dramatic move late in 1977 when it changed from adamant opposition to neutrality. In an internal memorandum, an officer of the Continental Group (can-makers) maintained that cans would not suffer any losses under a deposit law, although the company was urged to continue its opposition to any legislative action.

Considering the testimony given by these companies and the labor unions in past years, these changes in attitude by members of industry should have a significant effect on the debate during the next couple of years.

Several studies of the overall impact of a deposit system on employment have been made both nationally and in various states. All, including two studies based on actual experience in Oregon, have concluded that returnables result in a net increase in jobs. Estimates included net gains of 30,000 jobs (Department of Commerce study), 118,000 (Federal Energy Administration), and 138,000 (Wharton School of Business).

A correlative to these conclusions is the measurable *decrease* in employment in the beer and soft drink industries during the past 20 years, while consumption has increased dramatically and those industries have shifted to throwaway containers. The lower relative costs of transportation under a non-returnable system are an incentive for beverage companies to consolidate their operations and eliminate local or regional bottling plants. The soft drink industry, largely a franchise system, has done this to a lesser degree, but the brewing industry has consolidated considerably. In 1958 there were 765 breweries in the United States, but by 1974 only 99 remained. The Department of Commerce reports that employment in the brewing industry decreased by 26,300 from 1958 to 1974.

"Returnable bottles create more jobs," says Anthony Sapienza, president of a brewery and soft drink workers' union in Cleveland, Ohio. An active supporter of deposit legislation both in Ohio and nationally for several years, he has watched the number of breweries in his area decline from 18 to one as the industry switched to throwaways.

Traditionally the AFL–CIO, representing glass, steel, and aluminum workers, has strenuously opposed deposit proposals. Only the retail clerks have challenged from within the nation's largest labor federation. But a more serious chink in the armor appeared in 1979, when the Maine AFL–CIO refused to support a repeal of that state's deposit law. The statewide labor group stated that workers had experienced no negative effects anywhere in the New England area as a result of the law.

The Opposition and Its Arguments

Opposition to deposit legislation is made up of the US Brewers' Association, the National Soft Drink Association, major steel and aluminum companies (with the recent defection of Alcoa), the Glass Packaging Institute, the Can Manufacturers Institute, the AFL–CIO (the brunt of its attack carried by the United Steelworkers and the glass bottle makers), beer distributors, grocers, and retail liquor dealers.

They use a variety of arguments against deposit laws. The most general objection is that a returnable container system would deprive the consumer of the freedom of choice and convenience claimed to be associated with the present system. Proponents of deposits respond that returnable beer bottles are not generally available and that a deposit system would add that economical package to the shelf while maintaining the option to buy cans. They add that the consumer has the choice of throwing a returnable away, but pays for it by giving up the refund; if a consumer chooses to act responsibly and return the container, it is more convenient to return it to his or her neighborhood store than to take it to a recycling center.

As mentioned earlier, the threat of job layoffs is usually a powerful argument. Sometimes a net job gain is conceded, but the contention is then made that all new jobs are low paid and result in a net decline in total payroll. Studies by the FEA and Congress do not bear this out.

In regard to energy and resource questions, the opposition takes certain sectors of the system out of context (energy in the distribution sector, water in the bottle washing process) to imply that a returnable system is wasteful, when net figures prove the contrary.

Retailers predict that a deposit system would create unmanageable storage and sanitation problems. It is clear that returnables would present retailers with additional and unrequested responsibilities; the debate revolves around whether they are manageable. Proponents point out that retailers have dealt with returnables for many years. A poll of Oregon grocers taken by Progressive Grocer, a trade publication, indicated that a majority would not favor the repeal of that state's deposit law. The executive secretary of the Vermont Retail Grocers' Association estimated that 95% of Vermont's grocers, after some adjustments, now favor the law. Thelobbyist who represented that association in fighting the proposal in the early 1970s has also changed his mind and testified in favor of a California law in 1979.

The Opposition's "Alternatives"

For the most obvious problems of litter and waste, opponents maintain that deposit legislation identifies "the right problem — but the wrong solution." They favor education, litter law enforcement, and more comprehensive litter pickup programs, contending that beverage containers are not a significant enough portion of the litter stream to justify singling them out. They favor current recycling efforts and the development of high-technology resource-recovery facilities, which would process municipal waste to recover some materials and produce energy fuels from the organic portion.

Proponents contend that there is not yet a commercial method of removing either glass or aluminum from mixed municipal waste, and that any such method would be energy-intensive.

In states where the passage of a deposit law seems within reach of proponents, opponents have designed proposals which they considered an alternative — taxing portions or all of the business community in order to increase litter pickup and help fund recycling and resource recovery. They have thus been pressured into paying attention to solid waste management, but are attempting to avoid an internalized system of waste reduction.

These alternative proposals are very sophisticated political instruments and have passed in eight states. The most ambitious was a "litter tax" passed in California in 1977: it taxed manufacturers, wholesalers, and retailers to the tune of $20 million per year. According to deposit advocate Omer Rains, a California State Senator, "It offers everything except the kitchen sink, when the whole purpose of the deposit concept is to offer the kitchen sink. A deposit provides an incentive to prevent littering in the first place, and to utilize the existing distribution system."

This point often gets lost as legislators scramble away from a controversial deposit bill to take refuge in a tax for which the business community "volunteers". Connecticut legislators called everyone's bluff and voted for both a deposit bill and for the "tax-to-clean-up" approach.

But the post-Proposition 13 atmosphere may hurt the credibility of some of these "alternatives". In Colorado the legislature allowed the industry-sponsored litter law to "self-destruct" after only two years.

In California, the "litter tax" which deposit opponents contended was "equitable" and welcomed by the business community bombed in 1979 when assessments went out and legislators were hit with what the Los Angeles *Times* described as a "storm of protest". The tax was quickly repealed and the general fund tapped. As 1980 approached, it appeared that criticisms of the litter program as an ineffective "hype" would result in a change of direction for California's litter law.

In a surprising display of unity, the President's Resource Conservation Committee recommended unanimously against the "litter tax" approach. Regardless of the substantive merits of variations on it, most solid waste experts agree that there is nothing incompatible between it and a deposit law, despite industry protests.

Subtly operating in the background of the battle over "alternatives" are industry front groups such as the national Keep America Beautiful organization and various affiliated state anti-litter leagues. These efforts draw the assistance of

---

ONE OF THE BEST WAYS of avoiding necessary and even urgent tasks is to seem to be busily employed on things that are already done.

J.K. Galbraith

---

otherwise innocent citizens into admirable litter pick-up projects and educational campaigns against littering, while carefully posing no threat to the continuation of throwaway containers.

Keep America Beautiful slipped its cover in 1976 when its chairman, William May (also chairman of the American Can Company), called on all members to crusade against the "communist" deposit proposals.

Legislative and Initiative Battles

The opposition "plays hard and for keeps," as a *Reader's Digest* editor commented in a 1976 article. The various opposition interests work separately on different legislators but also form coalitions, especially for initiative battles. They give them names such as Nebraskans for Freedom of Choice, the Consumer Information Committee, the Committee to Protect Jobs and the Use of Convenience Containers, and the Maine Citizens for Litter Control and Recycling.

These coalitions are able to coordinate the opposition's approaches to legislatures and the media. They mount effective campaigns by marshalling substantial financial resources and motivating their members with predictions of disaster. Deposit law support groups tend to be public interest organizations which seldom make deposit legislation their top priority. It is difficult for them to match the opposition's directed intensity. Consequently, most efforts to enact deposit laws have failed.

Tired of battling for legislative votes with sophisticated lobbyists—and eyeing public opinion polls which usually showed 70 to 80 percent support for container laws — proponents in some states have taken the initiative route. In seven different state elections they easily obtained the requisite signatures, took commanding leads in the polls until one month before the election, and then watched in frustrated horror as some of the most expensive campaigns in initiative history stole their leads in the last month. Television, radio, and newspaper ads, along with brochures handed out in grocery stores to all consumers, trumpeted the opposition's arguments. Outspent by professional campaign managers and public relations experts by margins as high as 60–1, deposit advocates have found themselves in the cold on election day. Deposit initiatives lost in Washington in 1970, in Massachusetts and Colorado in 1976, in Nebraska and Alaska in 1978, and in Ohio and Washington (again) in 1979.

The closest initiative loss was in Massachusetts in 1976, when a student-led campaign lost by less than one percent. A determined group of statewide supporters then returned to the legislature, where after two years of tie votes in the Senate, they were successful in passing a bill, only to have it vetoed by Governor Ed King. Newspaper editorials attacked the Governor for his special interest ties, and citizens are trying again in 1980.

Despite these setbacks, deposit advocates in Maine and Michigan organized well in 1976 and came within a one-to-15 ratio of their opponents' spending, and saw their initiatives succeed. Michigan is considered particularly significant because it is the most industrial and labor-oriented state to pass such a law. The United Auto Workers, a larger federation of unions than the AFL–CIO in that state, remained neutral in the debate.

In 1979 the Maine law was threatened by a repeal initiative organized by a group of beverage distributors and merchants. Labor opposed the repeal along with several prominent businesses, and Maine citizens, who had had a container deposit law for nearly two years, gave it a resounding 84% vote of confidence.

Meanwhile, supporters in some states have made their mark at the local level. So far, a dozen cities or counties have passed ordinances mandating returnable containers.

In Canada, a majority of the provinces have implemented deposit legislation. Friends of the Earth in Great Britain is leading the fight in that nation for such a law.

The National Scene and Outlook for the 80s

In Congress, the campaign to ban throwaways has been led by Senators Mark Hatfield (R-Oregon) and Bob

Packwood (R-Oregon) in the Senate and by Representative James Jefford (R-Vermont) in the House. Bills in both houses have been mired in committee since 1974.

"We think that a national law is still two or three years away," states Mark Sullivan, a lobbyist for the National Wildlife Federation, one of the most active supporting organizations. "We need to have another large state pass a bill."

Environmental Action, headquartered in Washington, D.C., has been the most active group. One of its lobbyists, Sandie Nelson, runs the four-year old National Clearinghouse on Deposit Legislation, which serves deposit proponents running state campaigns throughout the nation, making available studies and testimonies and cross-pollinating the accumulated wisdom.

A Montana initiative campaign is being planned for 1980, and Nelson predicts an imminent legislative victory in at least one New England state. Deposit law proponents around the nation are convinced that they will eventually win the long hard battle. The Coors Brewing Company suggests that it is "inevitable."

Henry King, president of the US Brewers' Association, discussed deposit legislation at a beer wholesalers' convention in 1976: "They think they can wait us out. I'm suggesting that if we stick together, they won't wait us out."

But the apostasy of Coors, Falstaff, Alcoa, and some soft drink bottlers scattered around the country must give King cause to wonder.

Deposit supporters are fond of referring to a 1975 column by conservative columnist James Kilpatrick, endorsing their efforts. Kilpatrick ended his comments with:

Some day, thousands of years hence, archaeologists from a distant galaxy may stumble over the dead planet Earth. "Alighting from their spacecraft, they would explore what obviously had been roads and highways, and they would be puzzled by millions of identical small green artifacts.

"The archaeologists would take these to be symbols of the religion practiced by the vanished race of Americans. No deposit, no return. Surely, it would seem to me, our civilization could leave something more meaningful behind."

1980 Is the Year of the Coast

by Elizabeth Kaplan

America's 88,000 miles of coastline are now exploited to the limits of their capacity. The bluffs, beaches, bays, and rich estuaries that provided food, recreation, habitat for wildlife, and constantly changing patterns of beauty cannot continue to absorb the pressures of humanity's voracious use. It has become increasingly clear that the 1972 Coastal Zone Management Act has done little to slow the degradation of the coast and that more must be done to save what is left of our unspoiled shoreline.

In 1979, several national environmental groups formed the Coast Alliance, a coalition that would bring about new initiatives for the coastline of America—Atlantic, Gulf, Pacific, and Great Lakes. The Alliance named Friends of the Earth's Rafe Pomerance as chairman and launched an unprecedented agenda for saving the coast, beginning in 1980, which was designated the Year of the Coast.

Since then, the Coast Alliance has grown to include labor, fishing, urban and scientific groups.

The Alliance's goals are:

- To inform the public of the immense value of the coast and its resources, and the need for rescuing it from further degradation;
- To encourage groups and individuals across the country to work for the protection of coastal resources and to promote beneficial uses of the coast;
- To encourage local, state, and federal governments to strengthen protection for coastal ecosystems;
- To protect human life and the public purse by discouraging private development and public investment in coastal flood and erosion-prone areas;
- To encourage public access to coastal resources.

The national campaign has recharged the energies of those veterans who have been fighting coastal battles for years and has drawn in new recruits to the effort—and it has heightened public awareness that the coast is in serious trouble and urgently needs our attention. In many states— Mississippi, Alaska and Maine, for instance—new state-level Coast Alliances have sprung up. Veteran organizations like California's Coastal Alliance, which has been in the vanguard for years, are taking new strength from the national campaign.

Year of the Coast provides an opportunity to finish old business and launch new efforts. It is a year when we hope that Marine Sanctuaries will be established around the Santa Barbara Channel Islands and at Point Reyes and Monterey Bay, California, all areas incredibly rich in marine mammals and bird life. During 1980, passage of the Barrier Islands bill could save St. Phillips, a magnificent undeveloped barrier island off North Carolina from subdivision at the hands of noted developer Charles Turner. The last of the world's Bowhead whales, threatened by oil and gas development in the Beaufort Sea, off northern Alaska, could receive Marine Sanctuary protection. Winter navigation could be banned on the Great Lakes. The possibilities are exciting—and a little overwhelming.

More than ever, grassroots folk must take the lead in making things happen for the environment, as they influence their public officials at all levels. Problems with the coast are primarily land-use problems. In large part, they must be addressed through local zoning ordinances, state implementation of the Coastal Zone Management (CZM) program, the regional decisions of the Environmental Protection Agency in granting permits, and local decisions on whether to dredge or not, build jetties or not, enforce pollution laws or not. There will be no quick fix from Washington for the problems of the coast, but the Alliance can provide vital resource information, contacts with knowledgable people on a variety of issues, names of other people in one's area working on these issues, ideas for Year of the Coast projects and advice on how to organize around local issues.

The National Agenda: Legislation

The Coast Alliance's legislative package comprises a five-year agenda. First to move will be amendments to the Coastal Zone Management Act, which must be reauthorized in 1980. Twenty of the 35 coastal states and territories have approved CZM plans and are beginning to implement them. The quality of these plans varies considerably, and more citizen involvement is urgently needed in the struggle to develop strong local and regional plans within the state plans. (If you can help organize support in your state or district, send a postcard to Elizabeth Kaplan, at FOE's Washington, DC, office, 530 Seventh Street, SE, Washington, DC 20003).

Barrier islands, like St. Phillips, mentioned above, were an item on the coast agenda early in 1980, as well. Representative Phillip Burton held hearings in late March on a bill to prevent federal subsidies to development on barrier islands, and early in the year, the Interior Department released a long-awaited study on barrier islands.

The Alliance's legislative initiatives also include protecting fish habitat (against pollution, developments like oil drilling, and other threats; fisheries laws and regulations already protect many species from overfishing); increasing funds for access and transportation to coastal recreation areas; improving flood insurance and disaster relief programs; using tax measures to discourage development in critical coastal areas; and increasing funds to redevelop waterfronts in coastal cities.

Federal Programs

In his August, 1979, Environmental Message, President Carter directed the National Oceanic and Atmospheric Administration to conduct a review of federal programs to ascertain which (if any) are fostering harmful development in the coast. FOE staffers are working closely with NOAA on the study. They have recommended that NOAA look at the following programs:

1. Corps of Engineers Erosion Control Project, in which millions are spent on bulkheads, jetties and replenishing beaches each year to the detriment of natural beach systems vital to the health of the coast;

2. Outer Continental Shelf leasing program, specifically the stipulations for environmental safeguards and the adequacy of monitoring for the health of the ecosystem in lease areas;

3. Federal disaster relief and flood insurance programs that encourage repeated development in flood plains;

4. Environmental Protection Agency's construction grants program for sewage treatment plants, which can encourage development in coastal areas;

5. Economic development grants programs and highway grants programs which may violate the President's Executive Orders requiring that federal dollars not be spent

to fill wetlands or encourage development in floodplains;

6. The Forest Service's clear-cutting practices in the Pacific Northwest, where lumbering along streams is silting up vital salmon spawning streams.

In addition, FOE staff and others are meeting with the heads of major federal agencies such as the Park Service, NOAA, EPA, and the Fish and Wildlife Service to suggest specific actions these agencies can take during 1980 that would enhance the protection of coastal resources and the public's awareness of the importance of the coast to our quality of life.

Littoral Facts

- There are about 88,000 miles of US coastline including the Great Lakes. Alaska's coastline makes up about a third of the total.
- Sixty percent of the US population lives in counties bordering the coast, and the number is expected to rise to 75 percent by 1990.
- Two thirds of edible fish species spend part of their lives in coastal estuaries.
- In 1976, six billion pounds of fish and shellfish, worth more than $5.5 billion, were harvested by more than 250,000 American fishermen.
- Between 1966 and 1975, $226 in potential revenue was lost when pollution forced the closure of shellfish harvesting grounds.
- More than 100 new fossil fuel and nuclear plants are scheduled to be built in coastal areas by 1995. The new Energy Mobilization Board may speed this schedule considerably.
- Routine flushing of tankers accounts for three fourths of the oil that goes into the ocean each year.
- Today's total annual harvest of Chesapeake Bay oysters is only half what it was a century ago.
- Between 1954 and 1978, it is estimated that 100,000 acres of wetlands were lost annually, or a total of 36 percent of the nation's wetlands.
- California has lost 75 percent of its wetlands since 1900.

The Alliance is planning a Crisis Center to house up-dated information that citizens can use for help in responding to crises such as oil spills, fish kills, dredging and filling of wetlands. The center will provide immediate access to organizations, scientists, press, lawyers, and economists who could be helpful in meeting such crises. During 1980 the Alliance plans to hold regional conferences with local groups on specific regional coastal issues, culminating in a documented analysis of the state of the coast by the end of 1980.

Suggestions
Here are some ideas that you can work on in your state:

• Bring together activist groups to form a Coast Alliance for political activity during 1980.

• Develop a strategy for protecting 10 percent of your state's coastline during 1980, including acquisition, management and easements.

• Find out if your state or locality has any dune protection ordinances. If not, information on this can be obtained from the American Littoral Society (201) 291–0055, which is working on such an ordinance for New Jersey.

• If your state has an approved CZM plan, get involved in its implementation. Find out if your state is actually going to protect "areas of particular concern." Help shape the local and regional plans. Contact FOE's Northwest Office (4512 University Way, NE, Seattle, WA 98105) for advice in this area.

• Develop a network of coast watchers to keep an eye on development, oil spills, dredging, filling, and permitting processes, and to alert others for quick response to crises. A model was devised by the Barrier Islands Workshop. For details and assistance, contact the Coast Alliance, at FOE Washington, DC

• Find out what procedures your regional Army Corps of Engineers office uses to give permits for filling in wetland areas. You might discover that they are overburdened with applications and are processing them on a rubber stamp basis.

• If you are in a high hazard area, flood insurance, Small Business Loans and disaster relief may be costing instead of providing dollars to rebuild in flood-prone areas.

Gather information from your regional Small Business Administration and Flood Insurance Agency offices and build a case. Work with the Alliance to change both regulations and legislation governing these program.

• Survey your region to see how accessible the beaches are. Pressure local and state officials to remedy shortages.

For more specific ideas, order "202 Questions for the Endangered Coastal Zone" ($1.00, from the American Littoral Society, Sandy Hook, Highlands, NJ 07732).

For more information on the Year of the Coast, write the Coast Alliance, 918 F St. NW, Washington, DC 20004.

The Key to Legislative Success: Electoral Politics

It's a frosty, Saturday morning when two cars pull up to incumbent Supervisor A. F. Tower's campaign headquarters on Irving Street. Parked, the car doors swing open and nine people pile out, some rubbing their hands together and all breathing out white plumes.

They enter the office and identify themselves. They're environmentalists and they've come to lend Tower—who is a strong supporter of local environmental causes—a hand in her reelection bid.

For the next eight hours, they'll stuff envelopes, answer phones, type letters, call constituents, or walk precincts.

And for the next two years while Tower is in office, their help will be remembered.

It's 1980, election year. And the name of the game, like it or not, is electoral politics.

This and similar scenarios are being played out in cities, counties, and congressional districts across the country. Besides the political pinnacle of the White House, election day 1980 will determine the occupants of a whole slew of public offices.

Up for grabs will be the entire House of Representatives, one-third of the Senate, 13 governorships, and innumerable state and local posts. Voters will also decide the fate of numerous ballot initiatives, from bottlebills to nuclear waste controls.

Behind each of those races and ballot propositions is a campaign. And the moving force behind any successful political campaign, besides a well-stocked chest of money, is people. Volunteers. The grassroots.

In other words, in a healthy democracy where citizens participate and are not just led by government, the fate of each of those races rests in our hands.

"Politicians are not oriented to specific issues, nor even to the structure of government. Rather, they are oriented to people—the people who are going to put them back in office during the next election," says Carl Pope, head of the Sierra Club Committee on Political Education and director of the California League of Conservation Voters.

286

"They thus see their jobs as satisfying the people," he says, "specifically those segments of the public that are most involved in the electoral process, who have the loudest voice."

Pope believes in the electoral process—a system that by his own admission sometimes includes deception, blatant pretension, and disgusting displays of greed and power-grabbing.

The rationale is that it's all we have. And according to a recent poll, he is joined by almost three-fourths of the Sierra Club's members in thinking that the system, no matter how stodgy, is flexible enough to solve even the most serious flaws in our society.

Participating in that system, however, is far from being a favorite American pastime. According to Common Cause, two-thirds of Americans eligible to vote don't do so regularly.

Half can't name their representative. Nine out of ten are unable to identify anything their representative has ever done. Almost no one can cite any policy their representative espouses.

Even these statistics are lofty when compared to the number of citizens who get directly involved in the electoral process.

Politics is dirty business, the consensus also rings, best left in the hands of dirty politicians. Many public interest groups additionally feel that politics are necessarily divisive and bad news for group cohesiveness. They also fear that to lose a political campaign will have serious political repercussions best avoided by not getting involved at all.

The resultant political inactivity produces an interesting phenomenon: the fewer people who are involved in the electoral process, the more political clout those people have.

While eventually destructive to a democracy, this phenomenon translates into the practical ability of a handful of volunteer campaign workers, united around one cause, to have a considerable effect on an official's policy stands.

Campaign volunteers, and the candidates they're working for, know that their help can be more valuable than even the largest legal dollar contribution.

For instance, the nine Tower volunteers, working at the equivalent pay of $4 per hour, for four eight-hour days (two weekends), contribute the equivalent of a $1152 campaign contribution, $152 more than the law allows for cash contributions.

Recognizable as environmentalists (perhaps by wearing buttons that read, "Environmentalists for Tower"), their help will usually be rewarded with an open door and a receptive ear.

A case in point is Representative Jim Weaver from Oregon. Weaver's successful 1978 reelection campaign was viewed as one of the most important election results for environmentalists in the country.

Weaver, who is a consistent and able supporter of environmental causes representing a district loaded with industry, faced stiff opposition from a forest industry backed candidate. It was help from local environmentalists that tipped the election in Weaver's favor.

"When a public-interest congressman like Jim runs for office, traditional sources of funds from the monied interests are simply not available," says Ron Eachus, a Weaver assistant in Eugene.

"Thus, help from environmentalists—in the form of both individual contributions and commitmentsof human resources—has been critical.

"You develop associations, working political relationships, with people helping in your campaign. And while it's not a direct, 'you gave me money so I'll listen to what you say' sort of thing, there is a bond that is developed that, if maintained after the election, proves to be very effective in creating access."

Ken Kramer, legislative chairperson for the Sierra Club's Lone Star Chapter, agrees. In a chapter newsletter article, he asks why his chapter has not been more successful in its legislative efforts.

"There are many reasons," he writes, "but one of the most important is the failure of many Sierrans in Texas to understand the linkage between legislative lobbying and election-year politics.

"In other words, a legislator is more likely to listen to your viewpoint during a legislative session if you helped to elect him to the legislature in the first place."

Up against the electoral process, environmentalists face a blunt choice. Will those legislative ears hear arguments for a better environment? Or will the "other side" fill the vacuum left by our political absence?

According to the same Club member poll, the consensus is resoundingly for the former. Nine out of ten members believe the Club should become significantly involved in elections for public office.

(Seven out of ten support publishing evaluations of candidates' environmental stands; the other two go so far as supporting Club endorsements or opposition to candidates.)

Only 4% of the Club membership believes there should be no political involvement.

Here, then, are some ways to participate.

Taking the Political Plunge

All members of Congress have a primary interest in being reelected. Some members have no other interests.

former Rep. Frank Smith

The same, it seems, is true for most public officials, from city council members to the President.

Getting a candidate to accept your help is the easy part. The challenge is to find the right candidate (or issue), and to organize your group to lend that support.

Here are some tips from politically active Club leaders and other persons familiar with the tricks of the trade.

The first move is to stock your working library with three publications—the Club's *Political Handbook*, Common Cause's *Who Runs Congess?*, and *How You Can Influence Congess* (see *For More Information*). All three contain vital information on a wide range of political techniques from preparing voting charts to Club policy on endorsing candidates.

For personal advice, there are two people to get to know: Carl Pope, coordinator of the Sierra Club Committee on Political Education (which monitors all of the Club's political activities) and Marion Edey, head of the League of ConservationVoters in Washington, D.C.

You may also want to contact the Federal Election Commission and your state registrar of voters for technical information.

Also, don't forget the candidates. Needless to say, they more than anyone need to know the rules of the game, and can advise you on many of its murkier miens.

Next, do a careful assessment of your resources (both

financial and human) and draw up a campaign strategy.
Here are some questions to ask yourself.

*How much money do you have? Can you hold fund
raising events? Can you solicit members for special donations?*

*How will you publicize your group's views? Will you
produce voting charts (tallies)? Candidate profiles? Chapter
newsletter articles? Press releases?*

*Are there other local groups working on the same elec-
tions? Any possibilities of coalitions?*

*After the election, assuming your candidate wins, who
will take charge of keeping in touch, and working with that
official? What other techniques will you use to ensure that
your presence is viewed as consistent (one on which the
official can count in the next election)?*

By focusing on just the amount of work your group
can handle, and by distributing the work load, what seems
like an insuperable endeavor becomes miraculously manageable.

John Holtzclaw, a Club leader in the San Francisco,
California, Group, has long been active in local environmental issues. He's a strong believer in the legislative/electoral
connection, and has decided to focus his electoral efforts on
several key city board of supervisor races.

After adding all the factors up (including the incumbents' voting records and the challengers' chances at victory), he and two other group leaders chose three races
(backing an incumbent in one, and challengers in the others)
and went to work.

First, they talked the matter over with other group
leaders. They then contacted the candidates and got their
commitments on some ten local environmental issues, including public transit and open space.

They then obtained a list of Club members in those
districts, looked up their telephone numbers, and started
calling.

BEWARE of all enterprises that require new
clothes.

Henry David Thoreau

The pitch went like this:

"As you know, a runoff election is coming up on Tuesday. The Sierra Club doesn't endorse candidates, but one of the candidates in your district, A. F. Tower, has taken environmental positions for better transit, limiting auto use . . . But her opponent is well funded and she needs your help in her campaign. . . . You may work in the office, or make phone calls, or walk a precinct, or hand out literature — daytime, evenings, or weekends. Can you help? If yes, when will you go to her campaign headquarters? When you go, please identify yourself as an environmentalist."

John, who works full time as a private consultant, and the others did not have time to draw up voting charts, or elaborate candidate profiles, or to do any special mailing to members.

But they did manage to contact a couple hundred Club members (at a roughly 50 percent committal rate), of which as many as 30 or 40 ended up volunteering.

The result? One loss (the incumbent, along with all but one of the other incumbents, was defeated) and two wins (the challengers they supported won handily).

"Our efforts paid off really well," says Holtzclaw, "and we're now thinking about setting up a local League of Conservation Voters to do even more visible electoral work."

What about the loss? "Well, it's true that he won't be terribly receptive to our views, but he never was. At least now he knows that we are a political force that, in order to stay in office, he'll have to deal with," Holtzclaw says.

Not all facets of election campaigns involve this degree of commitment. In fact, besides the initial organizing, the jobs that count most can be done with one eye shut—perfect for those capacious weekend afternoons.

"To do the work that is really necessary and appreciated," says Buck Parker, Club leader in Oregon and a six-year veteran of electoral politics, "you don't need any political experience whatsoever.

"When I'm working on a candidate's campaign, I often will be ringing doorbells, licking envelopes, stapling, packaging things up for bulk mailings, or sorting out envelopes for zip codes. Not exactly glamorous jobs, but these are the things that canidates need done and the things that they remember.

To volunteer is easy. Simply call up your candidate's campaign headquarters, ask their hours, and commit yourself. They'll be delighted.

A more effective volunteer tactic, however, is to do as the workers for Supervisor Tower did—assemble at a predesignated location, and show up enmasse at the headquarters as a unity of environmentalists.

This allows your group spokesperson to promise and deliver an impressive number of volunteer hours. And it gives your group added political clout.

If you are short on person hours, there's one last tool to wield—the mighty dollar.

"Environmentalists can't match the big dollar contributions that pour in from business and other special interests," says Carl Pope. "But the money we can raise, through fund raisers and individual donations, can be critical to a candidate's campaign. Just look at Jim Weaver."

There are two ways to supercharge your campaign contribution. First, be sure to take advantage of the tax laws. For every dollar up to 50 dollars (or 100 for a joint return) that you donate, the IRS will reimburse you for half by deducting it from your federal taxes.

Second, send along an explanation with your contribution. You might write, for example,

"I am so pleased with your support for the nuclear power moratorium legislation, S._____, that I am moved to make the enclosed donation to your reelection campaign . . ."

One last point is that politicians, and subsequently many of those involved in politics, take it all too seriously.

Politics is fun. It's social. It's people. Organizers and participants alike shouldn't worry about political events being too corny or loose. Just go out and do it.

For More Information

David Gardiner, Sierra Club, 530 Bush Street, San Francisco, California 94108; (415) 981–8634.

Marion Edey, League of Conservation Voters, 317 Pennsylvania Ave., S.E., Washington, D.C. 20003; (202) 547–7200.

(note: Marion can tell you if there is a local affiliated league in your state.)

Vicki Leonard, Dirty Dozen Campaign, Environmental Action, Rm. 731, 1346 Connecticut Avenue, N.W., Washington, D.C. 20036; phone (202) 833–1845.

Federal Election Commission, 1325 K Street, N.W., Washington, D.C. 20463; or call toll-free (800-424-9530).

Sierra Club Political Handbook—Tools For Activists, edited by Gene Coan, fifth edition, Sierra Club, Information Services, 530 Bush Street, San Francisco, California 94108. $1 postpaid.

The Almanac of American Politics 1980, Michael Barone, et al, E.P. Dutton, New York.

How You Can Influence Congress, George Alderson and Everett Sentman, 1979, Dutton, New York.

Who Runs Congress?, Mark Green, 3rd edition, 1979, Bantam Books, New York.

How You Can Beat Inflation and Help Save the World

Better Living Makes For a Better Earth

by Garrett De Bell

It is estimated that in 1980 the average family will spend $1000 more for energy than they did in 1979. Every way you save energy you save money; every way you save energy you help save the environment. It's a simple issue, and a big one.

Consider: if you happen to be in the market for a house and are able to choose one near your work, you can reduce the need to commute and the attendant waste of energy and pollution of air, and you reduce the expense of maintaining a commuter car—an expense second only to housing for many, even after they invest in a new fuel-efficient car (with a $6000 price tag). If you walk—public transportation with zero start-up costs—or bike to work you will benefit as much in better health and a healthier pocketbook as the environment will from less need to find, pump, transport, burn and spill nonrenewable oil. Or you can save energy and money by taking public transportation to work. If this isn't practical in your situation, set up car pools or convince your employer to set up van pools for commuters. (The company provides the van; the employees share driving and gas expense, which are tax free if IRS conditions are met.) You don't have to be an environmentalist to adopt appropriate transportation, you just have to be a non-millionaire with some sense and better places to spend your shrinking income than at the gas station.

Housing that is easiest on energy is housing that already exists. This means restoring and using dilapidated buildings, and old warehouses and firehouses, rather than starting from scratch, which in the extreme requires removing land from agriculture or wildlife, and putting in roads, sewers, water and utility lines. Only when housing is in an unacceptable location—such as a floodplain—should it be demolished.

New construction should be high density, clustered as condominiums, apartments, etc., and not located on prime agricultural or wildlife areas. For instance, if the San Francisco Bay Area were being built from square one, the commercial and residential areas would be in a belt or in clusters around the base of the hills, and the flatlands would be left to agriculture and the ridges to wildlife and watershed. The economy of San Francisco, currently geared to tourism, would be enhanced by such a setting, while at the same time the city would conserve energy, the residents' lives would be more self-sufficient and their surroundings would be higher quality.

The options of future construction will be dictated more and more by economics as detached single family homes on large lots go beyond most people's means.

New construction should have good, cost-efficient, passive solar design—which is the housing equivalent of standing in the sun when you're cold, in the shade when you're warm—rather than using increasingly expensive heaters and air conditioners. New construction in cold climates should have north walls insulated to a high R factor, a minimum of windows on the north; good attic, wall and floor insulation throughout; lots of glass facing south with the roof designed or deciduous trees set to block the sun in the summer and let it in during the winter; good weatherstripping and caulking (and when you caulk, invest in a top-of-the-line silicone that lasts forever rather than a latex that will have to be replaced every five years or so); double or triple glazed or storm windows. Some of this can be retrofitted to existing housing, particularly attic and floor insulation, caulking and weatherstriping. Excellent books on home energy conservation are put out by Sunset Books and Consumers' Union.

A simple, less-hassle lifestyle will also be the cheapest and will tend to enrich one's life while reducing the impact of inflation on you — and reducing inflation overall. Act right and grow rich.

Old Way	New Way
Big car for all transportation	Walk, bike, use public transportation and limited use of an efficient car (rent rather than buy for infrequent use)
Large house on single lot in new subdivision	Clustered townhouse, restored building or building as either apartment or co-op
Living far out in the suburbs	Living near work
Using the elevator all the time	Walking three or four flights of stairs.
Old-fashioned showerhead	New 3 gallon/minute showerhead—saves energy as well as water
Regular toilet	New water-saving flush toilet
All electric house: luxury appliances, instant-on large color TV, no-frost refrigerator	Home with electricity only for lighting, electronics, perhaps cooking. Heating from wood stove burning mostly scrap, logging slash; "logs" made from pressed slash; solar water heater; passive solar design in any new construction. Energy-efficient appliances
Drafty house	Well-caulked, insulated, weather-stripped house
Mechanized recreation: snowmobiling, motorboating, dune buggying, dirt biking, off-roading, flying, porno movies	Snowshoeing, cross country skiing, sailing, rowing, bicycling, hiking, running, walking, hang-gliding, sex
Having lots of kids	Having two, one, no kids, or adopting

GDB

A Dozen Tips:

1. Your second biggest expense after housing is probably your car(s). You can save an astonishing amount of money and energy by reducing your dependence on the automobile.

2. Make sure your water heater is efficient (install an insulating jacket) and set at the lowest temperature that works, generally about 120 degrees. This not only saves energy but is much safer; there is less chance of scalding a young, infirm or disabled person.

3. Insulating pipes can be as easy as zipping on a foam tube available in most hardware stores.

4. Low flow showerheads provide just as good a shower. Measure your current showerhead with a bucket and watch. Any flow over three gallons per minute is high. Most plumbing supply shops carry a variety of low-flow showerheads. Usually you can install them yourself as easily as screwing in a lightbulb. If you have more than one bathroom, buy one at a time and measure it when you get home. If the first one doesn't cut flow to three gallons per minute or less, try another kind next.

5. Lighting can be converted to fluorescent for most uses. New fixtures cost twenty dollars or less and each will use about one tenth the electricity of a comparable incandescent. Many existing fixtures and lamps can take one of the new screw-in fluorescents.

6. Check energy-saving features of any new appliances you buy. A label detailing energy use should be on each by the time you read this. Check it.

7. Set back your thermostat. Zone the house so that you can always heat (or cool) the central core and occasionally the rooms that are only used once in a while. If you're in an area where you can count on wood, get a good wood-burning stove and make it the basis for heating at least, and maybe cooking, too. Develop the skills and acquire the tools ˌunmechanized, like a hand saw) you'll need to gather wood yourself. Good firewood is expensive but hundreds of cords of wood are free for the taking in most logging areas of national forests.

8. If you buy firewood, order it in the spring and summer. In the late fall demand is high and so are prices. Use solar energy to make the wood more efficient: let it stand until it's really dry so you get the full fuel value (rather

than using some of the fire's heat to drive off water in green logs). And cover your firewood during damp weather.

9. Close the fireplace damper when there is no fire.

10. Experiment with simple "fixes" like leaving the hot water in the tub after your shower or bath so the heat of it will reduce your need to use expensive fuels.

11. Solar energy could be installed now to save you money and provide security against the possibility of rolling brown-outs and fuel shortages in the future. If you live in parts of the country with lots of sun and little wood, there are relatively inexpensive solar cookers that you might choose. In a few areas, and for people with a high degree of mechanical ability, wind power, water power, or methane gas from waste are definite possibilities.

12. Do any landscaping with plants native to your area. They won't require artificial support like extra water and fertilizer. This saves water, energy, chemicals, and, you get a care-free backyard.

Money-Maker

New Business
To Preserve the Environment

The environmental movement is sometimes blamed for the collapse of whole industries — like automobiles and nuclear power — but let us note that many new enterprises have sprung up over the decade of the seventies because of the concerns, perceived new responsibilities, and opportunities presented by the environmental crisis. And opportunities still abound.

If Japanese and European car producers are outselling American factories it is because in their home territories gas for $1.25/gallon would be a dream, not a nightmare, and they geared their transportation to the fact long ago. The most traditional economics of supply and demand, not widespread recognition of the earth's limits, brought about that switch. Ford may be closing factories, but Honda plans to assemble 10,000 small cars a month in a new plant in Ohio; and near New York City, General Motors has converted a facility so old that its original use was to build steam-driven vehicles nearly one hundred years ago, and is working day and night turning out small, front-wheel-drive cars.

In addition there's a new spirit of Small Business at work. A lot of it centers around the ancient economics (and fun) of "do-it-yourself." For instance, when the back-to-the-land gang found they couldn't afford to call in a plumber (who pound for pound costs about the same as winter asparagus) they got books from the library and experimented and learned to fix their own leaky faucets. And then learned to build their own cabinets. And then how to rewire a refrigerator. And pretty soon the handyman got a contractor's license and went into business for himself.

A lot of it centers around solar power, which is turning into a real growth industry. And it too can begin with do-it-yourself. Someone begins tinkering just to try to cut his heating bill, and pretty soon he's retrofitting other houses, then designing new houses.

There is a Sufi maxim that if the horse is so wild it runs backward, then point its tail in the direction you want to go. As an example of this we have Howard Ruff getting rich off the prospect of coming bad times.

But we suggest that instead of stocking a cabin in the woods with expensive dried foods, you may be able to help prevent the bad times by pooling your resources with your neighbors to start a new business to preserve the environment.

AW

4 Gas-Savers That Really Work

by Paul Weissler

IN THE YEARS since the original gasoline crisis of 1974, Mechanix Illustrated (MI) has tested well over a dozen gadgets which were claimed to be fuel-savers.

Some of these gadgets were inexpensive; others weren't. In the end, they all shared one trait—not a one of them worked. One of our editors was quoted recently in a national news story as saying the magazine had never found a gas-saving gadget that really saved gas.

Well, there *are* some gadgets that really do save gasoline. We've found exactly four. None is as dramatic and exciting as the claims by the failures ("Increases Gas Mileage by 20%"), all do not conserve total energy and we'd hesitate to argue cost-effectiveness (whether you save money, as well) on all of them. But purely in terms of giving your car more miles to the gallon, all four *do* work.

The fuel-saving, bolt-on gadgets listed in order of lowest cost to highest are an air-conditioner cutout switch, a block heater, an electric cooling fan and a front spoiler.

The least expensive of the four is the vacuum-actuated switch that cuts out the air conditioning on acceleration and other low-vacuum conditions. Called the Pass-Master, the device is installed in series with the wire to the air-conditioner compressor and connected to a source of engine vacuum. The way it saves gas is obvious—you get less air conditioning for less engine load and better economy.

Pass-Master was tested by the Dept. of Transportation, using test procedures of the EPA. In those tests, fuel savings ranged from about 6 percent on a Pinto to more than 12 percent on a Cutlass, for an average of over 9 percent. With that kind of savings, the $12 price should be worth it.

The price for that saving is a warmer car, since shutting the A/C whenever the throttle is open wide raises passenger compartment temperature. But it's raised only about 4° on a 95° day. That's not even worth opening your shirt collar for.

To install a Pass-Master, cut the wire that goes to the

compressor clutch and splice in the two wires from the gadget. Then connect the vacuum hose from the Pass-Master to some source of engine vacuum.

If you want the A/C to cut out only when you're accelerating or climbing a hill, connect the hose to a vacuum source on the intake manifold or the base of the carburetor *below* the throttle plate. You can be sure of what you have by checking with a vacuum gauge. If you get a vacuum reading with the engine idling, you're hooked into manifold vacuum.

If there's no reading, blip the throttle linkage open. Now if you get a reading, you've got carburetor port vacuum. That's where to connect the Pass-Master if you want your A/C to cut out while the engine's at idle for even better economy.

As obvious as the way the A/C cutout switch works is how subtle is the way the block heater works. And the fact that the heater works while the engine is off makes the whole thing as clear as a wet road through a cracked windshield on a foggy night.

If your engine is warm all night, it's more efficient when you start off in the morning. The choke opens immediately to lean out the fuel mixture. And the engine parts and lube oil are also warm so the engine runs easily right away, instead of struggling through those first few miles while it's cold. Of all types of block heaters, the most efficient is the one we chose, a small gadget, from Phillips Industries, that goes into the water jacket in the engine block. When you park your car for the night, plug the wire from the heater into an electric outlet and the engine is toasty and ready to go in the morning.

Our heater is small enough to fit in a freeze-out plug hole and still pack a 400-watt punch. Since the heater is in the engine block, the heat it produces is transferred quickly all over the engine. If you live in the cold northland and do a lot of short-trip, cold-engine driving, the little gadget can make a real improvement.

The thing is, though the coolant heater lets you use less *gas* you may still end up using more total energy (paying more money) if you add gas and electric bills together. But even with the thing running all night, it should consume less than two bits worth of electricity. At that rate it should take less than ¼ gal. of gasoline, at a buck per, to pay for the electricity. How much gas you save depends on the temperatures.

The coolant heater offers some nice bonuses, too. Blowby is reduced and engine-oil contamination is cut, so oil and engine life is extended. Also, the hot coolant means instant warmth from the heater. That alone can make the $15 to $17 heater and its electricity worth it to plenty of folks.

A thermostatically-controlled electric cooling fan is another gadget that provides real fuel-economy benefits. These fans are turning up on more and more new cars, especially transverse-engine front drives, usually because the engine mounting makes it more practical than an engine-driven fan. But you can buy one in kit form under the Electra-Fan name.

A thermostatic electric fan cycles itself on and off as needed. It comes on only when engine coolant is hot. You decide how hot is hot by adjusting a thermostat. A plain-vanilla fixed cooling fan, on the other hand, is on all the time, using 7 hp or more. That's wasted power when the engine is cold and when the car is cruising faster than 30 mph. At high speeds the air going through the radiator cools it off.

Government studies show a likely 2-percent-overall improvement with one of these fans. MI tests of Electra-Fan showed a 15.7 percent hike in highway driving, 9 percent in suburban/highway operation.

Many cars already have part-time cooling fans in the form of thermostatically-controlled clutch fans. These fans save gas over the fixed type, too, but government studies show a savings of ½ percent for the clutch models.

The big saving, besides being while cruising on the highway, is during cold weather, when your engine doesn't come close to getting very hot.

The Electra-Fan kit lists for $100 but is usually sold for $49.95 or $59.95. The installation can be a bit tricky (see Nov. '78 MI) but nothing any backyard mechanic worth his torque wrench can't handle.

Our last gas-saving gadget is a fooler. Spoilers are nice-looking items and lots of folks like them on their cars because they spruce up a rig. Few think of them as gas-saving gadgets. But they are.

Another Gas-Saver That Really Works

The president of the New York Runners Club, Fred Lebow, ran everywhere in February, 1979 — to and from his office, business meetings, luncheon appointments, dinner parties, and concerts, and to Central Park, where he officiated at four Road Runners Club races. He avoided public transportation the entire month, found it necessary to ride in cars twice, was turned away from one restaurant because he lacked the proper attire, flew to New Orleans and back, and calculated that the experiment had resulted in a net saving of sixty hours and around two hundred dollars in transportation costs and dry-cleaning expenses. . . . Fred Lebow is convinced that when large companies get around to providing employees with locker rooms and shower facilities the city will be a more civilized place.

The New Yorker
(April 14, 1980)

Carmakers know that slippery cars, ones with good aerodynamics, use less gas than others. Anything that helps a car cut through the wind, especially at highway speeds, helps the mill under the hood use less fuel.

And, believe it or not, it's been found that the air moving *under* the car can be as big a drag as the air *over* it.

Front spoilers act as air dams, directing air over a car's top and around its sides, instead of letting it go turbulently under the rig. Rear spoilers pick up the airstream as it goes over the top of the car and direct it away, reducing drag even more.

Front and rear spoilers do save gas. How much, though, depends on how streamlined your car already is and how much highway driving you do. Government studies found a 2-percent saving. But if you drive a Model T or a 4WD or some other rig that's 1½ ft. off the ground and about as aerodynamic as a bookcase, don't look for any improvements, other than in appearance.

But for other rigs the improvement from spoilers may

be more than the government studies indicate. Herb Adams, whose Monterey, Calif., shop modifies Firebirds and Trans Ams, says the spoilers on those cars are worth ½ mpg, or about 5 percent in highway operation. Adams should know; he was heavily involved in aerodynamics studies as a Pontiac engineer in the early '70s.

The importers of Kamei spoilers (made for European and Japanese cars and Omni/Horizon) say that wind-tunnel work they did in Germany showed a 3- to 6- percent boost, or 1 to almost 2 mpg. Kamei spoilers range in price from $65 for a Honda Civic to $125 for a BMW. Even with gas at a buck a gallon some of them may never pay for themselves. But besides helping mileage, they help your car's looks, and that's something people pay plenty more for.

In addition to these four add-ons, you may be able to get a gas-mileage improvement by retrofitting an electronic ignition to a car with breaker points. The EI system won't improve gas mileage over a properly-tuned engine, but if you tend to run your tune-up intervals long, it may keep all plugs firing when breaker points wouldn't. Retrofit EI systems list for $70 to more than $100, so look for a big discount before you buy.

In any case, be realistic when shopping for bolt-on gas-mileage improvers. Moderate but worthwhile improvements are possible with the devices mentioned here; others of similar value may hit the market. But the only miracle from gadgets promising miracles is that so many people believe the promises.

Money-Maker

Encore!

by Kathy Evans

California is blessed with a rich and bountiful grape harvest, and Californians celebrate the harvest by consuming 94 million gallons of wine annually. Bottling this wine uses more than 150,000 tons of glass, most of which is thrown away after just one use.

Producing these bottles requires:

    100,000 tons sand
     32,475 tons soda ash
     32,625 tons limestone
     11,325 tons feldspar
        1.7 billion gallons water
        2.6 trillion Btus energy (enough for 20,000 California households for a year).

Manufacturing the glass also generates 28,000 ton of mining wastes and 2,085 tons of air pollutants.

If recycled glass were to replace 50% of the raw materials in the manufacturing process, water consumption and mining wastes would be reduced by 50% and air pollution by 14%, with a small savings in energy. If refillable containers were used, mineral consumption and waste generation could be reduced by 70% and energy use reduced by 40% (return transportation included).

Recycling is a worthwhile endeavor, but reuse has tremendously more potential for reducing waste and saving energy. The Ecology Center in Berkeley and other environmental organizations, which established recycling programs in the early 1970s, thought that this potential could be demonstrated.

Wine-bottle reuse is not a new idea. In 1942 the U.S. government mandated the standardized "Victory Bottle." After World War II there were ten reuse centers in the Los Angeles area alone. Single use came about only with proprietary — exclusive — bottle design. (Today an estimated 50% of all wine bottles produced are proprietary.)

With a $24,000 grant from Alameda County general revenue sharing funds, the Ecology Center established EN-CORE! (the Environmental Container Reuse Program) in February, 1975; since then ENCORE! wineries, recycling centers, restaurants, stores, concerned groups and individuals have demonstrated that glass bottles can be washed and reused on a large scale—and make money doing it.

The process is simple: used wine bottles are collected and brought to a processing facility. There they are sorted, washed and sterilized in custom-engineered bottle washers. The clean bottles are packed into new cartons and distributed to participating wineries.

Wine bottles were chosen for the ENCORE! demonstration because they are somewhat more standardized than other glass containers and because of the proximity of a thriving wine industry. Most northern California wineries are within 100 miles of the Berkeley area. Although we originally intended to expand the program to other types of containers, the demand for reusable wine bottles has been so strong that we've pretty much stuck to wine bottles. ENCORE! has, however, washed quantities of juice jugs, vegetable oil bottles and laboratory jars for special customers.

The operation was set up in an industrial area of Berkeley in a 7,000-square-foot warehouse that was generally well equipped with drains, gas and water piping. Our money was limited, so we bought only used equipment. Start-up equipment included: a one-gallon milk-bottle washer adapted (by us) to wash 4/5th quart, 1/2-gallon and one-gallon bottles; a 15-horsepower steam generator; a forklift; and a 60″ baler for used corrugated cases. A bottom stapler for constructing new cartons was soon added. The cost of this equipment was $11,000 (in 1975). The Ecology Center already owned a 1960 Ford propane-powered 20-foot flatbed truck, used for other recycling programs. The truck was put into full-time use by the ENCORE! operation; although it may soon be retired, it remains the program's only vehicle and is used almost daily for roundtrips of 150–200 miles to deliver clean bottles and pick up used ones. All the original equipment is still in use, except for the box stapler which has been replaced with an automatic, air-powered box former.

Bottles are supplied by northern California wineries, recycling organizations, restaurants and individuals. The program paid a delivered price of 25¢/case ($40/ton) during the first year. Bottles are also brought to ENCORE! for "custom washing." These are washed, sterilized and returned to customers, usually in the same cardboard cases in which they were brought.

ENCORE! bottles are significantly lower in price than new glass—from 10% to 30% cheaper. The strong support of several winemakers committed to the idea of reuse helped persuade others to try the program. Soon, virtually all northern California wineries participated in one way or another: selling ENCORE! their empty bottles, buying revitalized bottles, or by having their bottles customwashed.

The quality of reused bottles is excellent, perhaps better than new glass. Weak or defective bottles are generally broken or discarded during the first filling and are not available for reuse. The many quality controls insure a fine product: The bottles soak for a minimum of 5 minutes in a 70°C, 3 1/2% caustic soda solution (for sterilization) with 1/2% sodium tripolyphosphate (a wetting agent). The soak tank is constantly monitored for proper concentrations and temperatures. Each bottle is individually hand-inspected for chips or other defects, label or glue residue, etc. Samples are periodically sent to a private laboratory to test for bacteria or other organic material.

During the first year of operation, ENCORE! became self-supporting with an average of six full-time employees, an inventory of 10,000 cases of wine bottles, and sales exceeding 8,000 cases monthly. A year-end analysis indicated that it is both economically and environmentally sound to reuse wine bottles and that although economics favor bottle-washing at winery facilities, the program can be carried out by independently controlled facilities in full accordance with the California health and safety code. The study further showed that the ENCORE! process requires 75% of the water and only 35% of the energy (transportation and handling included) required to manufacture new glass. Each 100,000 cases of bottles reused also saves approximately 5,000 cubic yards of post-consumer waste.

After 2 years of operation ENCORE! had outgrown its warehouse and moved to a 15,000 square-foot building with

---

THAT MAN is richest whose pleasures are cheapest.

Henry David Thoreau

10,000 square feet of yard space in Emeryville, a neighboring industrial area. Shortly thereafter (during the West Coast drought) a water-recycling system was installed to further decrease the water required.

After settling comfortably into the new location, EN-CORE! co-managers Dick Evans and Peter Heylin began planning for the future; 1978 was to be a landmark year for the program. Another used bottle-washer was purchased to wash 4/5th-quart bottles exclusively. The original machine was then re-converted to wash only 1/2-gallon and one-gallon sizes for which it was better suited. The new machine has a larger capacity and personnel requirements and is operated for one shift per day. When the original machine is used, the staff is spread over a two-shift day.

1978 was also the year the wine industry began to convert to metric measure bottles. The 4/5th quart was replaced by 750ml, the 1/2 gallon by 1.5 liter, and the one-gallon size by either 3-liter or 4-liter bottles. Although the bottle-washing machines could easily accommodate the similar bottles, inventory control was a challenge for both the ENCORE! staff and the bottle suppliers.

In the summer of 1978, the Ecology Center received a modest grant from the federal Department of Energy to install heat exchangers and solar collectors to reduce the amount of natural gas required for heating water. The heat exchangers preheat the fresh rinse water by piping it counter to the heated, outgoing waste water. This warms the water approximately 13°F above its incoming temperature. After it leaves the heat exchangers, the fresh water flows to the washing machines or through the solar panels, depending on weather conditions.

By late 1978, ENCORE! was processing 17,000 cases (100 tons) per month. The program was a successful demonstration of the economic and environmental benefits of re-use, and the Board of Directors of the Ecology Center decided to sell the operation to a corporation formed by the program's co-managers.

Now a private company, ENCORE! washes 20,000 cases of bottles per month and employs eleven people. Prices paid for bottles have increased to an average of 54¢ per case ($90/ton) while wholesale prices for revitalized bottles have increased less than those for new glass. The purchase of used bottles sends $7,400 per month into the local area, supporting or supplementing many individuals and providing an economically attractive market for community recycling centers.

At a volume of 20,000 cases per month, ENCORE! recovers 1,500 tons of bottles per year. This amounts to a 1% reduction in the need for new wine bottles in California and saves 16 billion BTU's generated by fossil fuels and more than 4 million gallons of water per year. As the supply of used bottles increases, even more resource conservation will be realized.

To this end, ENCORE! is developing ways to make bottle recovery more convenient and economical for suppliers. With a grant from the California State Solid Waste Management Board, ENCORE! bought collapsible wooden bins that can be transported and stored flat when empty and that hold about 40 cases of bottles without cardboard cases. Eliminating the use of cases provides several advantages: protection from rain is not required, sorting and storage are cleaner and easier, and larger quantities of bottles can be conveniently delivered at one time.

ENCORE! has also designed and built an automatic decorking machine that provides an economic alternative to breaking bottles at wineries when defective merchandise is reprocessed or discarded. The resulting empty bottles are then sold to ENCORE! or custom washed and returned to the winery.

The program has not been without its problems, but the struggles have generally been no greater than those of establishing any small business and there is the consolation of doing good.

Indeed, the reuse message is spreading. Requests for information and assistance have come from all over the United States and beyond. Bottle reuse facilities could become at least as common as they were only 20 years ago, when 98% of all soft drinks and 58% of beer were sold in returnable containers. National container deposit legislation would encourage even more reuse and save significant amounts of fossil fuels. Better yet, standardization of all glass containers (beverage bottles, mayonnaise jars, salad oil and ketchup bottles, etc.) would promote local washing facilities, which would in turn enhance local economies by providing jobs and lower prices.

Economically and environmentally, new wine in old bottles makes sense.

Efficient Home-Heating Fireplace

There are three kinds of home-heating fires.

1. *Inefficient and non-polluting*: the old fashioned open masonry fireplace. It takes air from the (warm) room and uses it to combust the wood, then sends the air up the stack. The net production of heat in the room is about zero and the fire is only a nice luxury out of step with the times. At least this kind of fireplace is relatively non-polluting as the fire burns hot with plenty of air so little smoke (from unburned wood) is produced.

2. *Efficient and polluting*: an airtight stove. If the air inlet is set so too little air gets to the fire smoke results, not as harmful as pollutants like sulphur dioxide, but objectionable. Inadequate air for combustion is, in the words of the operator's of industrial boilers, "too little excess air" (the amount beyond the minimum to combust all the wood— assuming each oxygen molecule lined up right with each fuel molecule so no vaporized fuel made in the stack becomes smoke, but rather meets an oxygen molecule, burns and gives up efficient heat and produces CO_2 and H_2O). A smokey stove is also a dangerous one, particularly if it is the wrong kind of chimney, because the smoke condenses on the walls of a cool chimney as creosote, and creosote causes chimney fires. This is not to condemn wood stoves, only to caution that they are not foolproof and with them a fool can pollute the air, bother neighbors with smoke, waste heat, and risk his house.

3. *Efficient and non-polluting*: either a fireplace stove, or stove with an external source of combustion air regulated to provide enough oxygen to ensure complete combustion without wasting expensive heated air from the room. A recent article in *Popular Science* rated the Thermograte fireplace stove as five times more efficient than an ordinary fireplace with 57% of the heat being delivered to the room.

Only number three is part of the environmental lifestyle, and then only when the wood is obtained in an acceptable manner.

GDB

How to Make Sure Your Woodburning Stove Is Part of the Solution

Fire shines like gold right now, but is home-heating with wood ecologically sound? Yes and no, depending on where and how you get your wood and how you burn it.

The Right Way

Using a truck you have anyway for wood hauling is efficient, as is sharing a truck with someone who has regular need for it (you pay for gas, or provide the equipment for woodcutting as your share).

Using cull trees—the trees cut to make room and to release nutrients, water and light so the remaining trees grow—from commercial logging.

Getting wood from a sustained-yield woodlot or using the limbs and slash from logging, tree removal, etc. It is surprising how many people who burn wood only use the regular-sized rounds and logs. Limbs burn just as well and need only to be cut, not split, as they are already the right diameter.

The Wrong Way

Buying a ½-ton pickup as your regular vehicle instead of an economy car, solely to haul firewood. You're better off buying heating fuel or cord wood. It would be cheaper and save more energy than using the pickup.

Cutting dead snags that are homes for such hole-nesting birds as woodpeckers, some owls, chickadees, nuthatches, bluebirds, and even flying squirrels.

Cutting perfectly healthy trees when there is no silvicultural (tree-farming) need or other reason for removal.

The ideal would be to hand-cut and split your own wood, using scrap or dead and down timber. But don't take it all because a clean forest is a sterile one—many animals depend on logs for shelter. (Large logs with lots of bark are more important to animals than logs of smaller diameter.) You probably won't supply all your wood by hand cutting, but maybe 10%, and you can cut a little each day as exercise rather than laying in the whole supply in a few fall weekends. As the saying goes, cutting your own wood warms you twice.

GDB

Save Water, Save Money

by David Gaines

Saving water saves the energy that would otherwise be consumed in water conveyance, distribution and treatment, and in home water heating. The California Department of Water Resources calculates that modest domestic water conservation would save the equivalent of over eight million barrels of oil per year.

We could extend our discussion of water conservation to many pages on water-saving appliances, drought-resistant landscaping, night-time watering, drip irrigation, large scale wastewater recycling, and other important topics. But let's leave that for another article, and turn to some readily available means of reducing water consumption inside our own homes.

Reducing interior consumption from 80 gallons to 50 gallons of water a day may only require a simple, inexpensive flow-restricting device in your shower and a water-filled plastic container in your toilet tank. A few small changes in personal habits—such as shutting off the tap when brushing teeth, taking shorter showers, or even bathing with a friend—can save much more. The replacement of water-guzzling toilets and appliances with new, water-saving models will pay for itself in water and energy savings.

We use most of our household water to carry away wastes. Fully 95 percent ends up in the sewer. As 75 percent is used in the bathroom, it is there we look first for means to conserve.

Five to seven gallons of water gush through the typical flush toilet at every flushing. The simplest means to conserve flush water is to flush less often. You can easily and effectively save much more by placing water-filled plastic containers, weighted down with pebbles, into your toilet tanks. Two one-quart soap or bleach bottles will displace one-half gallon of water and save that much at every flushing. Plastic containers are better than ordinary building bricks, which, while they displace about a quart of water, may disintegrate and clog your plumbing. If you must use a brick, obtain a more expensive, ceramic model.

Toilet dams, flushing valve sleeves and adjustable

float assemblies are commercially available water-saving devices that do much the same thing as displacement containers. In typical commodes, a somewhat greater, one-to-two-gallon-per-flush savings may be achieved without impeding the toilet's ability to do its job. Toilet dams, which cost about $6, are pieces of flexible plastic that can be wedged into the tank on either side of the flush valve, holding back "reservoirs" of water at each flush. A flushing valve sleeve is a three-inch ring that fits around the flushing valve and prevents the last few inches of tank water from flushing into the bowl. Adjustable float assemblies allow the water level in the tank to be reduced as desired. These devices are easily installed and are available at most large hardware and plumbing supply outlets.

Far more effective, but more costly, is the replacement of a water-consumptive toilet with one of the shallow-trap models now on the market. Toilets that use 3½ gallons per flush are available new for less than $50. Ultra-saving designs, such as those manufactured by Ifö Cascade of Sweden, cost over $200, but flush efficiently on only 1½ gallons of water.

Your best efforts to conserve flush water will come to naught, however, if you have a leaky toilet. To find out, add a few drops of coloring to the tank water. If there is a leak, colored water will show up in the bowl. A worn or poorly seated tank ball or a defective toilet tank valve can silently leak many hundreds of gallons of water a day.

Of course the most effective water-saving alternative is a dry toilet that does not use water at all. These range from pit outhouses and chemical toilets to energy-wasteful incineration and oil flush toilets. An especially promising development is the composting privy, which naturally decomposes feces, urine, paper and kitchen garbage into an odorless, humus-like residue that can be safely used to fertilize non-edible plants and fruit trees. Composting privies are suitable for urban as well as rural households, but are relatively expensive (unless you do it yourself), and do require the same modest labor and attention as ordinary aerobic compost piles. Composting privies are still so new that many health and sanitation departments do no yet sanction their use. For more information on composting privies and other dry toilet alternatives, refer to the references listed at the end of this article.

As about 30 percent of interior water is consumed by showering and bathing, it is there we look next for ways to conserve. Just taking shorter showers, washing hands in the basin instead of under a running faucet, washing dishes in a dish pan instead of under running water, and so forth can save hundreds of gallons a day. These savings can be greatly augmented through the use of flow restrictors, aerators or water-saving heads on showers and sink faucets.

Flow restrictors are inexpensive valves that are easily installed in flow lines behind faucets and shower heads. They reduce water use by up to 50 percent.

Aerators are equally simple, inexpensive devices, that are usually thread-mounted on the ends of faucets. By mixing air with water as it leaves the tap, aerators reduce water use by as much as one-third. Because wettability is increased and splash is decreased, less water is required for rinsing and washing.

Water-saving shower heads also create an aerated spray and reduce flow rates to as low as one-half gallon per minute, one-twentieth that of some standard models. These heads, which cost as little as $13 for two-gallon-per-minute designs, quickly pay for themselves in water-heating energy savings.

The value of these water-saving devices, however, can be more than cancelled by a plumbing leak. Up to 1000 gallons a day can drip from a single leaky faucet down the drain. Usually it is the hot water faucet that starts to leak because the heat accelerates the wear on the washer. With the cost of heating water soaring it is time well spent to replace washers when they start to leak, or at regular intervals to prevent leaks. Since you have to drain the pipes for some plumbing repairs, this is a good time to go through and fix all washers, an easy job for anyone with reasonable skill.

Choose washing machines and dishwashers based on energy and water usage and you will save plenty. Newly required labels on appliances make this easier, and reading Consumers Reports will help you save water, energy, and money.

Dirty household water, except that from toilets, can also be reused for flushing toilets and watering yards and gardens. The technology to safely recycle this "greywater" is rapidly developing, and the first home greywater recycling systems are now on the market. Greywater systems,

New Industrial Park

It is more than ironic that we have problems such as thermal pollution—the undesirable heating of water by wastes from power plants and some other large industries—at the same time that a major use of our precious fuel reserves is simply to create heat. Similarly the collection and transportation of water for long distances to provide such services as car washes, and things that do not require drinking quality water, is a stupid misuse of resources. As we start rebuilding the decayed areas of our cities, there could be comprehensive utilization of the waste heat from energy consuming industries by those industries that require only low grade heat. The industries could be grouped into parks—as they have tended to cluster lately—but parks designed to maximize the resources used in industry. The park could be located in an area where the sewage treatment for the region is located. The sewage effluent could be treated to a standard for many uses such as washing the buses of the local mass transit system and various other industrial processes not dependent on high quality drinking water.

Our environmental problems are inter-related and as we look toward the future we need to seek ways where the solutions of one can help solve those of another.

GDB

like composting privies, are promising innovations in water-saving domestic plumbing that have yet to be sanctioned by many health and sanitation departments. For more information, refer to the references listed at the end of this article.

For further water conservation information. . . .

Contact your local water utility. They should have free pamphlets and other materials on water-saving techniques. If they don't, complain! An excellent primer for children (and adults, too!) is *The Captain Hydro Water Conservation Workbook* (first published by the East Bay Municipal Utility District, P.O. Box 24055, Oakland, CA).

North Marin's *Little Compendium of Water-Saving Ideas* ably and critically skims the cream from the vast technical literature on domestic water conservation available for $7 postpaid from North Marin County Water District, P.O. Box 146, Novato, CA 94947). The Compendium describes and evaluates water-saving devices, reviews case examples of their use, includes a valuable bibliography of 114 references, and lists retail outlets and wholesale distributors of water-saving equipment, not only in California, but across the United States.

In *Goodby to the Flush Toilet: Water-Saving Alternatives to Cesspools, Septic Tanks, and Sewers,* Carol Hupping Stoner has edited informative essays on bathroom history, composting privies, greywater recycling and water conservation (1977; Rodale Press; $6.95 paperback). Additional, essential information, especially for the do-it-your-selfer, may be found in Sim Van der Ryn's *The Toilet Papers: Designs to Recycle Human Waste and Water—Dry Toilets, Greywater Systems and Urban Sewage (1978; Capra Press; $3.95 paperback).*

Health:
The Next Challenge

by David Lenderts

There are now two clear divisions of medicine that overlap only at the convenience of corporate and political powers.

One division is the diagnosis-and-treatment form of medicine — or what, by usurping the name, has become known simply as "medicine."

The other is known variously as population medicine, environmental medicine, preventive medicine — or public health. This division looks at the frequency and distribution of disease in a population of people and its social and economic causes, such as inadequate nutrition, poor working conditions, environmental pollution, poverty, etc.

The split in medicine came about after World War I when public health was taken from the curriculum of medical schools and placed in its own schools. Medical students were exposed to public health topics less and less and concentrated on diagnosis and treatment of already-existing disease in individuals. Individuals were in a better position to purchase their health care than were whole communities and medicine became a saleable item used primarily by those who could afford it. Medicine thus came to directly compete with environmental medicine in the private marketplace, and for public funding for research and development. So, while federal allocations for health-related research and development are over $2 billion per year, they go primarily toward more powerful tools of diagnosis and treatment rather than toward prevention.

With the transformation of medicine into a competitive industry has come evidence that the benefits of medicine have been arrested, and often even reversed.

Before the industrial revolution of the late 19th and early 20th centuries diseases were largely beyond our understanding or control. People were carried off in millions by the smallest of nature's organisms. Bacteria, viruses, rickettsia and parasites caused infections such as plague, tuberculosis, typhus, syphilis, cholera, smallpox, polio, influenza, yellow fever, and malaria. They were responsible, along with famine and natural disasters, for nearly all human fatalities. People often died at an early age. Some of these diseases occurred in global epidemics which killed millions of people in a matter of months. Infectious diseases and malnutrition are still responsible for the vast majority of deaths and debilitation in parts of the world where the industrial revolution has failed to reach. Yet, a dramatic change occurred in the rest of the world. The tables compare causes of mortality in the U.S. in 1974; present American mortality causes are representative of all the developed world.

Infectious diseases have been eliminated as a major cause of mortality—and they have been replaced by the so-called "diseases of civilization." The prevailing assumption is that diagnostic and therapeutic methods are responsible for eliminating infectious diseases' mortal effects. And it is felt that the diseases which have now moved up on the chart can be subdued in the same way.

Neither assumption is true.

Actually, the death rates from tuberculosis, cholera, dysentery, and typhoid peaked and declined *before* modern therapies were applied. And the "combined death rate from scarlet fever, diphtheria, whooping cough and measles among children up to 15 years shows that nearly 90% of the total decline in mortality between 1860 and 1965 had occurred *before* the introduction of antibiotics and widespread immunization."[1]

The decline is attributed, in part, to a spontaneous decrease in the ability of infectious organisms to cause fatal disease, to improved housing and better education, and even more, to increased human resistance created by better nutrition and better sanitation. This is how environmental medicine has influenced health.

Let us look at each of the current major causes of mortality in America and describe briefly their causes.

Diseases of the heart. Most heart disease results from clogging of the arteries that supply blood to the heart. This clogging is the cause of "heart attacks," in which the heart muscle no longer gets enough blood for itself and therefore cannot pump blood to the body. The chief causes of this disease are: diets high in animal fats and highly refined foods, including sugar; obesity from overeating; lack of exercise; emotional stress; smoking; high blood pressure; and diabetes, another disease which, in adults, is related primarily to overnutrition.

Cancer. Cancer researchers are in almost complete agreement that 70% to 90% of human cancers are induced by natural and, primarily, human-made environmental factors. Most cancers are therefore preventable. Erik Eckholm, in a Worldwatch Paper, writes: "Diet, cigarette smoking, and alcohol consumption; pollutants in air, water, food, and soil; toxic chemicals in workplaces or manufactured products; and exposure to sunlight, and ionizing radiation all influence cancer rates. Rooted in cultural habits and technological patterns, cancer is, as one researcher put it, a 'social disease.' "[2]

Strokes. Strokes are caused when arteries supplying blood to the brain either become clogged or rupture. The factors are about the same as for heart disease.

Accidents. Altogether 120,000 persons die every year from accidents and 45,000,000 are injured. About 49,000 die each year, and five million are disabled to some degree in auto accidents. In just two years auto accidents cause more American deaths than did ten years of war in Viet Nam. Half the auto deaths are caused by drunken drivers. (In Sweden, the per-capita rate of car-related deaths is far below ours. But drinking drivers there are subject to very tough law enforcement and stiff penalties, and there is good driver education for all drivers.)

Influenza and pneumonia. These are terminal events for many elderly or chronically ill persons; they probably cannot be significantly changed.

Cirrhosis of the liver. This is caused by alcoholism. Alcoholism has been called the largest untreated treatable disease—and "preventable" might be a better word. Ten million Americans are alcoholics. Another 8-20 million people are classified as having moderate to severe drinking problems. Drinking can produce cirrhosis, cause accidents, suicide, and homicide, and induce cancer—seen in this combination, alcohol ranks behind heart disease and cancer as the number three disease killer in the nation. As a symptom and cause of social chaos it is unsurpassed—and yet each year $250 million is spent on advertising and $10.5 *billion* is spent on consuming alcohol in the U.S. Arteriosclerosis has the same causes as heart disease and stroke, but it causes mortality by its effects in arteries other than in the heart and brain.

Diseases of infancy. Many are caused by birth defects that are related to mutagenic pollutants in the environment.

Mortality, Ten Leading Causes of Death, Age Group and Sex, 1974

	All Ages		Age 1–14		Age 15–34	
	Male	**Female**	**Male**	**Female**	**Male**	**Female**
1.	Heart Diseases 411,492	Heart Diseases 326,679	Accidents 7,252	Accidents 3,667	Accidents 30,389	Accidents 7,247
2.	Cancer 196,746	Cancer 163,726	Cancer 1,595	Cancer 1,191	Homicide 8,940	Cancer 3,783
3.	Stroke 90,394	Stroke 117,030	Congenital Anomalies 1,038	Congenital Anomalies 971	Suicide 6,782	Homicide 2,344
4.	Accidents 73,209	Accidents 31,413	Pneumonia, Influenza 589	Pneumonia, Influenza 519	Cancer 3,774	Suicide 2,161
5.	Pneumonia, Influenza 29,787	Pneumonia, Influenza 24,990	Homicide 411	Heart Diseases 304	Heart Diseases 2,552	Heart Diseases 1,333
6.	Cirrhosis of Liver 21,806	Diabetes 22,193	Heart Diseases 310	Homicide 284	Cirrhosis of Liver 893	Stroke 800
7.	Suicide 18,595	Arterio-sclerosis 19,010	Stroke 198	Cystic Fibrosis 163	Pneumonia, Influenza 817	Pneumonia, Influenza 601
8.	Homicide 16,747	Diseases of Infancy 12,069	Meningitis 165	Stroke 158	Stroke 790	Cirrhosis of Liver 519
9.	Diseases of Infancy 16,717	Cirrhosis of Liver 11,513	Suicide 145	Cerebral Palsy 134	Congenital Anomalies 598	Congenital Anomalies 487
10.	Emphysema 15,794	Suicide 7,088	Cerebral Palsy 142	Meningitis 127	Diabetes 380	Complicat of Pregnancy 384

Source: Vital Statistics of the United States, 1974.

Age 35–54		Age 55–74		Age 75+	
ale	**Female**	**Male**	**Female**	**Male**	**Female**
eart seases ,066	Cancer 28,961	Heart Diseases 199,960	Heart Diseases 104,867	Heart Diseases 159,182	Heart Diseases 204,900
ncer ,330	Heart Diseases 14,923	Cancer 109,548	Cancer 80,553	Cancer 54,415	Stroke 80,024
cidents ,697	Stroke 5,618	Stroke 34,351	Stroke 30,349	Stroke 49,129	Cancer 49,571
rhosis Liver ?38	Accidents 4,767	Accidents 12,884	Diabetes 9,737	Pneumonia, Influenza 15,076	Arterio-sclerosis 16,535
oke 24	Cirrhosis of Liver 4,704	Cirrhosis of Liver 10,795	Accidents 6,420	Arterio-sclerosis 9,967	Pneumonia, Influenza 15,940
cide 88	Suicide 2,892	Pneumonia, Influenza 9,336	Cirrhosis of Liver 5,339	Accidents 7,095	Diabetes 10,210
nicide 62	Diabetes 1,809	Emphysema 9,184	Pneumonia, Influenza 5,167	Emphysema 5,684	Accidents 8,672
umonia, uenza 97	Pneumonia, Influenza 1,605	Diabetes 7,496	Arterio-sclerosis 2,361	Diabetes 5,364	Hernia & Intestinal Obstruction 2,077
betes 54	Homicide 1,267	Suicide 4,723	Emphysema 2,361	Hyper-tension 1,740	Hyper-tension 2,040
hysema	Nephritis 550	Arterio-sclerosis 3,063	Suicide 1,670	Nephritis 1,578	Gastritis 2,002

Emphysema. It is caused primarily by smoking and by air pollution, and it ranks as number twelve. If smoking were eliminated, a fifth of all cancers would be eliminated, worldwide. Americans spend $10 billion per year on tobacco; $100 billion is spent worldwide each year. The Department of Agriculture spends $50 million each year in price supports, research, export promotion, and other programs to support the tobacco industry. The Massachusetts Public Health Association estimated that smokers in that state cost the public half a billion dollars each year in costs for fire protection, fire damage, treating smoke-induced diseases and in costs of lost working time owing to smoke-related diseases. Extrapolated to the rest of the country, the costs come to $19 billion per year.

OUR HEALTH is influenced less by doctors, drugs, and spiraling medical expenditures than by our social and physical environments. Indeed, in creating its way of life, each society creates its way of death.

Erik P. Eckholm

The effect of environmental factors on present mortality and disability and the availability of means to prevent these diseases are readily apparent. Yet, according to President Carter, when America spent $130 billion on health care in 1977, 40 cents per health dollar were spent on hospitalization, 3 cents on disease prevention, less than a half cent on health education, and a quarter of a cent on environmental health.[3]

Out of all this, we find medicine gearing up to fight harder a war which its own interests contribute to. Better we should change our health-producing priorities. It must be clear by now that this writer expects the next big advance in keeping people healthy to come in the realms of how they live their lives, and how we, as a society, manage the environmental conditions under which we live.

Medicine has become a huge enterprise. It is to health as the agribusiness industry is to farming. The medical industry comprises chemical companies, which manufacture diagnostic chemicals and pharmaceutical drugs for therapy. There are medical and hospital equipment manufacturers and specialized architecture firms and construction companies that design and build the buildings in which the equipment is used. There are corporatehospital owners and administrators, government health-care administrators and government regulators. There are health insurance companies and finally, the schools of medicine, nursing, and laboratory diagnosis, and the physicians, nurses and technicians whom they produce.

By itself and through corporate interlocks, the medical enterprise is part of the corporate state which, through its advertising and marketing arms, convinces Americans to buy the products it creates and to accept the inevitable pollution and social disruption. The medical industry's structure and function resemble very strongly the monopoly of the traditional energy industry. In medicine as in energy the trend has centered on more complex, arcane and expensive technologies which consume nonrenewable resources.

But health problems can be solved by applying simple laws and modest technology based on knowledge we already have. Thus, for potential heart disease victims, the most significant development in the last decade has not been the increased use of coronary artery surgeries to bypass arteries clogged by a combination of poor diet, stress and cigarette smoking, but the spontaneous advent and growth of running and other excerise, and the rejection by many people of processed and polluted food. The latter factors had more to do with the 20% decrease in the death rate from heart attacks in the U.S. since 1965 than any others.

The technological-treatment orientation in medicine is indicated by the awarding of the 1979 Nobel Prize in medicine to the two inventors of the "CAT" (Computerized Axial Tomography) scanner. This is a sophisticated x-ray device which gives clear pictures of internal organs. Its proper and prudent use may replace some risky diagnostic tests and eliminate the need for some exploratory surgery. Yet, its high purchase price (up to $800,000) and maintenance and operation costs make it prone to overuse. Other less expensive devices, such as ultra-sound, it is argued, expose patients to no x-rays, are less expensive (CAT scans cost four hundred dollars) and give comparable diagnostic results.

In energy, the corporate direction has been to develop more sources of non-renewable energy. In medicine it is more visits to the doctor, more drugs and surgeries, more diagnostic and therapeutic equipment, and expensive national illness insurance which gives everyone access to *treatment* from cradle to grave. But what was the question?

Medicine is more and more controlled by centralized corporate and government institutions and is less and less in the hands of those seeking health and paying for the health system. Medicine is increasingly difficult to understand, and people undergoing diagnostic tests and therapy usually have only a dim understanding of the relative hazards involved in what they are being subjected to. Medicine is increasingly authoritarian and people are too often treated as objects ("the stomach in bed two"), passive carriers of interesting disease processes, or simply as "crocks," "hystericals," or "complainers" who are only in the way of their treatment or are out to exploit the system. The poor and uneducated— who are, more often than not, the victims of the system of which medicine is a part—are usually resented the most and treated the worst. People are often disliked when they take too active and inquisitive involvement in their disease process and care. Physicians are often not to be questioned or criticized. Their judgment is authoritative and final and few options are given the patient.

Then there is the matter of medicine as a market commodity—a consumer item. The pursuit and sale of the item creates its own illnesses both directly and indirectly. People come to equate the number of pills they take or the thoroughness of diagnostic attempts (blood and urine tests, EKG's, x-rays) with a guarantee of better health. They are directly harmed by a common litany of excessive tests and therapies: unnecessary surgery, adverse reactions to drugs (at least a million and a half persons are admitted to hospitals each year because of adverse side effects from medications[4]), servere infections which occur because of a person's hospitalization, and diagnosis of non-diseases which result in people being labelled as sick. Many people have been wrongly diagnosed, for example, as having heart disease and a "murmur" and thereafter are treated as physical incompetents or social outcasts, when actually they had innocent murmurs that were not pathological. Several texts have been written on physician-induced diseases.

Yet, one must say that doctors are often forced, in

self-defense, to do unnecessary and potentially dangerous tests and therapies. If the patient, for some reason, feels that the physician's efforts were inadequate, the result may be a malpractice suit. People are not taught enough about their bodies and disease processes to be able to tolerate rather minor and short-lived discomfort. Exaggerated expectations of what physicians can actually do are quite common. In these ways, the legal profession and lack of patient education have increased alienation and consumption by turning physician and patient against each other.

It is all part of the tragedy of the selling of medical treatment to the public rather than education, prevention,

---

"IT IS NOT the fault of our doctors that the medical service of the community, as at present provided for, is a murderous absurdity. That any sane nation, having observed that you could provide for the supply of bread by giving bakers a pecuniary interest in baking for you, should go on to give a surgeon a pecuniary interest in cutting off your leg, is enough to make one dispair of political humanity. But that is precisely what we have done. And the more appalling the mutilation, the more the mutilator is paid. He who corrects the ingrowing toe-nail receives a few shillings; he who cuts your inside out receives hundreds of guineas, except when he does it to a poor person for practice.

"Scandalized voices murmur that these operations are necessary. They may be. It may also be necessary to hang a man or pull down a house. But we take good care not to make the hangman and the housebreaker the judges of that. If we did, no man's neck would be safe and no man's house stable. But we do make the doctor the judge, and fine him anything from sixpence to several hundred guineas if he decides in our favor."

George Bernard Shaw (1911)

and self-help. Much of the public has come to think that any physical or psychological state other than "normal," as defined by the medical industry, can benefit from treatment. The drug companies have certainly sold this notion, suggesting medication to cure all of the following: occasional sleeplessness; minor pain, anxiety, grief; alteration in sex drive; early awakening; appetite disturbances; constipation; weakness and fatigue; headaches; indigestion; irritability; palpitations (increased awareness of heartbeat); crying; feelings of guilt, unreality, hopelessness, unworthiness; rumination over the past, present or future; indecisiveness; excitement; nasal stuffiness; cough; and poor memory. Nearly all these experiences are a normal part of life. If prolonged or severe, most of them are symptoms caused by job-related stress, poor food, crowding, pollution, alienation, and all the extras of a lifestyle produced by materialism and industrialism. Yet these experiences have become yet another corporate market.

Ivan Illich has observed that, "An advanced industrial society is sick-making because it disables people to cope with their environment and, when they break down, it substitutes a 'clinical' prosthesis for the broken relationships. People would rebel against such an environment if medicine did not explain their biological disorientation as a defect in their health, rather than as a defect in the way of life which is imposed on them and which they impose on themselves".[5] In this way medicine indirectly acts to relieve people of social and political responsibility to change the system which makes them ill. It makes people seem like innocent victims of biological mechanisms rather than of society. Tranquilizers are substituted for action, and victims are given the official medical pabulum of "disability" so that they will be pacified. Thus their illness is turned into more material for another institutional enterprise. People who are angered, sickened and impaired by their industrial labor and leisure can often escape only into a life under medical supervision and are therefore reduced and disqualified from the political struggle for a healthier world. ("Make a fuss and your disability will get cut off.") By minimizing personal responsibility and self-help people lose their ability to cope by always relying upon others for warnings as to what is harmful or not. Then they often create problems by seeing therapists too much or too little because they fail to distinguish between harmless and harmful conditions.

Finally, the "services" approach to medicine will bankrupt treasuries everywhere because it is too expensive. Just as defense spending is concentrated on purchasing tools of war rather than programs to ensure pease, so the medical industry promotes "health" by increasing the tools to fight a war against existing disease rather than by preventing it.[6] The saddest example is the American Cancer Society's Seven Warning Signals for cancer. The Society has educated the public to look for them, but the signs become present only after one has cancer that needs treatment.

1. Ivan Illich, *Medical Nemesis: The Expropriation of Health*, (Bantam Books, New York 1976), p. 6
2. Erik P. Eckholm, *The Picture of Health: Environmental Sources of Disease* (W.W. Norton Co. New York 1977), p. 90
3. Speech by President Carter April 25, 1977.
4. Richard Burack M.D., *The New Handbook of Prescription Drugs* (Ballantine, New York 1976), p. 41
5. Ivan Illich, *loc. cit.*
6. Rick J. Carlson, *The End of Medicine,* (Wiley, New York 1975)

Suggested further reading
The Holistic Health Handbook, by The Berkeley Holistic Health Center, And/Or Press, Berkeley, 1978.
Medical Self Care, (journal) PO Box 717, Inverness, California 94937.
Well Being, (journal) 40 East 42nd St, Suite 921, New York, New York 10017.
The Tranquilizing of America, by Richard Hughes and Robert Brewin, Harcourt, Brace, Jovanovich, New York, 1975.
The Politics of Cancer, by Samuel Epstein, Sierra Club, San Francisco, 1978.
The New Handbook of Prescription Drugs, by Richard Burack, Ballantine Books, New York, 1976.
Medical Nemisis, by Ivan Illich, Bantam Books, New York, 1976.
The Picture of Health, by Erik P. Eckholm, W.W. Norton Company, New York, 1977.
The End of Medicine, by Rick J. Carlson, John Wiley and Sons, New York, 1975.
Knowledge and Power, by Colin Norman, Worldwatch Institute, Washington, DC, 1979.
The New American Medicine Show, Irving Byle MD, Unity Press, Santa Cruz, 1979.
Women and the Crisis in Sex Hormones, by Barbara Seaman and Gideon Seaman, Rawson Associates, New York, 1977.
Getting Clear: Body Work For Women, by Anne Kent Rush, Random House, New York, 1973.
Our Bodies, Ourselves, by Boston Women's Health Book Collective, Simon & Schuster, New York, 1979.

How Healthy is Your Life-Style?

RISK CATEGORY	NO RISK	SLIGHT RISK
Smoking	No smoking or stopped for at least 10 years	Less than 10 cigar-ettes, 5 pipes or cigars a day
Alcohol	Nondrinker	Stopped drinker
Trimness	Lean	Slightly plump
Physical Activity	Walk more than 2 miles a day or climb 20 or more flights of stairs a day	Walk 1.5-2 miles a day or climb 15-20 flights of stairs a day
Prescription Drugs	With doctor's consent following orders carefully	Take medication daily without side effects
Nonprescription Drugs	Use occasionally only for short periods. Label warnings heeded	
Alcohol and Driving— Boats, Cars, Motor-cycles, Snowmobiles	Never drink. Drive only with safety aids—seat belt, helmet, life jacket	Never drive after drinking without safety aids
Motor Vehicle Safety	Always wear seat belt	Wear seat belt more than half of the time
Water Safety— Swimming and Boating	Qualified expert	Know how to swim and the safety rules
Blood Cholesterol	Less than 180	180–220
Blood Pressure	120/80 or less	120/80-140/90
Blood Sugar	Less than 120, 2 hours after a meal of syrup and pancakes	Between 110 and 130 2 hours after meals; checked each 3 months
For Women Only		
Breast Check For Lumps	Monthly self-exam and yearly check by physician	Monthly self-exam but no doctor exam
Pap Smear	Every year	Every 3 years

Note: Some risk factors are more important than others, and so it is not possible to score the results of this self-analysis accurately. But for a longer and healthier than average life, try to change your health habits so you will be in the categories on this page rather than the opposite one.

SUBSTANTIAL RISK	HEAVY RISK	DANGEROUS RISK
...lf pack a day	1 pack a day	2 or more packs a day
...ss than 6 drinks ...r week	More than 6 drinks per week	More than 2 drinks per day
...oderately obese	Considerably obese	Grossly obese
...lk only 0.5 to 1.5 ...les a day or ...mb only 5—15 ...hts of stairs a day	Walk only 2–5 blocks a day or climb 2—4 flights of stairs a day	Walk less than 2 blocks a day or climb less than 2 flights of stairs a day
...e medication when ...ded with few ...e effects	Use sleeping and nerve pills regularly without doctor's supervision	Without doctor's consent, mix with other drugs or alcohol
		Continuing use, alcohol used or auto driven despite label warnings
...ve after 2 drinks with ...ety aids	Drive after 2 drinks without safety aids	Drive after more than 2 drinks without safety aids
...ar seat belt as a ...ver half of the time	Wear seat belt as a passenger half of the time	Wear seat belt less than half of the time
...ow how to swim and ...y swim after 1 drink ...nerve drug	Do not know how to swim but use life jacket half of the time.	Do not know how to swim; never use life jacket
...–280	280–320	320 and up
.../90–160/100	160/100–180/105	Above 180/105
...od sugar more than ...l without diet ...trol	Blood sugar more than 150 without diet control, doctor's care	Diabetes without doctor's care at less than 45 years of age
...-exam 2–3 times ...ar but no doc- ...s exam	1 time a year by a doctor	Never
...y 4 years	Never	Never; non-menstrual bleeding

...chart was prepared by Pamela Hall under the supervision of Drs. Lewis C. Robbins and Jack H. ...of Methodist Hospital, Indianapolis, developers of the Health Hazard Appraisal system.

Feeding the Future

by Nikki and David Goldbeck

An interest in diet and nutrition can be both a selfish and a selfless concern, for the modern techniques that are supposed to supply food for mankind now seem to be linked to many of our personal, social, and economic problems.

Consider modern feed-lot techniques which fatten animals in less time but produce meat that contains residues of feed additives (particularly the highly suspect hormone DES), and meat so fatty that it is increasingly thought of as a contributor to obesity, heart disease, and cancer.

Consider white flour, pasta, bread, rice, and over-processed vegetables and fruits; while these foods have been suspected for a long time as being poor sources of nutrition, they are now viewed with increased concern because of their lack of fiber, a potential cause of digestive illnesses ranging from simple constipation to cancer of the bowel.

Consider a food supply containing artificial flavors, colors, sweeteners, preservatives, and the like, whose safety is constantly in doubt and whose use allows manufacturers to employ inferior raw ingredients.

Consider FDA and the USDA, the two federal agencies we have entrusted with the tough job of protecting and policing our food supply; both are so corrupted by the interests they were intended to oversee that the regulators are now controlled by those who were to be regulated.

Consider the "Green Revolution," industrial farming techniques which use so much energy that our homes, factories, and cars must now compete with our stomachs for fuel. This agricultural situation is due largely to our dependence on artificial fertilizers—chemicals that require vast amounts of fuel for their manufacture. It is understandable that chemical fertilizers are needed to supplement the available natural ones, but at present we ignore 1.6 billion tons of animal wastes and an equal amount of human waste— enough waste, once treated, to fertilize at least half of America's farmland. "Farming uses more petroleum than any other industry," state two Cornell researchers writing in *Science* magazine.

Consider the separation of suppliers, growers, processors, warehouses, wholesalers, retailers, and consumers, which adds an enormous surcharge to food costs and a needless drain on our limited fossil fuels. Several studies have shown transportation to be the second largest energy user in our food production system.

Because energy-intensive farming techniques were developed for large-scale farming, government farm policies favor the factory-farm. With lack of federal and academic support, more than 2,000 farms have been closing down each week since the 1940's; farms that provide employment and high-quality local produce with minimum energy input. As one observer has put it, ". . .the small farmer is no longer an agricultural problem; he is a welfare problem."

Money-Maker

An Environmental General Store Franchise

As each of us tries to develop a personal lifestyle that is satisfying as well as environmentally responsible, it is a burden to have to evaluate each product in it. We don't have the time—or the ability—to discover which refrigerator uses the least energy over its lifespan, is easiest to repair and can be recycled when worn out, that doesn't contribute to fluorocarbon pollution of the atmosphere through leaking refrigerant, etc.

Consumer Reports is some help and publishes good evaluations of the energy and water use of such products as refrigerators and washing machines but the Consumers Union has distressing lack of environmental perspective in evaluating products that most environmentalists consider totally inappropriate or unnecessary.

We need an environmental general store that would do the evaluating and selecting and wouldn't stock products that don't fit in an environmentally sound society. Some small stores like this exist—the Whole Earth Access Store in Berkeley is one—but we need a national chain on the scale of, and in competition with, Sears.

GDB

Although a few states, including North Dakota, Kansas, and Minnesota, have laws that prohibit or curtail corporate farming, lack of public interest has kept a Federal Family Farm Anti-Trust Act in congressional committee.

In much the same way, our national encouragement of a diet high in meat has brought about inefficient use of our remaining farmland. Much of the valuable crops produced on the land, like soy and grain, are fed not to people but to cattle. Professor Georg Borgstrom of the University of Michigan estimates that the developed world, which makes up only 28 percent of the world's population, consumes three fourths of the world's fish supply and two thirds of the world's grain—not as human food, but indirectly, through the meat we eat.

One reason why we eat what we eat, is the tantalizing packaging that surrounds factory foods, nine tenths of which you throw away when you get home. It is estimated that merely cutting packaging in half would save 200,000 barrels of oil each day.

America's food advertising, which uses high-powered media techniques, exposes children to an average of twenty TV commercials an hour, half of which sell edibles on the basis of their "sweetened, sugared, or crisped quality." The billions of dollars spent each year on public relations and advertising have so perverted our eating habits that many people now prefer the taste of factory-made foods to their real counterparts. As Dr. Ross Hume Hall has written in his excellent book *Food for Nought/The Decline in Nutrition:*

> When food technologists began to separate nutrition from palatability, they also undermined the ability of the human senses to assess the quality of the food. Texture, color, odor, taste, and feel of natural food are all human guides, not only to the nutritional value of food, but also to its safety. At one time, one could use one's own senses to determine accurately the freshness of food, but man's senses no longer guide him in his choice of food items.

A U.S. Senate Report (1973) established that there were more than 12 million malnourished people in this country, spanning all economic sectors. This malnutrition can be directly linked to one of America's most tragic faces, that of the retarded child. Because of improper diet during pregnancy and infancy, the national incidence of learning dis-

Quick Cheap Whole Foods At Home

One of the main drawbacks about cooking with whole foods like brown rice, wheat berries, peas, beans, etc., is that they take so long. Traditional recipes for legumes, for instance, call for overnight soaking and hours on the stove. A lot of us just don't have a full day to prepare one dinner. So to save energy—your own and your cooking fuel—try an old-fashioned pressure cooker (available in modern stores). Hours of cooking can be reduced to minutes.

Unfortunately pressure cookers got a bad name when they were abused by institutions like schools to produce stringy beef and tasteless vegetables. So good recipes with them are hard to find. Therefore, you get to experiment. And find that the artichoke—a seeming natural—doesn't cook evenly in them. Apparently all those layers of leaves make an insulating wall around the heart. And the eggplant, which is delicious steamed, bursts in a pressure cooker.

One of the best sources for cooking in a pressure cooker is *From Julia Child's Kitchen*. The French Chef whose name is synonymous with extravagant, difficult-to-prepare meals has some of the best recipes for "earthy alternatives," as she calls them, in print. She provides a basic procedure for all legumes, except the small flageolets, in the pressure cooker. With her method, you can have beans on the table in an hour and a half—with only about five minutes total time cooking on the stove. To further conserve energy Mrs. Child suggests that you prepare a big potful of plain beans, perhaps during the time while you're in the kitchen fixing another meal anyway, and then dress them up later. You can keep them handy to toss into salads, soups, or stews, or in one of her marvelous concoctions with tomatoes, onions, garlic, herbs, meats, cream or cheese. The same book has a recipe for pressure-cooked potatoes or beef stew.

Another good source is Margaret Gin's *One Pot Meals*. She has a few recipes for pressure-cooked bean dishes (most of them calling for some meat) and many recipes for meat and vegetable stews.

AW

abilities, social maladjustment, and neurologic disorders is increasing rather than diminishing.

And, saddest of all, we are now in the business of exporting food technology, so that American cola drinks are available even in remote villages; improperly prepared infant formula is replacing mother's milk in underdeveloped countries; and, in an attempt to emulate the American lifestyle, many nations are forsaking their traditional diet and are encouraging in its place a fatty meat regimen.

The unequal distribution of food throughout the world, according to the noted biologist Dr. Barry Commoner, has had a significant effect on one of our most pressing problems: overpopulation. In his article "How Poverty Breeds Overpopulation (and not the other way around)," Dr. Commoner explains that in poor societies children, particularly male children, are an important source of wealth, one of the only chances to advance one's economic condition. However, when "quality of life," of which food and nutrition are basic elements, improves, population growth levels off. "The sense of well being and security in the future" leads people "voluntarily to restrict the production of children. . . ." Think about it; if food is more equitably distributed, eventually it will have to be shared by fewer people.

Managing Your Own Food Supply

by Ray Wolf

Home food production—that's what this part of the book is all about. And it just might be the most important part of the whole book; at least it might be for many people. Why? Because when you have a hand (or two) in the production of the food you eat, you're getting right down to the basics. You're working from the beginning of the production line, helping to create something from basic raw materials. You're planting seeds and multiplying them maybe a thousandfold. Think what this means in terms of savings at the store, the purity and quality of the food you eat, reduced demand on natural resources, and reduced demands on food supplies around the world.

Growing vegetable products is possible for most everyone with even a little bit of land (or rooftop or sunny porch). The returns from a garden can be terrific. The food you get from it can be worth many times the money, energy, and time that went into preparing, maintaining, and harvesting it. A great many people who've never gardened before are beginning to realize just this. And so are one-time leisure gardeners who now look at gardening as the way to food production. Gardens have become bigger and more productive, and gardeners are now taking their hobby more seriously. Today's vegetable gardens are earning the place that victory gardens enjoyed during World War II; they're at the center of self sufficiency and food security.

In this chapter we will be limiting our discussion to vegetable growing only. While many people raise their own grains and dried beans, that requires additional space and equipment. For those with the space for such an undertaking, there is ample information available.

Gardening is a low-input, soft technology in that it requires human labor and cooperation with the land, not massive machines and use of fossil fuels to force the land to do the unnatural. While large-scale agriculture is currently being damned as an energy user instead of being an energy producer, gardening is just about at the top of the efficiency scale. By working with nature and using a minimal amount of inputs, you convert solar energy into an abundance of energy in the form of food for you and your family. Organic gardening doesn't depend on chemical fertilizers and pesticides; instead you produce most of your own fertilizer from the waste your household produces and from animal manures, and you rely on improved methods of planting and good soil health to keep insects under control. Organic gardening is the most natural relationship you can have with the earth. You work with nature to provide food to support life.

Organic Gardening and Farming magazine polled 20 gardeners (see Table) to find their yearly gardening expenses and value of the food they grow, and it discovered that these good gardeners saved on the average about $300 a year. The National Garden Bureau designed an average vegetable garden for a family of four and calculated that it would save a family $350 a year.

And gardens will become increasingly important as money-savers as food prices rise. As Robert Rodale explained in his June 1974 OGF editorial, "Organic Living Helps You Fight Inflation," home-grown food is inflation-proof food. If the price of store-bought vegetables goes up, that only means that the vegetables you grow yourself are worth more. They certainly won't cost you more to grow (except for maybe a slight increase in the cost of seed), especially if you garden organically, because you don't have to buy more fertilizers (which are also becoming more expensive as food costs rise). The wastes that your family and its land produce become the raw materials for your garden, the only cost being your own labor. And an organic garden is easier and less expensive to work than a chemically fertilized one. Humus-rich soil is productive beyond the level of a regular garden, and natural approaches to the control of destructive insect and disease levels can mean less money spent for expensive pest sprays and dusts.

Average Cost-Value of 20 Organic Gardens*

Yearly garden expenses	Value of food grown	No. in family	Percentage of food grown
$54	$538	3—4 people	60 percent

*The gardens ranged from $100-value kitchen gardens to $2,000 whoppers that feed a large family and more. Eliminating the gardens over $1,000 leaves an average food saving of about $300.

The Importance Of Advanced Planning

It's how and when a garden is planted that contributes most to food savings, and the actual quantity and quality of the harvest. Many gardens, especially beginners' gardens, are haphazardly planted. Because of this, the yield is not what it could be, and much of the garden space is wasted. A well-planted and well-cared for small garden will outyield a poorly run, large plot. Since the small plot will require less work, that's what you want to shoot for; to get the most vegetables possible out of the least amount of space.

There are few things as enjoyable as planning a garden. You start off by ordering seed catalogs. Soon you'll be busily flipping through them and finding literally dozens of varieties you "have always wanted to try." Go ahead and do some window shopping; learn what each company offers, and who seeems to specialize in what vegetables, disease resistant varieties, short season varieties, and who has the best selection of each vegetable. Since you'll be doing this during the dead of winter, enjoy yourself—take your time.

Before ordering seeds, decide what foods you and your family eat and make a list. At this stage of the game, you are only interested in what foods you want to grow, not how much or where to grow them. Spend a little time to make sure your list is complete. Don't forget to include those foods you like but seldom get to enjoy due to their cost in the store; your garden will provide these treats for next to nothing. Once your list is complete, set it aside.

Next, carefully analyze and determine how much garden you can handle. This requires two measurements: the first is how much space you have that you are willing to put into garden, and the second is how much energy you are willing to put into gardening. Most people end up with about two acres of space and one-quarter acre of ambition. Once you decide how much work you are willing to do and how much space you have, you will probably have to compromise a bit to decide just how large a garden you end up with. Remember, you can start small and always expand. The thing you want to avoid is having more garden than you can take care of. Remember when computing your estimated work load that not only does the garden take work, it makes it. When you decide how many tomato plants you want to weed and stake, don't forget that you will also be canning the tomatoes when they ripen.

Grow Vertically

Whether in containers or a regular garden, one sure way to save space and improve performance is to grow your vegetables up, not out. It will not only save gardening space, but training plants upward will expose more vegetables to the sun for quicker ripening and increased yields. Additionally, it will prevent vegetables from rotting on the moist ground, possibly picking up soilborne diseases and being exposed to insect and rodent damage.

IT IS EASY in the world to live after the world's opinion; it is easy in solitude to live after our own; but the great man is he who in the midst of the crowd keeps with perfect sweetness the independence of solitude.

Ralph Waldo Emerson

A good vertical gardener takes a look at a fence 5 by 20 feet and sees 100 square feet of gardening space. Any plants that vine on the ground can usually be trained, or tied to a vertical growing area.

If you don't have any vertical areas with good sun exposure, vertical growing cages are easily built with standard construction grade reinforcing wire, or any other wire with openings large enough for you to harvest through. To build a simple growing tower, form the wire into a circle with a 30-inch diameter. Staple the wire to 8-foot wooden stakes, leaving about 3 feet of stake at the bottom for hammering into the ground, and to allow you room to reach under the wire cage. The cages can either be permanent, or you can take them down every year. Squash, cucumbers, and small melons all do well in such a tower, as do tomatoes, and, of course, pole beans and peas.

Growing vertically usually requires that you pay a bit more attention to your plants, especially when they start producing. Cucumbers often have to be tied in slings, and branches producing tomatoes have to be better supported to hold the weight of the fruit. One point many people forget is that a vertical garden in a container must be watered more often and usually side-dressed with fertilizer during the season, or watered with a manure tea, to compensate for the reduced root zone and the heavy production of a vertical garden.

By building walls, with wire loosely attached to one side, lined with plastic, and filled with soil, a wall of vegetation can be planted through holes in the retaining plastic. Such a planting wall works especially well for loose-leaf lettuce, tomatoes, cucumbers, and peppers, but not root crops.

Vertical gardening can be anything from a simple stand to set containers on to a suspended platform with plants growing up the suspenders, or hanging over the edge of the platform. But in most cases, it will be staking something to a fence, or erecting a trellis to train crops into the air instead of letting them wander around the garden. One final word of caution: Varieties that produce especially heavy fruit should not be grown vertically, unless special precautions are taken to support the weight.

Soil, Lifeblood Of The Garden

No matter how well you plan and maintain your garden, if you have poor soil, you'll have a poor garden. Luckily, you can always improve your soil through the addition of organic soil conditioners.

If soil is the heart of your garden, then humus is the heart of your soil. Good garden soil consists of about 5 percent humus. Most soils are from 1 to 2 percent humus, while native prairie soils may be 10 percent humus, and land that has been continuously farmed with chemicals may have as little as ½ or even ¼ of 1 percent humus.

There are two ways you can add humus to your soil. You can either grow it there, or you can put it there. Most gardeners will use both these methods, in that you may actually grow a cover crop or a green manure crop to add humus to the soil (roots of vegetables left in the soil add humus), and you will also be adding humus to the soil in the form of compost, animal manures, and soil conditioners. The higher your organic matter content, the easier tight clay soils are to work and the better the drainage. In light sandy soils, organic matter holds moisture and nutrients in the root zone. Organic matter holds moisture in all soils and allows air to penetrate and stimulate root growth.

Herbs, Their Companions and Their Uses

Herb	Companions and Effects
Basil	Companion to tomatoes; improves growth and flavor. Repels flies and mosquitoes. DISLIKES rue intensely.
Beebalm	Companion to tomatoes; improves growth and flavor.
Borage	Companion to tomatoes, squash, and strawberries; deters tomato worm; improves growth and flavor.
Caraway	Plant here and there; loosens soil.
Catnip	Plant in borders; deters flea beetle.
Camomile	Companion to cabbages and onions; improves growth and flavor.
Chervil	Companion to radishes; improves growth and flavor.
Chives	Companion to carrots; improves growth and flavor.
Dead Nettle	Companion to potatoes; deters potato bug; improves growth and flavor.
Dill	Companion to cabbage; improves growth and health of cabbage. DISLIKES carrots.
Fennel	Plant away from gardens. Most plants dislike it.
Flax	Companion to carrots, potatoes; deters potato bug. Improves growth and flavor.
Garlic	Plant near roses and raspberries; deters Japanese beetle; improves growth and health.
Horseradish	Plant at corners of potato patch to deter potato bug.
Henbit	General insect repellent.
Hyssop	Deters cabbage moth; companion to cabbage and grapes. DISLIKES radishes.
Lemon Balm	Sprinkle throughout garden.
Lovage	Improves flavor and health of plants if planted here and there.
Marigolds	The workhorse of the pest deterrents. Plant throughout garden; it discourages Mexican bean beetles, nematodes, and other insects.
Mint	Companion to cabbage and tomatoes; improves health and flavor; deters white cabbage moth.
Marjoram	Here and there in garden; improves flavors.
Mole Plant	Deters moles and mice if planted here and there.
Nasturtium	Companion to radishes, cabbage, and cucurbits; plant under fruit trees. Deters aphids, squash bugs, striped pumpkin beetles. Improves growth and flavor.
Petunia	Protects beans.

Herb	Companions and Effects
Pot Marigold	Companion to tomatoes, but plant elsewhere in garden too. Deters asparagus beetle, tomato worm, and general garden pests.
Peppermint	Planted among cabbages, it repels the white cabbage butterfly.
Rosemary	Companion to cabbage, beans, carrots, and sage; deters cabbage moth, bean beetles, and carrot fly.
Rue	Plant near roses and raspberries; deters Japanese beetle. DISLIKES sweet basil.
Sage	Plant with rosemary, cabbage, and carrots. Deters cabbage moth, carrot fly. KEEP AWAY from cucumbers.
Southernwood	Plant here and there in garden; companion to cabbage; improves growth and flavor; deters cabbage moth.
Summer Savory	Plant with beans and onions; improves growth and flavor. Deters bean beetles.
Tansy	Plant under fruit trees; companion to roses and raspberries. Deters flying insects, Japanese beetles, striped cucumber beetles, squash bugs, ants.
Tarragon	Good throughout garden.
Thyme	Here and there in garden. It deters cabbage worm.
Valerian	Good anywhere in garden.
Wormwood	As a border, it keeps animals from the garden.
Yarrow	Plant along borders, paths, near aromatic herbs; enhances essential oil production.

This information was collected from many sources, most notably the Bio-Dynamic Association and the Herb Society of America.

In an organic garden your first concern is soil building; the vegetables will do just fine on their own if you have proper soil. The main tool you will have at your disposal to build soil quality is compost.

To the compost pile comes all your organic leavings: kitchen garbage, pulled weeds, spoiled hay, leaves, and manure. From the pile comes all the major and minor nutrients your garden vegetables need.

A list of compost's major benefits to gardens includes:

• It is food for soil organisms which, during the growing year, feed the plants the nutrients they need.

• Plants thrive in a loose, crumbly, humusy soil, and compost conditions the soil, making it loose and fluffy so that it absorbs water and yet is well drained.

• Soil health requires thriving colonies of bacteria, fungi, and earthworms. Compost feeds these organisms, which in turn aerate and enrich the soil with nitrogen and other elements.

• Trace elements not provided in chemical fertilizers are included in compost. Without these elements imbalance occurs, causing lower yields.

• Weed seeds that often heavily infest all kinds of manure are killed by the high temperatures in compost.

• Soil conditioned by compost allows for stronger root systems. This in turn means healthier, drought-resistant plants.

• A compost pile gives you top-quality potting and seed-flat soil for your house and greenhouse.

• Compost costs very little and often nothing.

• Using waste from around the house means energy saving, in an age when this kind of practice is vital to everyone.

After the condition of your soil, the next limiting factor you have to worry about is soil pH. A correct pH is necessary for plants to absorb nutrients needed for growth.

The letters pH refer to the potential hydrogen and indicate soil alkalinity or acidity. The pH scale ranges from zero to 14, from acid to alkaline. Seven on the scale is neutral. Soils testing 4 to 5 are very acid or sour, and relatively few plants will tolerate them. Similarly, soils of over 7¾ are too alkaline or sweet for most plants to thrive. A large number of commonly grown plants prefer a pH range of 6 to 7½. Testing soil for pH is not a highly technical operation; there are simple, inexpensive kits that are easy to use. By adding various substances to the soil the gardener can adjust the pH to suit a crop. Table 4-10 gives the preferred pH of many commonly grown plants.

Compost, maple leaves, ground oyster shells, marl, and wood ashes all help to increase soil pH. Lime is the most often used as it is inexpensive and fast acting.

Aluminum sulfate is usually recommended to make soil more acid, but organic gardeners prefer generous applications of peat moss, rotted sawdust, cottonseed meal, pine needles, and oak leaves.

THE PHYSICIAN can bury his mistakes, but the architect can only advise his client to plant vines.

Frank Lloyd Wright

A simple soil test will quickly tell you the pH of your soil, and from there it is rather easy to correct. However, if your soil is low in organic matter, it isn't so easily corrected.

Compost is the best way to improve soil organic matter and still maintain a good soil pH. We should offer one word of caution about composting—it is habit forming. Many a gardener has started off with a casual compost pile only to turn into a fanatic about feeding the pile. It doesn't take long to reach the point where you won't throw away anything that could go to the pile, and eventually back to the soil.

These simple steps will help get you started in composting:

1. If possible, shred leaves, cornstalks, and other organic material. Matted clumps of leaves or grass clippings will not allow air to penetrate the pile nor provide the high temperatures needed for quick composting.

2. Scratch the soil where the pile is to be built with a pitchfork. This will expose the bottom of the pile to microorganisms and earthworms.

3. Place a layer of green matter—hay, shredded cornstalks, etc.—on the bare ground. This layer should be a foot thick and 8 feet in diameter for a 5-foot pile.

4. Cover the green matter with one-fifth as much manure as green matter. What you use depends on what kind of manure is available.

5. Place kitchen garbage on top of manure. This adds trace elements and increases the temperature of the bacterial "fire."

6. Sprinkle on a couple of shovelsful of rock powder and wood ashes. Use rock phosphate, potash, greensand, and crushed limestone. To avoid caking do not overuse these materials.

7. Cover the first layer with an inch or so of good soil providing more bacteria.

8. Water each layer of the pile thoroughly but do not saturate. Neither overly wet nor overly dry compost will work.

9. Lay down a number of small tree branches across the first layer. This provides air channels when removed later, or the pile can be lifted and shaken. Either method provides air, a necessary ingredient for bacterial action.

10. Put down remaining layers in same order as first. Three to five layers will make a 4- or 5-foot pile which is high enough to promote proper temperatures.

11. Top the pile with hay or other green matter and an inch or two of soil. Water the last time.

12. Turn the pile frequently if you want fast action; if you can wait till next year, don't turn at all. Check occasionally to see if it needs moisture.

13. Naturally you need not be as exact as this. The goal is to pile vegetation and manure together in a manner that permits air in the pile, and occasionally turn the pile to subject all parts of it to the high temperatures created within the pile.

If there is no yard where you can make compost, make it in garbage cans; this is the easiest and cleanest way. Here are some guidelines:

1. Use a galvanized garbage can with a good-fitting lid. Punch holes in the bottom and add a layer of gravel and about 3 inches of soil.

2. Add earthworms, preferably some of the red worms or red wigglers. Although they are not necessary, worms will speed up the proccss.

3. If your lot has good drainage, the can may be sunk in the ground to allow the worms to work through the winter, below the frost line. The can may also be kept in the cellar or on a balcony if set off the floor on some bricks with a pan underneath to catch any fluids dripping out. These fluids will be odorless and are good for house plant waterings.

4. Throw kitchen wastes into the can. Avoid all but very small amounts of grease or meat scraps. Chicken bones should be added, as they add calcium and can act as a filler in the soil if they don't completely decompose.

5. Odor is usually not a problem if each addition of

fresh garbage is covered with a sprinkling of soil or some type of organic matter like leaves, grass clippings, etc. Coffee grounds will act as a natural deodorant and should be included, and a shredded newspaper will take care of any odors almost immediately.

A regular 20-gallon can will just about hold the household waste of a family of four for six months. A good idea, if space permits, is to start one can in the fall, and as it fills up, start another can. This lets you treat your garden before the growing season, and again after the growing season.

Insect Control

More than anything else, insects are thought of as a sign of an unhealthy garden. A healthy garden has insects, but they're in a balance of beneficial insects and problem causers. That's what you want, a healthy balance of insects throughout the garden. That way, no one species ever becomes so populous that it can cause major problems.

By using chemical sprays, you not only destroy the pest you're after, but you kill off the beneficial insects as well. It is one of mother nature's general rules that problem insects have a shorter life span than do predatory insects. Thus, when you kill off all the insects, the problems causers reappear before their enemies do, compounding your insect problems.

The seven steps below will enable you to handle your garden insects in a much more efficient and, we believe, sane method.

1. Encourage soil health—Healthy soil and its dependent life is promoted by adding rich compost, mulch, green manures, animal manures, and natural rock powder fertilizers.

2. Interplant—Insect damage can be cut in half by inter-planting one crop with another. Intersperse the garden with strong herbs like dill, rosemary, summer savory, garlic, and thyme to confuse insects' senses and make it more difficult for them to find their favorite vegetable.

3. Plant pest-resistant varieties—Search out seed's of pest-resistant varieties. Practice crop rotation and stimulate vigorous plant growth by organic soil improvement, watering, and mulching.

4. Practice garden hygiene—Garden hygiene and good cultivation are preferable to poisons as pest control methods. A good tilling of the soil can kill a lot of pests. A healthy mix of good and harmful insects in the garden allows nature to set up her own delicate and effective checks and balances.

5. Biological controls—Biological controls can be the first line of defense against a pest population explosion. Ladybugs, green lacewing, praying mantis, and the trichogramma wasp are all beneficial and can be purchased from many sources. They should be released in late May or early June in order to meet the burgeoning pest populations. Birds are voracious bug-eaters and should be encouraged around the home and garden. Harmless snakes, toads, frogs, and salamanders all have a part in establishing natural control. A spray of *Bacillus thuringiensis,* known as BT (Thuricide, Dipel, Biotrol, and other trade names), is effective against caterpillars that attack members of the cabbage family. BT is also good against gypsy moth, tent caterpillar, and other tree-infesting crawlers. BT doesn't affect beneficial insects, humans, fish, or animals, nor does it build up in the soil. Another insect disease, milky spore disease (trade name Doom), keeps Japanese beetles in check.

6. Physical traps—Plastic jugs painted orange and coated with Tanglefoot and other tree stickum is a trap for flea beetles. The beetles are attracted by the color, jump on and stay on. Strips of plastic, wood, or cardboard painted yellow and coated with stickum controls white fly in the greenhouse.

7. Botanical poisons—As a last resort the gardener can turn to the botanical poisons—pyrethrum, rotenone, and ryania. These are made from plants and are effective, but they are poisons and rotenone is very toxic to fish. Heavy exposure can be mildly toxic to humans and animals, but they can be safely used and they quickly degrade, unlike the long-lasting chemical poisons.

Your garden should easily produce all you ask of it, with a minimal amount of labor. The best advice we can give a gardener is an ancient Chinese proverb, ''The best fertilizer is the farmer's shadow.'' This quite simply means that you have to pay attention to what's going on in the garden. If there is about to be an outbreak of insects, your garden will tell you if you are there to see the signs.

I HATE QUOTATIONS. TELL ME WHAT YOU KNOW.
Ralph Waldo Emerson

Money-Maker

Fast Natural Foods Restaurant Chain

The man was trying to sell steaks, but their price was going through the roof because the herds have dwindled as a result of the drought in the West. "So rather than raise the price to the customers in your restaurants," he was telling a room of about thirty people, "we've come up with some innovative new ways to cut the cost."

It sounded interesting. Although I'm not in the restaurant business and my presence at this "steak-tasting" was almost accidental, I'm all for innovative ways—new or old—to cut costs. The man explained that first of all the restaurants could shop more wisely. "Traditionally the price is lowest in January and February—why? Because in the summer months the American public goes on vacation and goes out to eat, and what they want is steaks."

Why? I wondered. I myself would rather eat almost anything than a steak. But the man didn't follow my train of curiosity. He went on to explain that the restaurants could buy an entire year's supply of meat at the bargain, winter rate. "How are you going to keep it?—when most freezing results in some deterioration after six months? With our exclusive process." He held up a thick red filet wrapped in plastic, snug as a void in a vacuum. "You'll notice that even though this meat has been sitting here for over three hours there is no loss of juice. So that when your broiler man puts it on the fire and sears it, the juice stays inside until the customer cuts into it and then it all comes boiling out onto his plate."

The man went on to explain other ways to shave prices by simply changing the way the meat is cut. "For instance, by leaving on this small piece of gristle—called 'the strap' in the business—you can still serve your customer an eight-ounce steak, and yet get one extra steak per tenderloin. For the filets what we do is cut them, freeze them, thaw them a little, then put them in a press so that they all come out a

uniform size, and the result then is you get an extra filet."
Between salad and the main course he showed us that with
his new hamburger patty machine he can get five patties to a
pound, and the customer still gets a portion the *size* of a
quarter-pounder.

And how did the steaks taste? I had the sirloin, and my
neighbor had the filet; they each tasted mostly like artificial
charcoal flavoring. Right next to my steak was a portion of
zucchini and crookneck squash, flavored with a little onion,
mushrooms and tomatoes, that looked like a still life and
tasted fresh and delicious. I would have traded all of my
beef for a little more of the veggies. Why is steak what the
American public wants for a treat?

Well, we all know some of the historical reasons, but
the reason I see when I go on vacation and stop in unfamiliar
restaurants is that steak is what's on the menu. Some restaurants won't allow you to eat at their tables unless you
order a main course, and they don't offer anything but meat.

And yet hearty soups with legumes and grains and
vegetables—a whole meal in a bowl—are simple to prepare,
can be made far in advance, leftovers can easily be held over
to the next day, and then extended if necessary with a few
more fresh vegetables. Of course there are restaurants offering meals like this—but they're mostly on one coast or the
other. Between the Appalachians and the Rockies, almost
anywhere along the highways, in the airports or train stations, what the American public gets is beef.

We need a fast natural foods chain offering good cheap
food, made with plenty of locally grown vegetables. It
would allow the creative restaurateur more profit, the customer lower prices, and be better for you and the earth.

AW

Principal Authors

GARRETT DE BELL has devoted his career to the environment. He is perhaps best known as editor of *The Environmental Handbook* and has written many articles on aspects of the environment. For the past few years he has been the Environmental Advisor to the Yosemite Park and Curry Company in Yosemite National Park, and in this role he has implemented many of the ideas advocated by environmentalists, such as a beverage container deposit program and an overall recycling program in Curry Company's operation. His academic background includes an A.B. in biology from Stanford University and a Ph.C. in zoology from U.C., Berkeley.

AUBREY WALLACE is the author of fiction and non-fiction, including articles on the environment, for many national magazines.

DAVID GANCHER, former Editor of *Not Man Apart*, is now the Managing Editor of *Sierra*, the bulletin of the Sierra Club. His background includes education at Reed College and San Francisco State, and service in the Peace Corps in Turkey.

ANNE EHRLICH is a senior research associate in biology at Stanford University, dividing her time between studies of the reproductive biology of insects and policy research in human nutrition and demography; a member of the executive committee of Friends of the Earth; and author of numerous works as well as co-author of *The End of Affluence, Ecoscience: Population, Resources, Environment,* and *The Golden Door: International Migrations, Mexico, and the United States.*

PAUL EHRLICH is Bing Professor of Population Studies at Stanford University, where his work on natural populations of butterflies, fishes, and other organisms has led him to a deep concern for the state of the earth's ecological systems. He has recently received the John Muir Award from the Sierra Club for his work, which includes more than 20 books, of which *The Population Bomb* is best known to the general public.

RON RUDOLPH has served in an advisory capacity to the U.S. Environmental Protection Agency, Bureau of Land Management, National Park Service, National Commission on Air Quality, and the California State Energy Commission and Department of Water Resources. He also was a member of the Air Pollution Task Force of the National Coal Policy Project from 1978 to 1980.

GARY SNYDER is a Pulitizer Prize-winning poet.

DAVID BURWELL is coauthor of *The End of the Road; A Citizen's Guide to Transportation Problemsolving,* published by the National Wildlife Federation and Environmental Action Foundation.

DAVID GAINES is head of the Mono Lake Committee, centered in Lee Vining, California.

JUDITH KUNOFSKY is the president of Zero Population Growth (1977–1980) and is the Population & Growth Policy Specialist for the Sierra Club.

MARC LAPPÉ is chief of the Hazard Alert System, California Department of Health Services, where he has been working in setting health policy for four years. He has a Ph.D. in experimental pathology, has been a cancer researcher and a fellow at Hastings Center in New York.

HAROLD GILLIAM is a staff writer on the environment for the *San Francisco Chronicle*.

AMORY LOVINS is the world's leading advocate of alternative energy planning and author of *Soft Energy Paths,* published by Friends of the Earth, Ballinger Publishing Company, and Harper and Row in the U.S.,